IMAGES
of America

LAUREL HILL CEMETERY

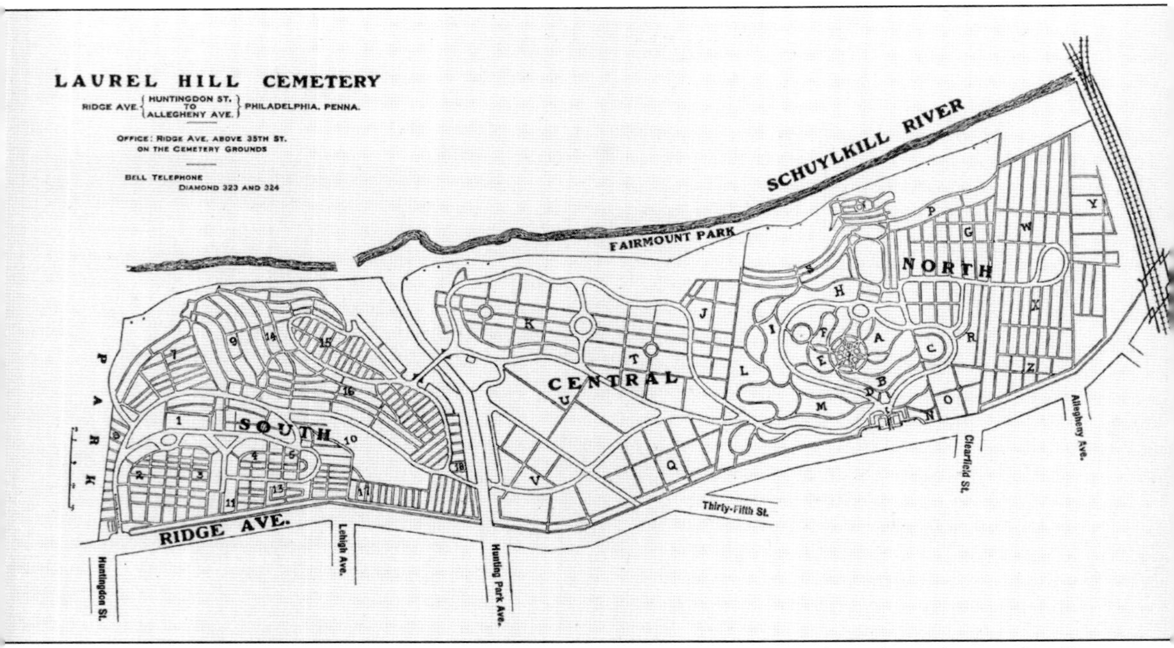

Laurel Hill Map. Prior to the creation of Central Laurel Hill, North and South Laurel Hill were completely separated from each other, requiring independent entrances, offices, and superintendents. This map delineates the individual sections. Not labeled is the Stoever tract, which comprises sections W through Z. (Laurel Hill Cemetery Company.)

On the Cover: "Millionaire's Row." Millionaire's Row in Section K of Central Laurel Hill is pictured here around 1930. (Laurel Hill Cemetery Company.)

IMAGES
of America

LAUREL HILL CEMETERY

Carol Yaster and Rachel Wolgemuth

ARCADIA
PUBLISHING

ISBN 978-1-4671-2655-7

Published by Arcadia Publishing
Charleston, South Carolina

Printed in the United States of America

Library of Congress Control Number: 2017931996

For all general information, please contact Arcadia Publishing:
Telephone 843-853-2070
Fax 843-853-0044
E-mail sales@arcadiapublishing.com
For customer service and orders:
Toll-Free 1-888-313-2665

Visit us on the Internet at www.arcadiapublishing.com

Contents

ACKNOWLEDGMENTS

This book is built on the research and support of countless others. It is impossible to know all the stories Laurel Hill has to tell, and we relied on many people to help bring these lives to light. We wish to thank Gwen Kaminski; David Gurmai; Russ Dodge; Anthony Waskie, PhD; E. David Horwitz, PhD; and Michael Brooks, PhD.

A thank-you goes to the staff of Laurel Hill Cemetery: Bill Doran, Emma Stern, Beth Savastana, Suhee You, and Nick McAllister.

We also relied upon the extensive research done by Aaron Wunsch, PhD.

A special thank-you goes to William J. Levant, Esq., for legal guidance above and beyond the call of duty.

We also wish to thank Wilson and Barbara Smith; Henry Disston Jr.; Gregg E. Gorton, MD; and Frank Rausch for supporting this project.

Thank you to Alexander "Pete" Hoskins, Deborah Cassidy, and Priyanka Setty for supporting this project and Caroline Anderson at Arcadia Publishing for answering countless questions.

Numerous institutions were kind enough to donate the use of images. Thank you to Leslie Morris-Smith of the Morris Arboretum of the University of Pennsylvania, Mark Lloyd of the University of Pennsylvania Archives, Nicole Joniec of the Library Company of Philadelphia, Kaitlyn Pettengill of the Historical Society of Pennsylvania, Marge Huang and Rose Chiango of the Philadelphia Museum of Art, Louis M. Iatarola of the Historical Society of Tacony, Nichole Calero and Nanci Young of Smith College, Joshua Caster of University of Nebraska-Lincoln, and Thomas Lisanti, David Rosado, and Andrea Felder of the New York Public Library.

Finally, thank you to our friends and families for supporting us and our love of cemeteries and Laurel Hill.

Unless otherwise noted, all images appear courtesy of Laurel Hill Cemetery Company.

Key to image credits:

HABS	Historic American Buildings Survey
HSP	Historical Society of Pennsylvania
LCP	Library Company of Philadelphia
LOC	Library of Congress Prints and Photographs Division
NLM	US National Library of Medicine
NYPL	The New York Public Library
UPENN	University of Pennsylvania Archives
WLHC	West Laurel Hill Cemetery

INTRODUCTION

Nearly two centuries ago, Americans living in urban areas found themselves dealing with the challenges that resulted from an increasingly industrialized society. To make room for the rapidly growing population and developing industries, old buildings were removed and the resulting open spaces became the sites of new factories, businesses, offices, and homes. There was little room for the dead, who were confined to crowded burial grounds within the bustling cities. Burials were often made in unmarked graves, with several unrelated deceased sometimes placed in one grave. The interments of the recently dead often disturbed previously buried bodies. Sometimes, only the very wealthy could escape these indignities. Graverobbing to obtain fresh corpses for use by medical students was a frequent occurrence. Disease, contamination, and fear of miasma led to concern over sanitary conditions as outbreaks of disease were attributed to these foul places.

In cities like Boston, Philadelphia, and Baltimore, reform-minded individuals looked for a new way to bury the dead, and with the opening of Mount Auburn Cemetery in Cambridge, Massachusetts, in 1831, the Rural Cemetery Movement was born. For the first time in America, the dead were buried well outside of city centers. Visiting loved ones' graves was encouraged, as was the placement of grave decorations and elaborate memorials. Families could be buried together in family plots. The word *cemetery* entered the popular lexicon. With gates, fences, superintendents, and rules regulating visitors' conduct, cemeteries began to transform into controlled and very pleasant spaces.

Rural cemeteries filled a greater role than just places to bury the dead, however. In an era before municipal parks, they became areas of recreation. Visitors traveled to see the trees and other horticultural offerings in these cultivated landscapes (often created by horticulture experts). With few museums and art galleries to visit, the rural cemeteries became outdoor museums, featuring memorials that were regarded as sculptural works of art. When visiting a major American city, a trip to that city's rural cemetery was a "must-see" attraction. In a time when Americans were struggling to lay claim to their heritage, the monuments both honored the dead and instructed the living. Memorials to the country's founders and Revolutionary War heroes became visible manifestations of the nation's values.

Philadelphia experienced its own challenges regarding the dead. In 1812, when the city banned all new burials in Philadelphia's public squares, the city's residents keenly felt that they were being forcibly separated from their ancestors. By the mid-1820s, Philadelphians addressed the crisis by organizing private burial grounds within the city. Finally, in 1836, citizens rioted at Sixth and Arch Streets when the owners of the burial ground located there arranged to sell the space to an expanding business. When the ground was opened to begin exhumation of the bodies, a mob stormed the burial ground, broke the workmen's tools, refilled the newly dug open pit, and threatened bodily harm to anyone who would attempt to reopen the graves. Rioting was a temporary solution, and it was not until John Jay Smith and his colleagues envisioned a burial ground beyond the city limits that this revolutionary form of burial would come to Philadelphia.

The chosen site of the new cemetery was three-and-a-half miles outside of what was the boundary of 1836 Philadelphia. The initial tract of land, referred to as Laurel, or the Laurels, was the former estate of Joseph Sims. It was comprised of 32 acres on either side of the Ridge Pike (now known as Ridge Avenue), a major artery leading northwest from Philadelphia. Other properties within the city limits were considered, but this site featured panoramic views of the Schuylkill River, with bluffs rising 120 feet above the water. While those buried there were largely Protestant and completely white, the cemetery was established with no direct religious or ethnic affiliation.

Like the other rural cemeteries, Laurel Hill featured works of art by well-known architects and artists, outstanding horticulture, beautiful views, and an impressive array of prominent citizens. Unlike Mount Auburn, however, Laurel Hill was designed to be a "private garden put to semi-public use." As a student and lover of horticulture, and someone intimately familiar with the great private gardens in Philadelphia, John Jay Smith supervised the plantings of additional trees and shrubs, even venturing into the countryside of New Jersey to bring back specimens. As the third rural cemetery in America, and second in a major city, Laurel Hill helped to shape how Philadelphians, and then Americans, would bury their dead for generations. Soon, the city had multiple rural cemeteries, some much closer to its center than Laurel Hill. Thousands of visitors came to the cemetery, both to pay tribute to loved ones and to admire the scenery.

This success led to the purchase of three additional tracts of land. In 1867, the cemetery found itself hemmed in by the Schuylkill River and the newly-created Fairmount Park. After more than 30 years of service, John Jay Smith resigned from the board of managers and moved even farther outside the city of Philadelphia to Montgomery County, where in 1869 he established a new cemetery: West Laurel Hill. While Laurel Hill's lot sales continued throughout the 19th century and into the 20th, the cemetery began a decline that would last another 100 years. Economic downturns and a decline in the surrounding neighborhoods, combined with fewer burials and even fewer lot sales, took their tolls on the cemetery. Age, weather, and vandalism resulted in destroyed monuments and stolen art. The cemetery became overgrown, and its gates were only opened for a few hours each week.

Despite Laurel Hill's condition, it was not totally forgotten. A group of Philadelphia educators began bringing groups of students to the cemetery. John Francis Marion, a local historian and author, began bringing his own groups to the cemetery. The creation of the Friends of Laurel Hill Cemetery in 1978 signaled the beginning of the cemetery's rebirth. While burials and memorialization remain part of the function of Laurel Hill in the 21st century, thousands of visitors now come to the cemetery for tours, concerts, photography, and physical recreation. In an urban environment, the cemetery is a green space and has returned to one of its 19th-century uses—that of a park. Laurel Hill has again become an important part of the cultural fabric of Philadelphia.

One

Origins of Laurel Hill Cemetery

When recounting the inspiration for creating Laurel Hill Cemetery, John Jay Smith recalled the difficulty of locating his daughter's grave in a downtown Quaker burial ground as his main motivation for beginning a new cemetery venture. Smith, an editor and horticulturist, was certainly also aware of the success of Mount Auburn Cemetery (founded in 1831). Whatever the motivators, in November 1835, Smith gathered a group of civically active men to discuss the potential of such a project. This group included former Philadelphia mayor Benjamin W. Richards, merchant Nathan Dunn, and druggist Frederick W. Brown. Also included in the initial meeting were lawyer Thomas I. Wharton, marble mason John Struthers, and architect William Strickland. Wharton declined to participate in the project, but the others decided to pursue the goal of establishing a rural cemetery in Philadelphia. With Smith as the secretary and Nathan Dunn as chairman, the men looked for an appropriate site, and in February 1836, Dunn made the initial purchase of land and financed the initial construction.

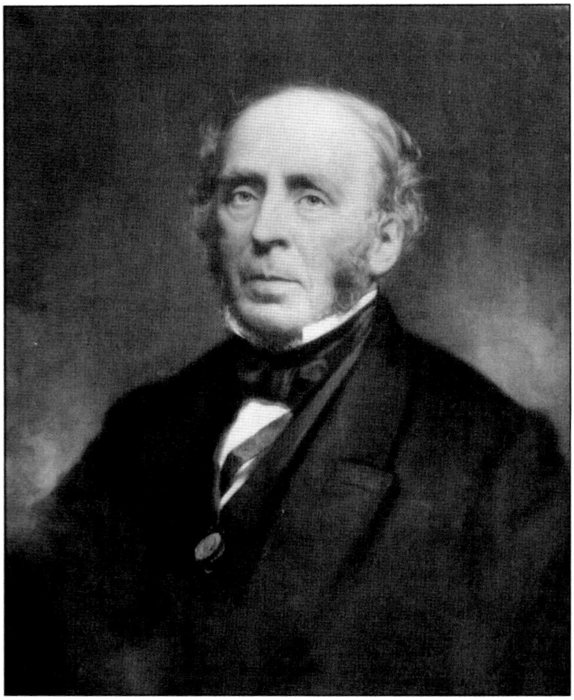

John Jay Smith. The driving force behind the creation of Laurel Hill and West Laurel Hill Cemeteries, Smith (1798–1881) was a librarian, publisher, and horticulturist. He supervised plantings at both cemeteries, served as president of the board of managers, and wrote the early Laurel Hill guidebooks and monument pattern books.

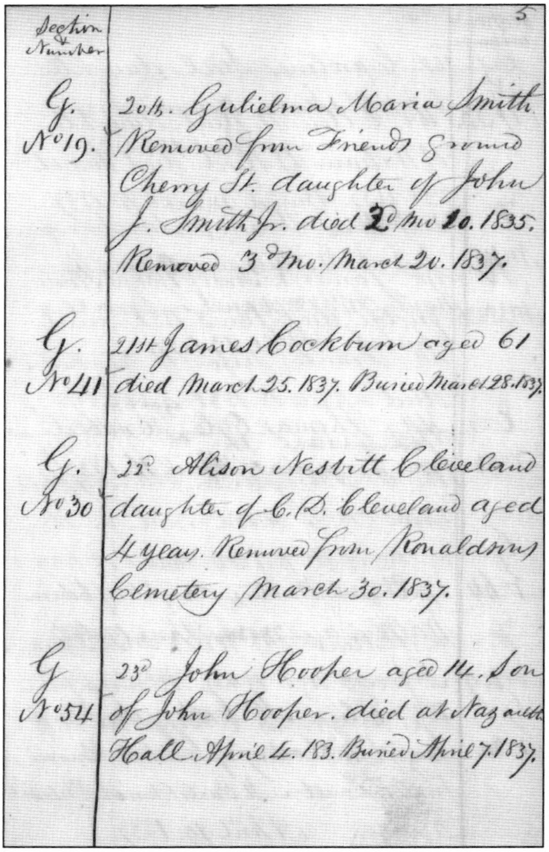

Section & Number

5

G. No 19. 20th. Gulielma Maria Smith Removed from Friends ground Cherry St. daughter of John J. Smith Jr. died 2d mo 10. 1835. Removed 3d mo./March 20. 1837.

G. No 41 21st James Cockburn aged 61 died March 25. 1837. Buried March 28. 1837.

G. No 30 22d Alison Nesbitt Cleveland daughter of C. D. Cleveland aged 4 years. Removed from Ronaldson's Cemetery March 30. 1837.

G No 54 23d John Hooper aged 14. Son of John Hooper. died at Nazareth Hall April 4. 183. Buried April 7. 1837.

Laurel Hill Interment Ledger, 1837. In his diary, John Jay Smith notes that on a visit to a Quaker burial ground in 1835, he "found it impossible to designate the resting place of a darling daughter," which impressed upon him the need for a new kind of cemetery. This Laurel Hill interment ledger shows the reburial of Smith's daughter in 1837. She was moved again to West Laurel Hill following his death.

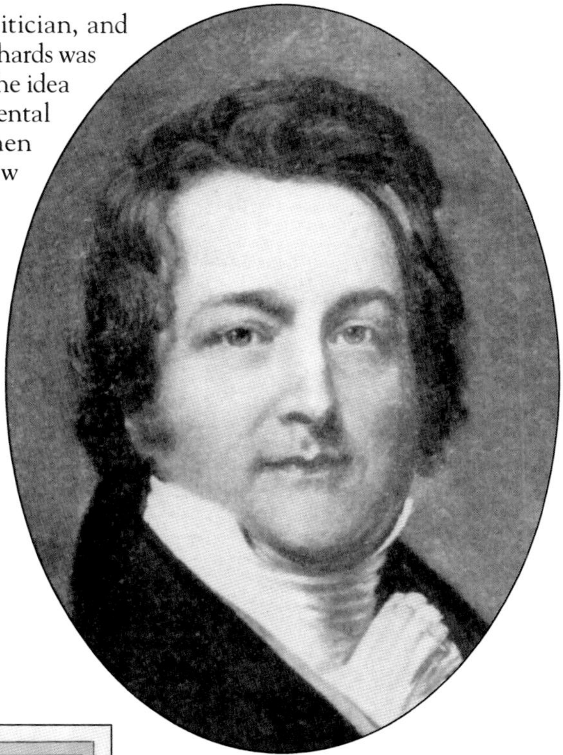

BENJAMIN WOOD RICHARDS. Lawyer, politician, and former Philadelphia mayor Benjamin W. Richards was among the first approached by Smith with the idea for a new cemetery. Richards was instrumental in reaching out to other civic-minded men in the effort to gain support for the new cemetery venture.

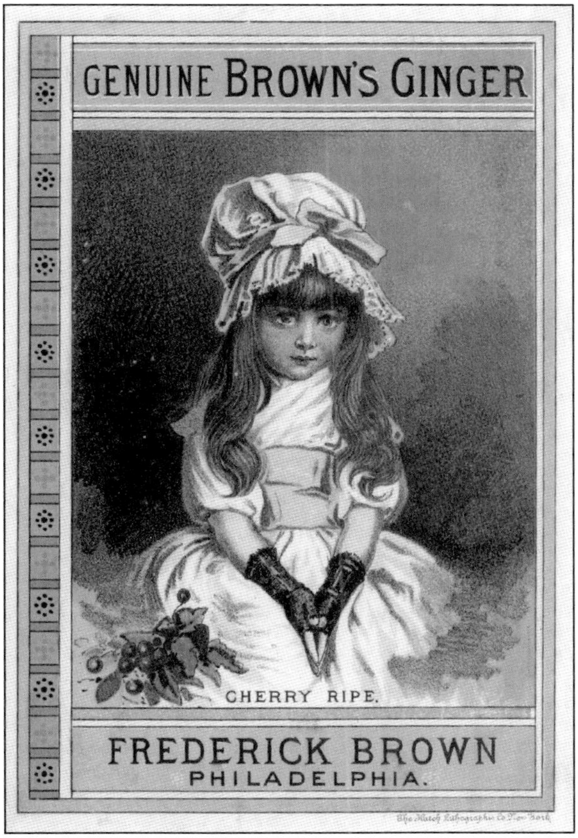

FREDERICK BROWN'S GINGER TRADE CARD, C. 1880. One of the original trustees, Frederick Brown was a druggist and patent medicine dealer whose original shop was located at Fifth and Chestnut Streets. This card claims Brown's Ginger would "make you take interest in life," along with keeping away the chills. (LCP.)

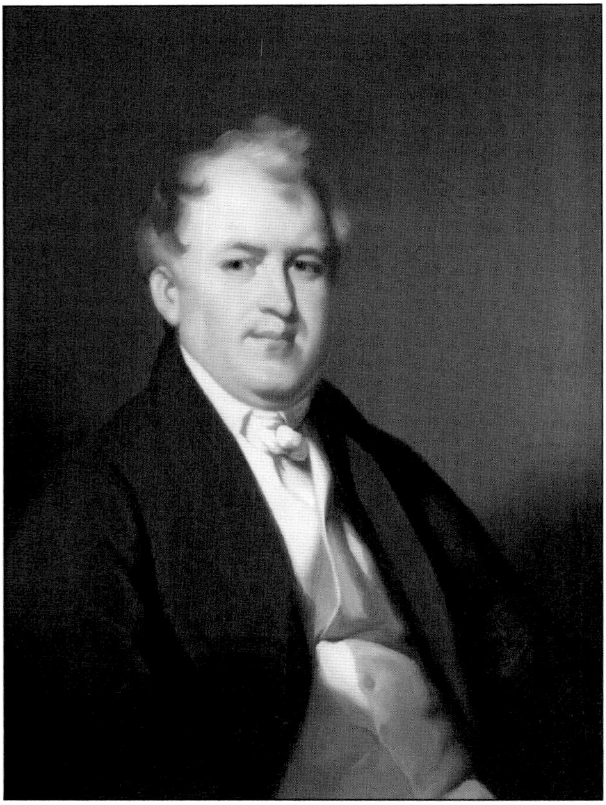

Nathan Dunn, c. 1830. Merchant Nathan Dunn financed much of the early development of Laurel Hill and acted as its first chairman. He was well known for his Chinese museum, which brought his collection of artifacts from China to a new audience in Philadelphia. (1970-89-1, Gift of Mrs. Joseph H. Gaskill, 1970, Philadelphia Museum of Art.)

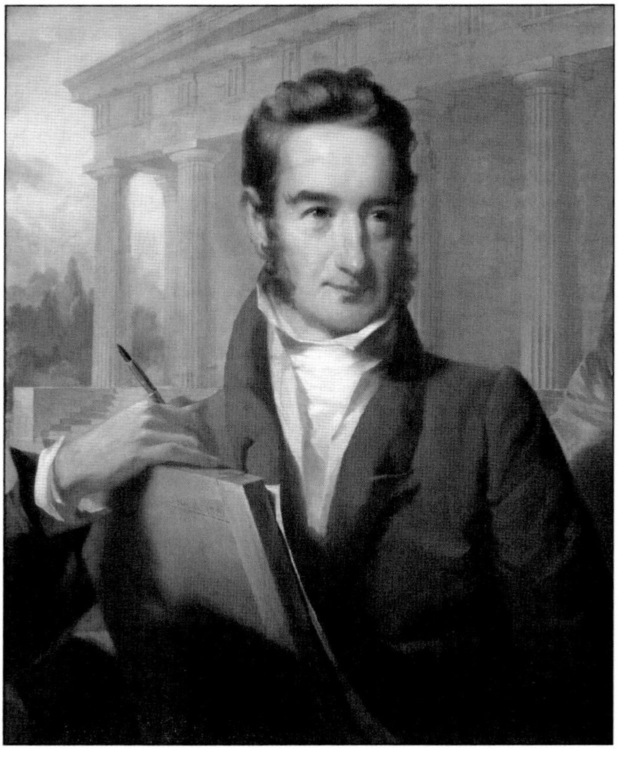

William Strickland, 1829. Architect William Strickland was involved in the earliest planning of Philadelphia's first rural cemetery; however, his design for the layout of the cemetery and gatehouse was rejected in favor of John Notman's. One of his last commissions was the Tennessee State Capitol. When he died in 1854, his body was placed in a crypt on the building's north wall. While Strickland is not buried at Laurel Hill, his family is. (Yale University Art Gallery.)

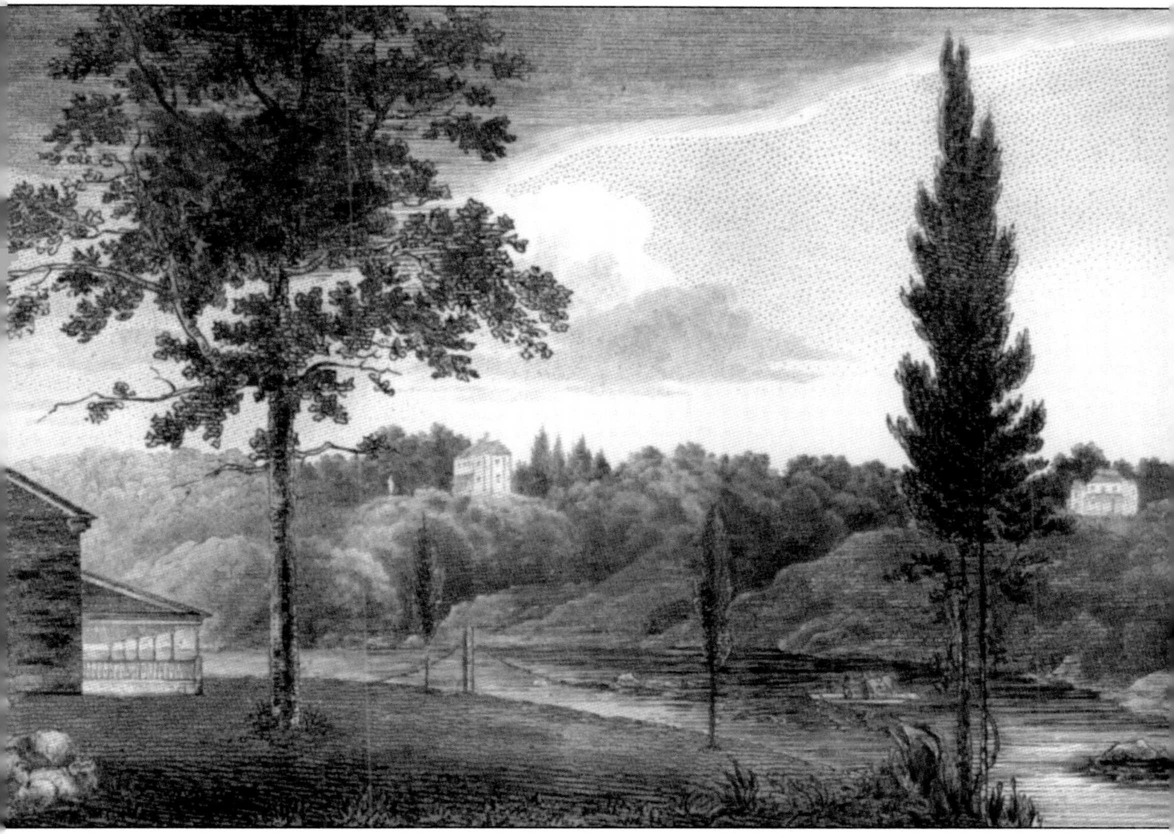

MENDENHALL FERRY, 1808. In the early 19th century, wealthy Philadelphians frequently owned estates in the countryside where they could escape the heat and bustle of the growing city. This engraving by William Birch depicts the country seats of Joseph Sims (left) and William Raele (right), both of which would eventually become part of Laurel Hill Cemetery. In the foreground is the Mendenhall Ferry, which was located across from the lane that ran between the Sims and Raele estates and led to Ridge Pike. (NYPL.)

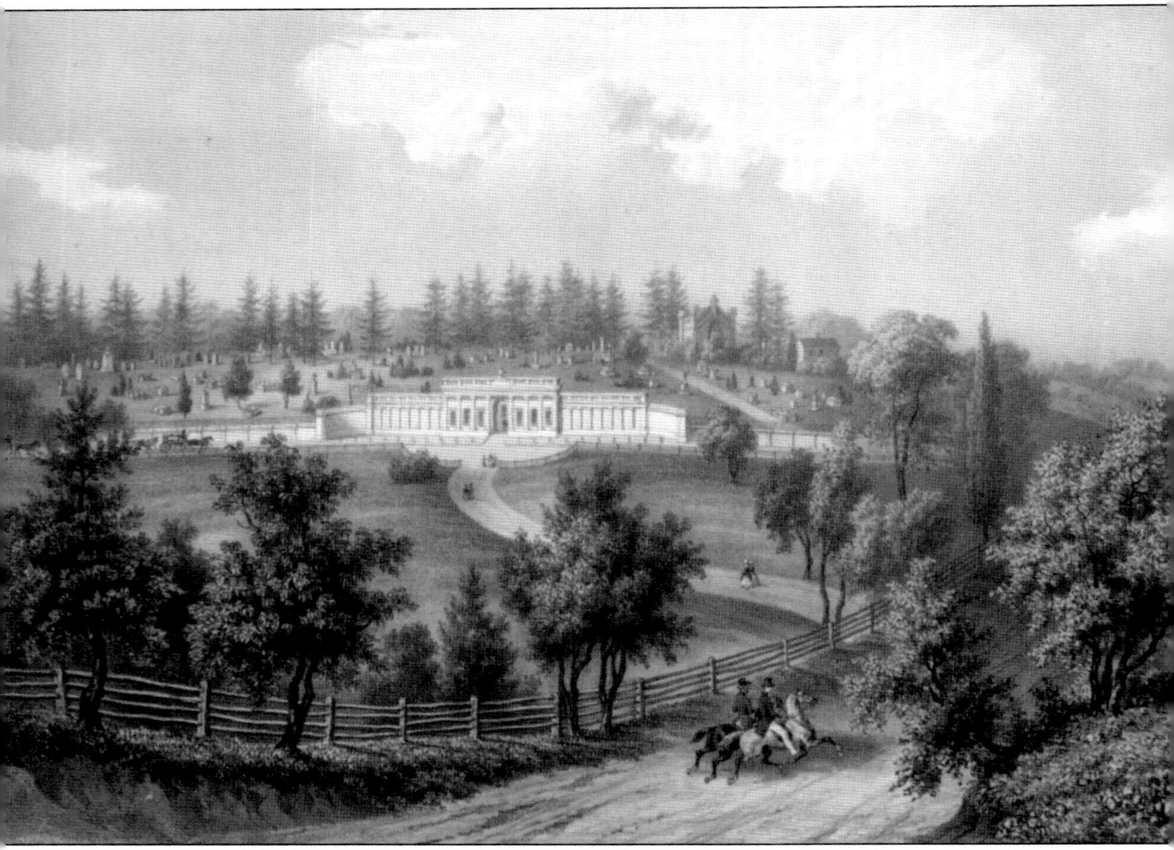

Lithograph of Laurel Hill Cemetery, c. 1848. This drawing by Augustus Köllner shows the roads leading to the cemetery's gatehouse, designed by John Notman. Within the cemetery, monuments are visible, as are the chapel and superintendent's house, which once stood in North Laurel Hill. (LOC.)

Two

North Laurel Hill

In looking for an appropriate site for the new cemetery, the founders sought a space far enough outside the city to prevent immediate encroachment yet close enough for funeral processions to reach it easily. It also needed to have geographical elements suitable for the creation of a picturesque site. After discovering that William Hamilton's estate, the Woodlands, was unavailable and that two others were unsuitable, the founders chose the 32-acre country seat of merchant Joseph Sims, which Nathan Dunn purchased for $15,200.

The former Sims property, known as "Laurel" or "Laurel Hill," had changed owners and uses several times in its history. It was rented as a farm and tavern, and in 1834 served as a Catholic boys' school. William Strickland and Thomas Ustick Walter were among the architects to submit designs for the new cemetery, but it was the Scottish architect John Notman whose design was selected. Notman's design for the cemetery included a gatehouse, superintendent's house, and chapel, along with paths and roadways. The cemetery retained the Sims mansion, stables, carriage house, and greenhouse. Surveyor Philip M. Price laid out Notman's design, which was likely inspired in part by Henry E. Kendall's plan for Kensal Green Cemetery near London. John Jay Smith completed the design with the addition of hundreds of new trees and shrubs. On October 19, 1836, the first burial occurred, that of a Quaker woman, Mercy Carlisle. By 1838, nearly half of the original surveyed lots had been sold. Additional burial space was created by demolishing the Sims mansion in 1844, but Laurel Hill needed additional space to continue to generate revenue.

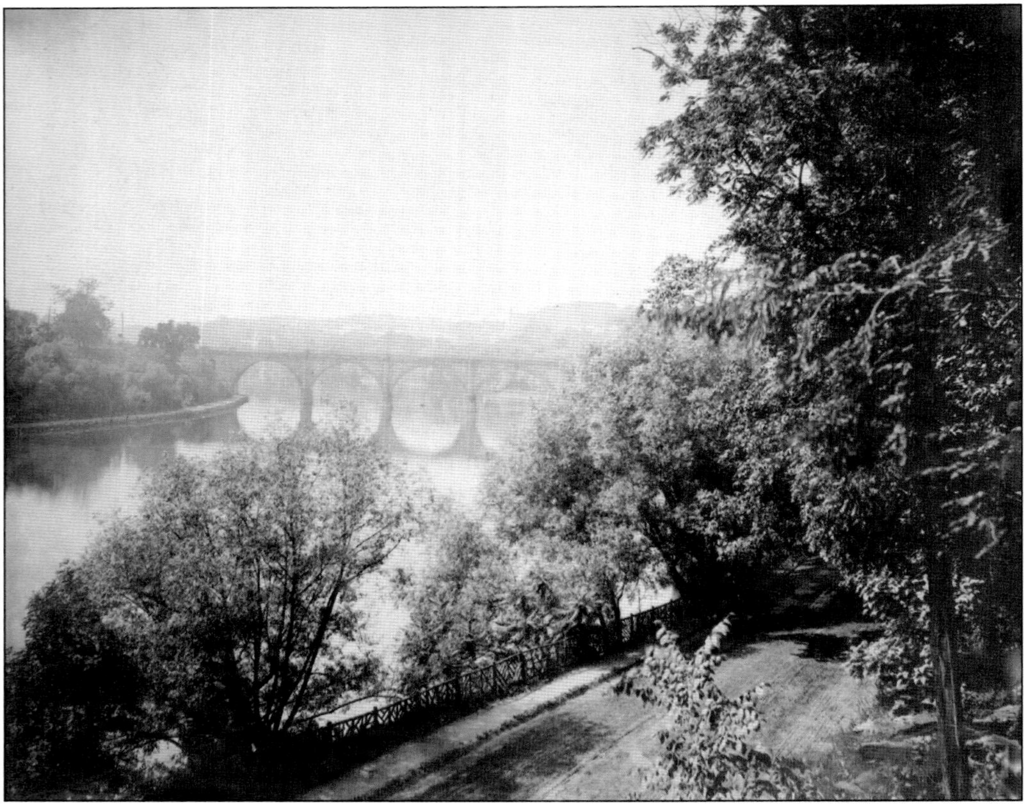

River View from North Laurel Hill, c. 1890. One of the required characteristics of American rural cemeteries was picturesque landscapes. With exceptional views of the Schuylkill River among its attributes, Laurel Hill was no exception. This image shows the upriver view from North Laurel Hill.

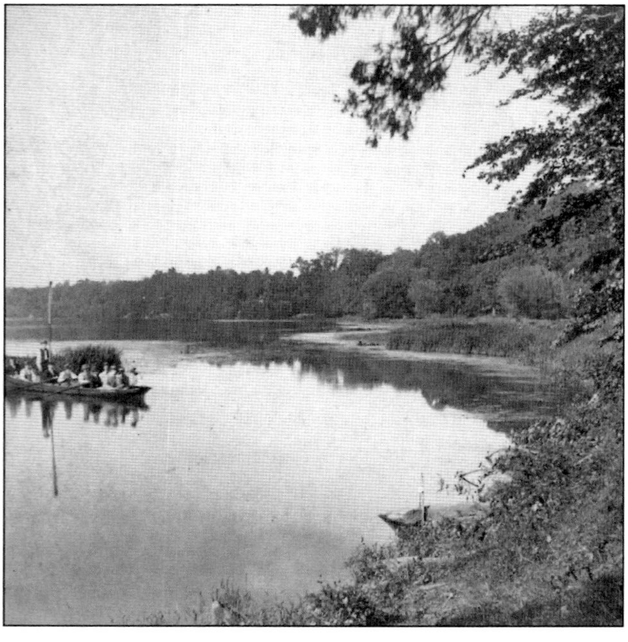

Landing on the Schuylkill River. Easy transportation to the cemetery was a requirement. In the years before Laurel Hill, steamboats made regular runs to landings along the Schuylkill River. The cemetery's main landing was located at the end of Nicetown Lane. While lot holders and visitors experienced a tranquil and leisurely ride down the river, once they reached the landing, they faced a difficult uphill trek to the cemetery.

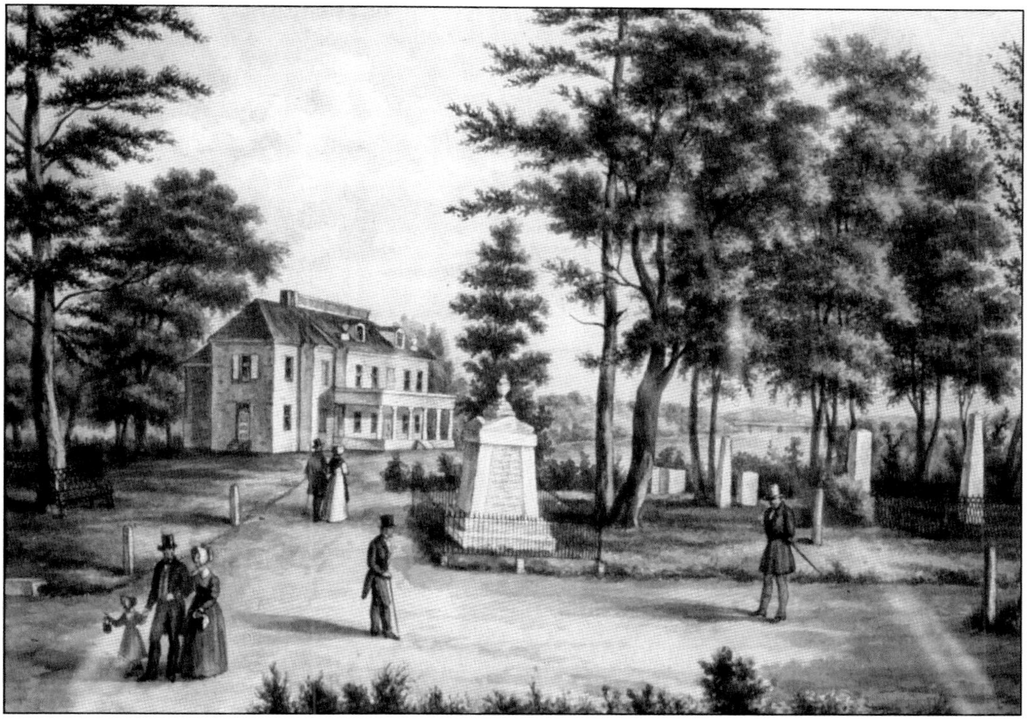

SIMS MANSION, 1841. This lithograph offers a rare glimpse of the Sims mansion, with the Mercer monument in the foreground. Cemetery managers initially elected to keep several buildings belonging to the estate, but by 1844, they voted to demolish the mansion, which was in a state of disrepair. Its woodwork was sold at auction, its stone was used to create terraces in Section S, and its basement was used for underground vaults.

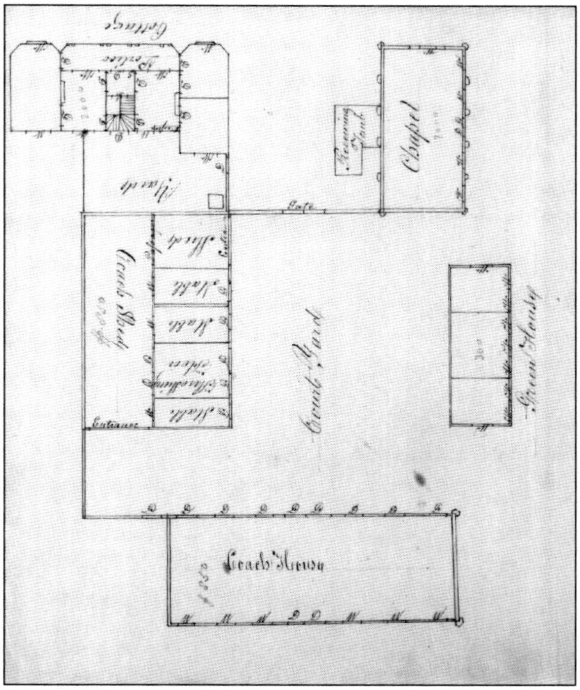

FRANKLIN FIRE INSURANCE POLICY, 1837. This insurance document shows the Sims property buildings, along with the newer additions made by the cemetery. The coach house, stables, and greenhouse were all part of the estate; however, most of these buildings were destroyed by fire in 1840. The chapel also likely preexisted the cemetery, but Notman made some alterations to the building, including the addition of a receiving tomb.

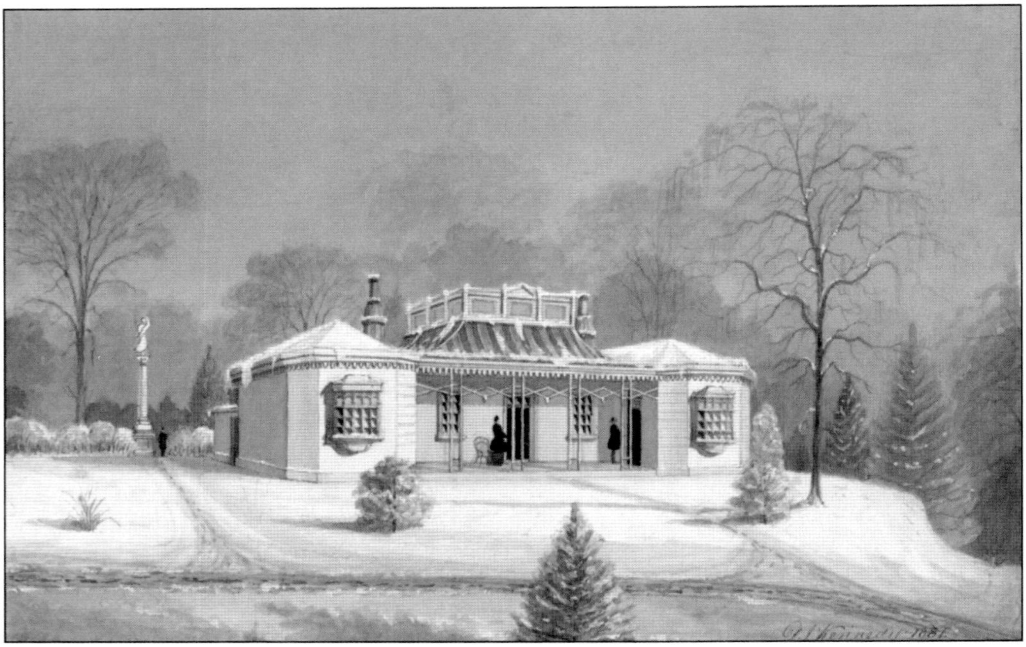

COTTAGE AND OFFICE AT NORTH LAUREL HILL. John Notman's original design for the cemetery included a cottage for Supt. Thomas Drinnan and his family. Done in a vaguely Oriental style, the cottage stood until the late 1840s, when it was demolished to create more space for burials. (HSP.)

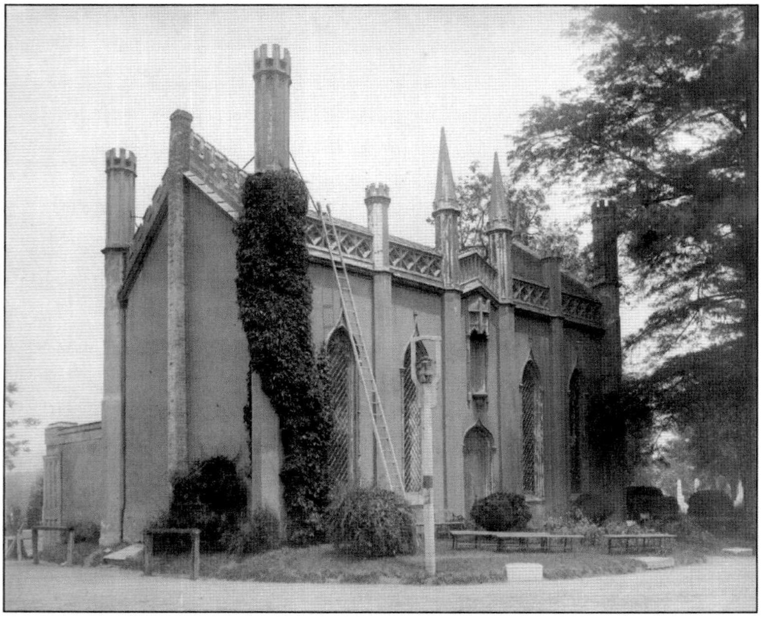

LAUREL HILL CHAPEL, C. 1880. Completed in 1838, this Gothic Revival chapel stood in what is now the Chapel Section of North Laurel Hill. Likely a redesign of an earlier structure, John Notman's alterations included a receiving tomb adjoining the rear wall. The chapel was used until 1884, when it was torn down to make room for additional burial space.

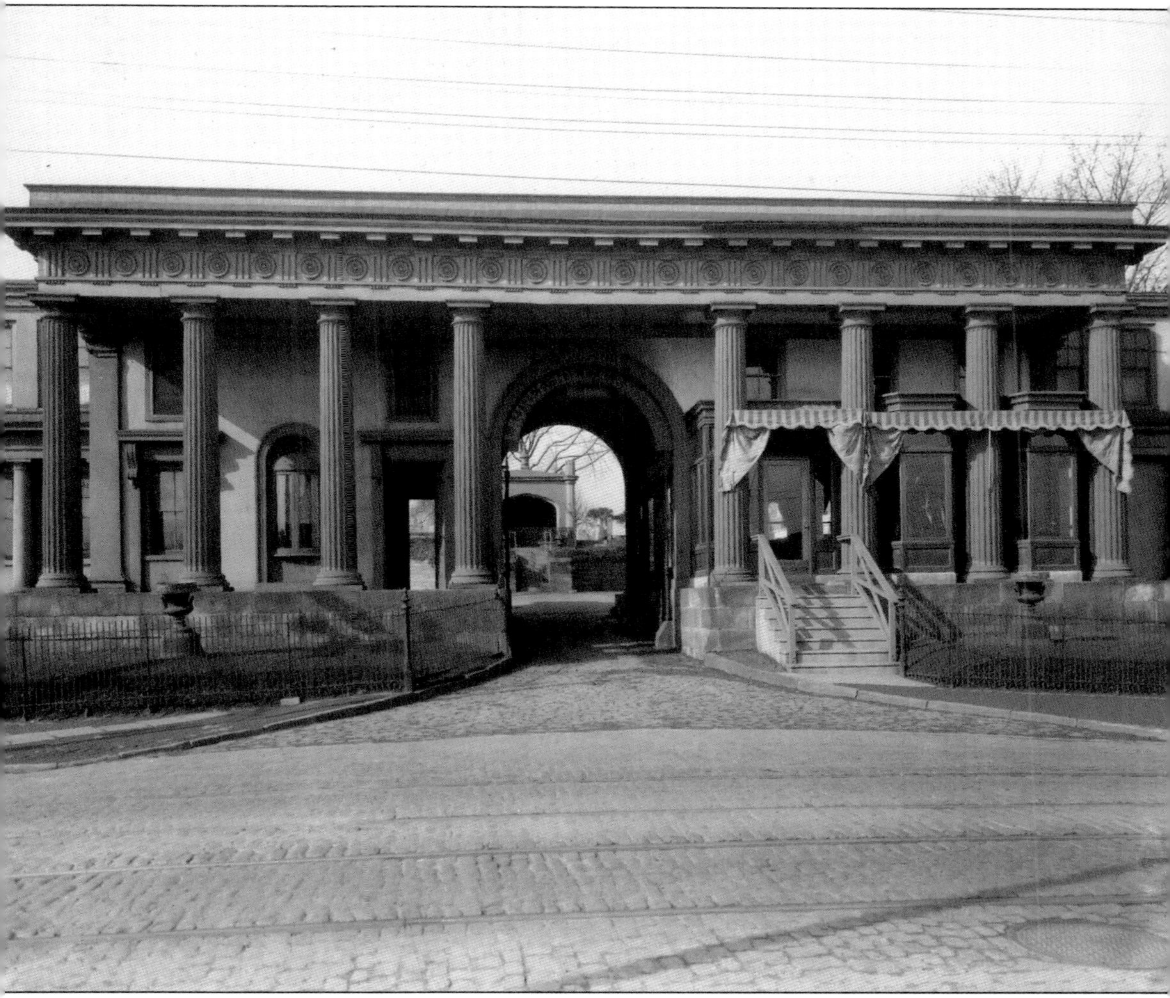

North Laurel Hill Gatehouse, 1927. The gatehouse, constructed in 1836, remains Notman's grandest contribution to the design of Laurel Hill. Originally housing a gardener's lodge and porter's lodge, the Roman Doric structure featured an arched passageway through the middle of the building. A large urn (now missing) on top defined the function of the space as a cemetery, and the building was flanked by two elevated walkways. Over time, significant renovations have altered the space, and it now houses an apartment and the cemetery's office. The gatehouse remains the primary entrance to the cemetery, welcoming visitors arriving on Ridge Avenue.

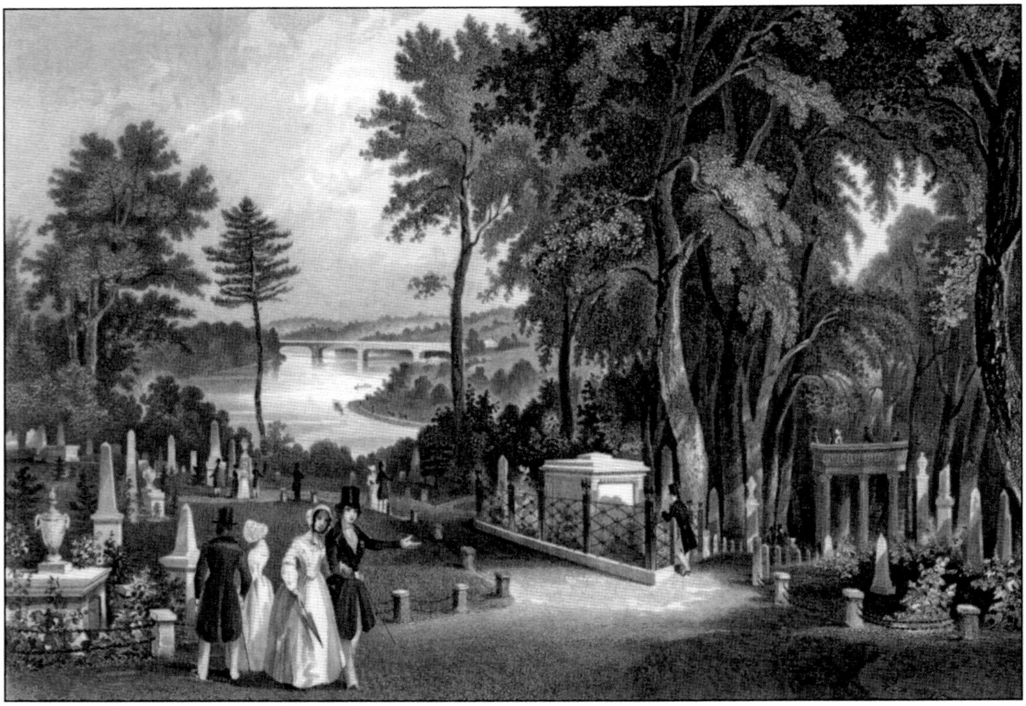

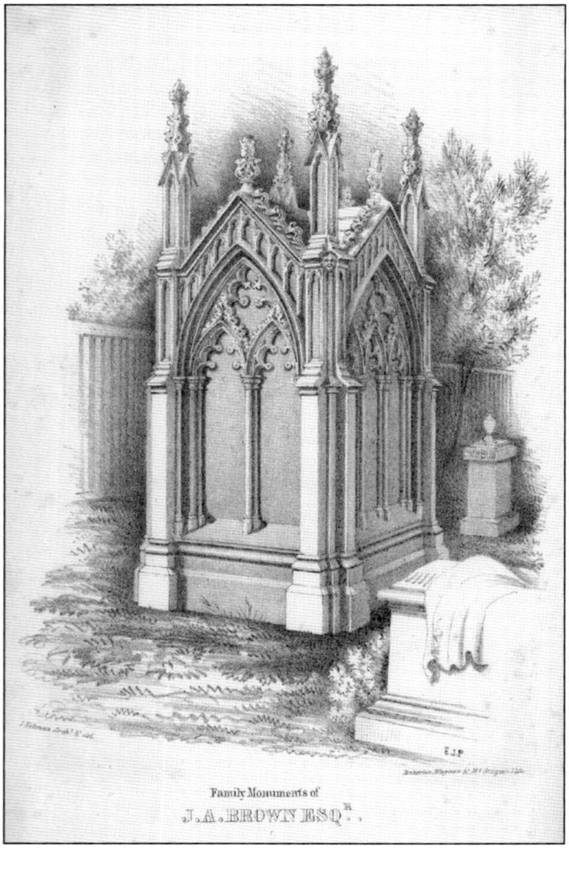

ENGRAVING IN *GODEY'S LADY'S BOOK*, 1844. In this illustration that appeared in the March 1844 edition of *Godey's Lady's Book*, visitors are shown strolling along the cemetery's paths amid beautiful trees and flowers. On the right is the observatory tower. This structure was a gazebo with an upper level that provided excellent views of the river. It was removed by 1850.

SKETCH OF BROWN MEMORIAL, 1844. John Jay Smith's *Guide to Laurel Hill Cemetery, near Philadelphia* acted both as a tour guidebook to attract visitors and a way to influence monument choices. With monuments designed by Notman, Struthers, and J.M. Hamilton, Smith hoped to cultivate a kind of sculpture gallery, and to avoid the dull uniformity of a cemetery of obelisks.

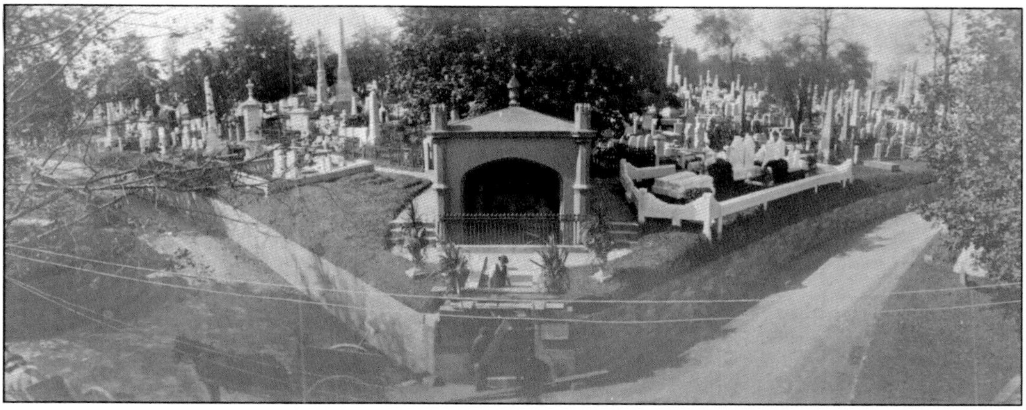

Old Mortality, 1903 (above) and 1910 (below). Designed by Scottish artist James Thom and purchased by the cemetery in 1837, the sculpture of *Old Mortality and His Pony* still greets visitors entering Laurel Hill through the gatehouse archway. The sculpture served both as an attraction for visitors and a symbol of the cemetery's commitment to maintaining a permanent space for the dead. The canopy that shelters the group was part of Notman's original cemetery design.

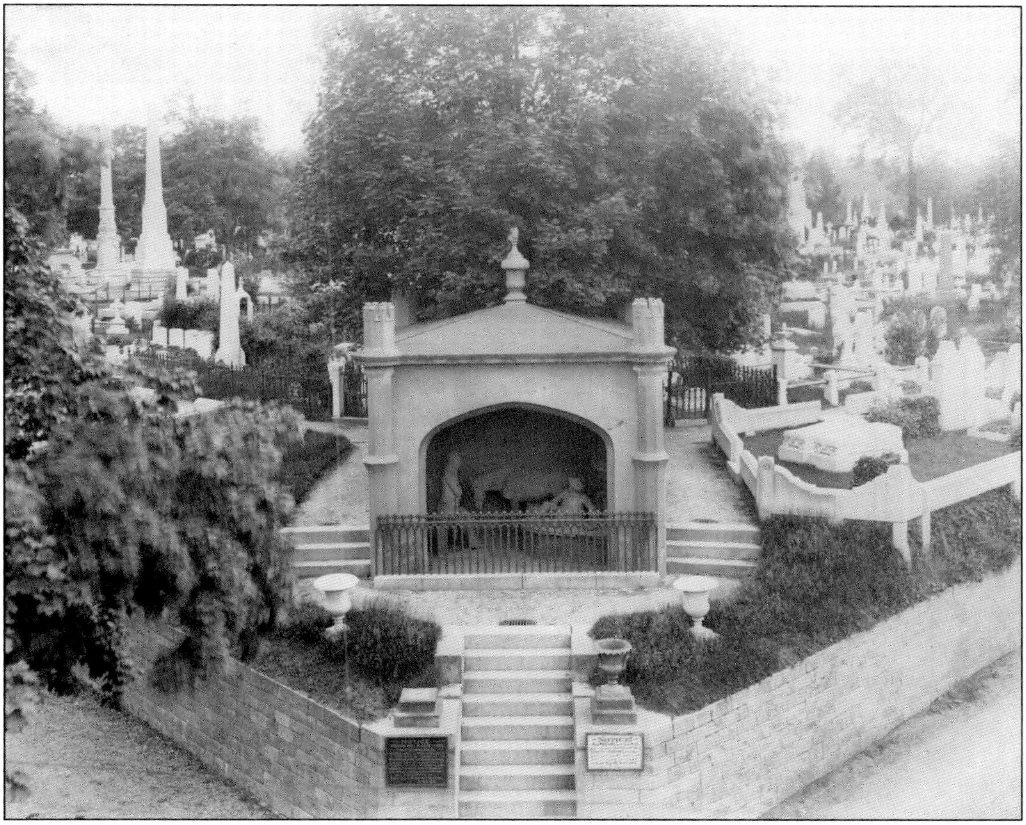

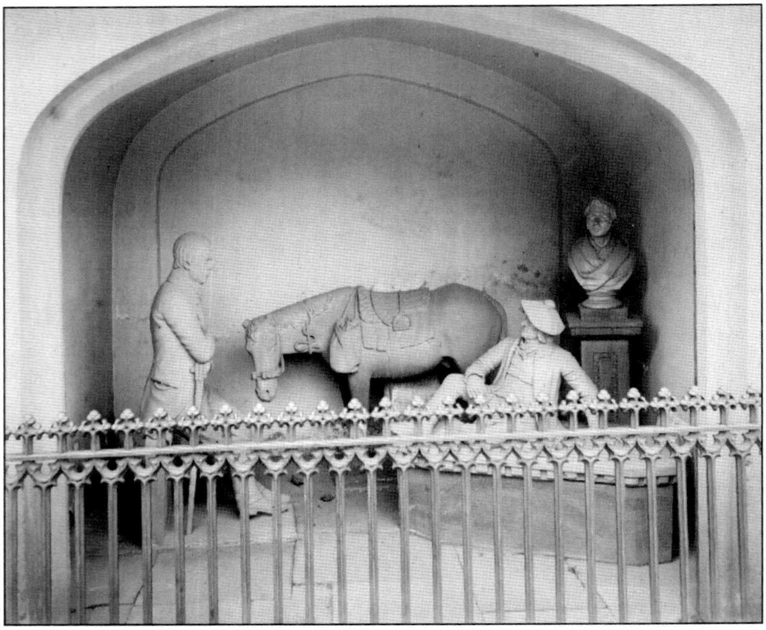

OLD MORTALITY, c. 1890. The scene depicts the story of the stone carver "Old Mortality," as told by Sir Walter Scott. In the tale, Old Mortality travels around Scotland re-carving inscriptions for murdered Presbyterians so they would never be forgotten. Thom brought the statues to America, but the pony was broken in transit and had to be re-carved prior to installation.

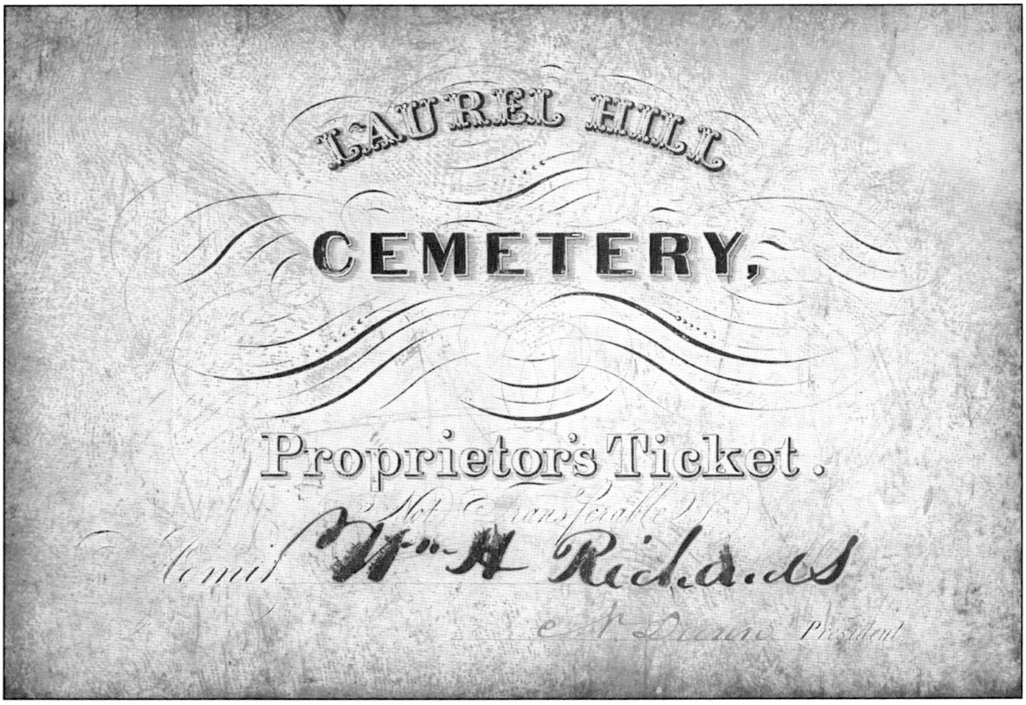

LAUREL HILL CEMETERY PROPRIETOR'S TICKET. In the 1840s, thousands of visitors came to Laurel Hill. The cemetery's managers became increasingly concerned about the number of "casual visitors" wandering through the cemetery until 1847, when it was decided to restrict weekend admittance to funerals and lot owners, who were issued an official ticket for admission.

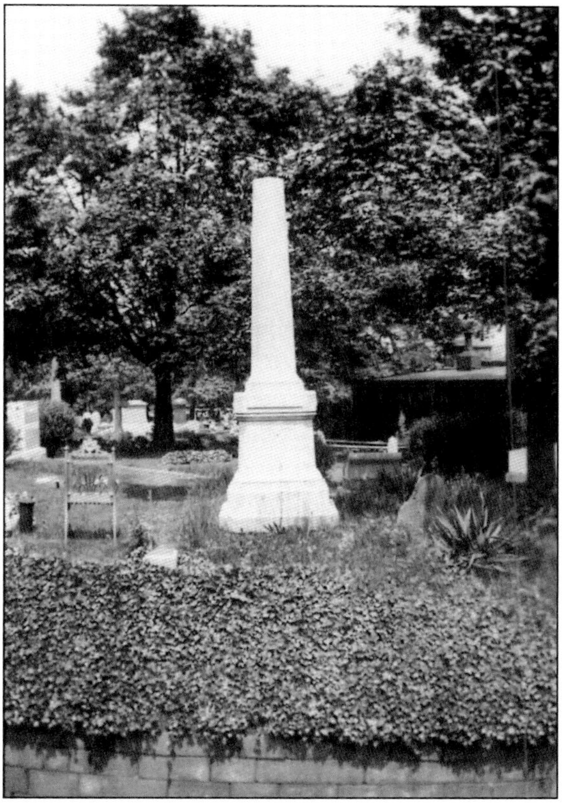

THOMAS GODFREY OBELISK, 1929. Thomas Godfrey was a glazier and mathematician. Around 1730, independently of each other, he and English mathematician John Hadley invented the octant, or mariner's quadrant. In 1838, Godfrey's remains, along with those of his parents, were moved to Laurel Hill from the farm in Germantown where they were originally buried.

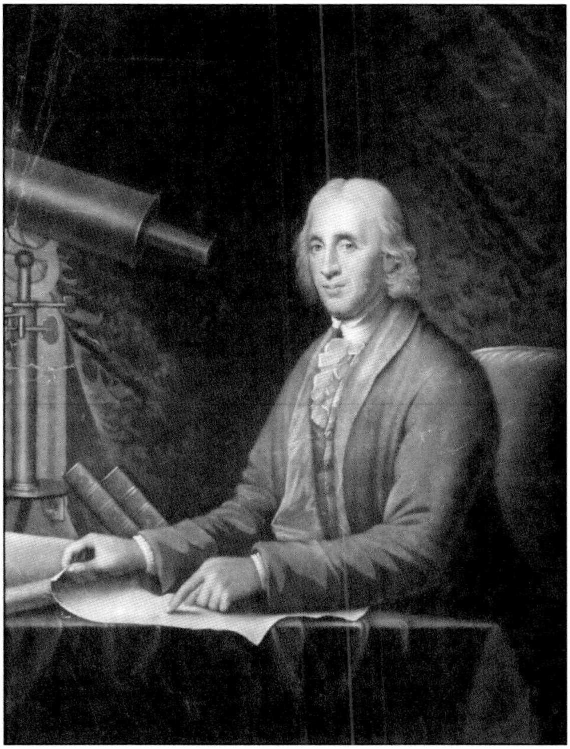

DAVID RITTENHOUSE PORTRAIT, 1796. One of the most prominent men of science in the 18th century, David Rittenhouse was a clockmaker, mathematician, and astronomer. Rittenhouse and Thomas Godfrey were to be two of the four scientific giants of Philadelphia honored by an enormous pyramid that was to stand in North Laurel Hill. The proposal failed, and the monument was never built. (NYPL.)

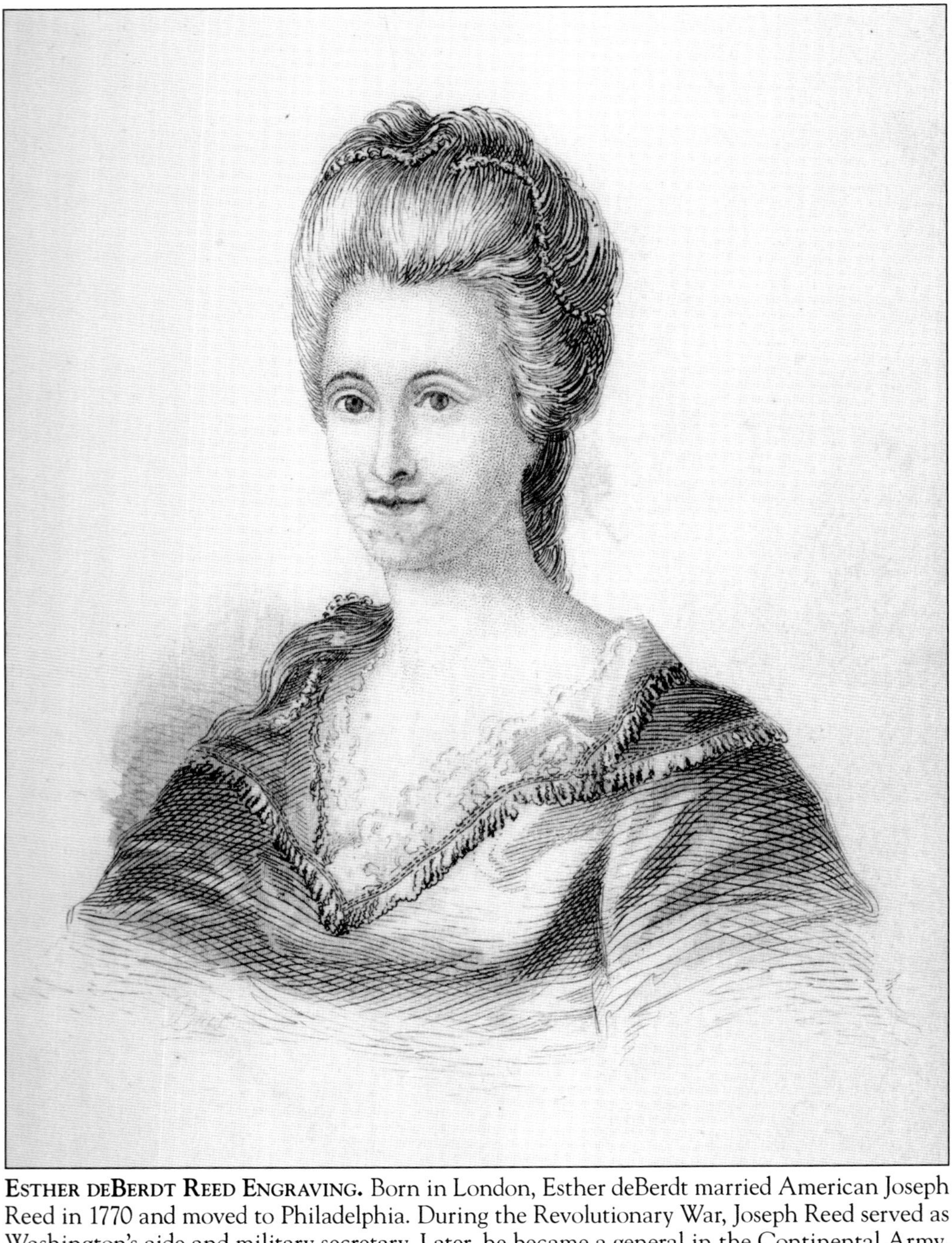

Esther deBerdt Reed Engraving. Born in London, Esther deBerdt married American Joseph Reed in 1770 and moved to Philadelphia. During the Revolutionary War, Joseph Reed served as Washington's aide and military secretary. Later, he became a general in the Continental Army. In 1778, Esther formed the Ladies of Philadelphia, an organization created to raise funds to help Washington's army. Walking door to door, they raised $300,000 in Continental currency. Esther wrote to Washington to tell him of her plan to give the money directly to the soldiers, but he urged her to put the money toward something the soldiers needed. She took his advice, and the women bought linen and sewing supplies to make new shirts for the men. Esther did not live to see the completion of the project. She died in September 1780, and was buried in the Second Presbyterian Churchyard. In 1868, Esther and Joseph's bodies were reinterred in Laurel Hill. (LCP).

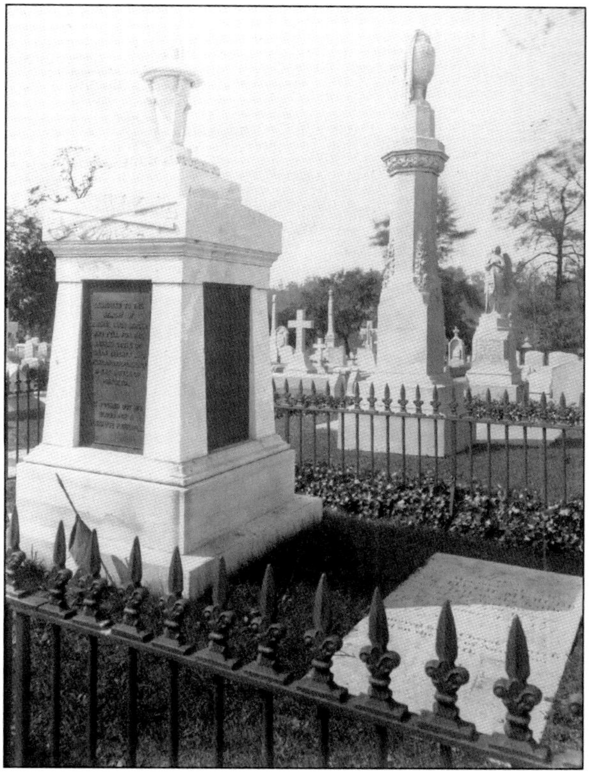

Gen. Hugh Mercer Memorial, 1928. Hugh Mercer was a physician and soldier who became a brigadier general in the Continental Army. He died on January 12, 1777, of wounds received at the Battle of Princeton. Originally buried at Christ Church Burial Ground in Philadelphia, his removal to Laurel Hill in 1840 was accompanied by a great deal of ceremony and publicity for the cemetery.

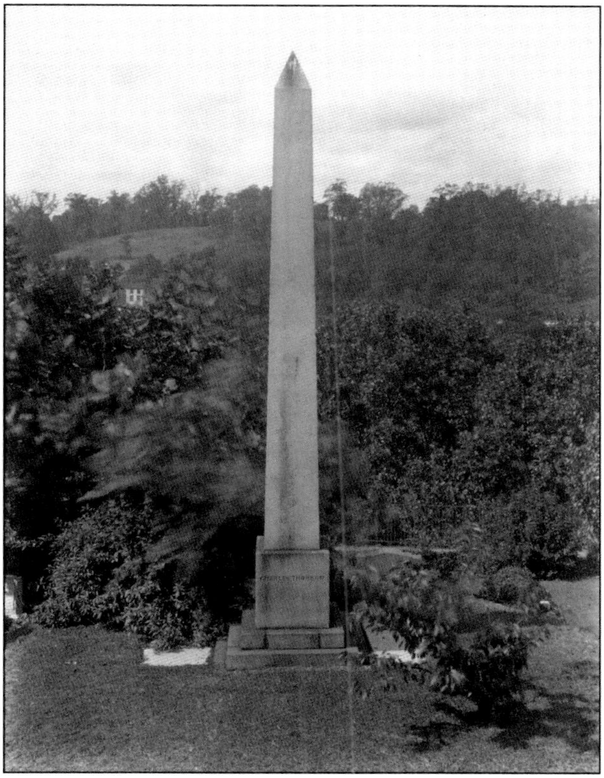

Charles Thomson Memorial, 1928. Laurel Hill's founders wanted to create a space of cultural and historical relevance and prestige. One way they attempted to do this was to transfer the bones of the famous dead from other areas. Charles Thomson, a leader in the American Revolution and secretary of the Continental Congress, was moved to Laurel Hill in 1838. A five-ton obelisk was installed to mark his lot.

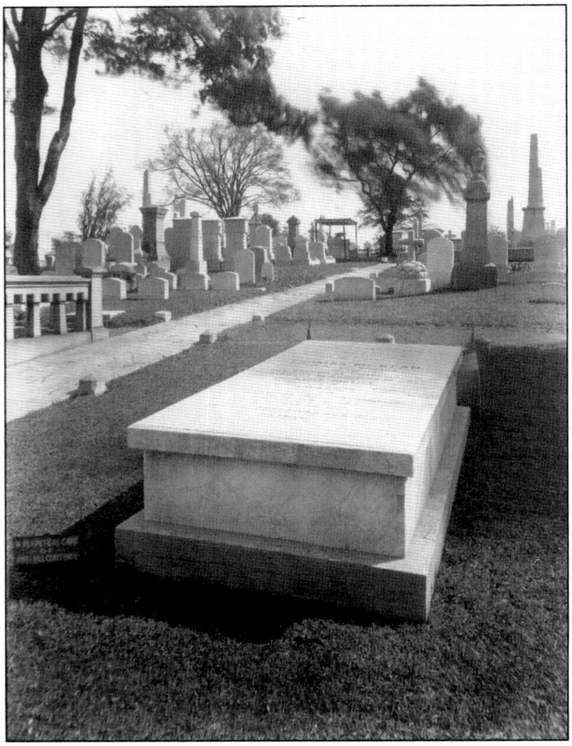

THOMAS MCKEAN MEMORIAL, 1928. Political leader Thomas McKean was born in Pennsylvania in 1734. As a member of the Continental Congress, McKean was a signer of the Declaration of Independence. He was a colonel in the Revolutionary War and played an important role in the drafting of the Delaware and Pennsylvania constitutions. McKean died in 1817 and was moved to Laurel Hill in 1843.

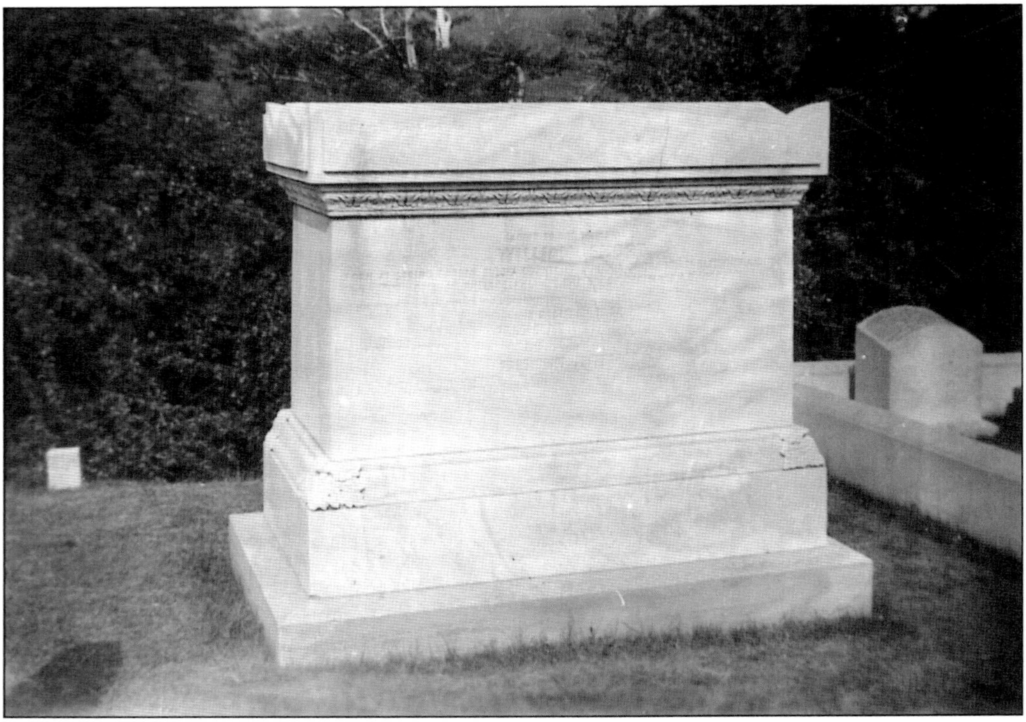

WILLIAM SHORT MEMORIAL, 1929. The man Thomas Jefferson referred to as his "adoptive son," William Short, was a lawyer who served as Jefferson's private secretary during his years in France. Short and Jefferson maintained a lifelong friendship, corresponding on a wide range of topics.

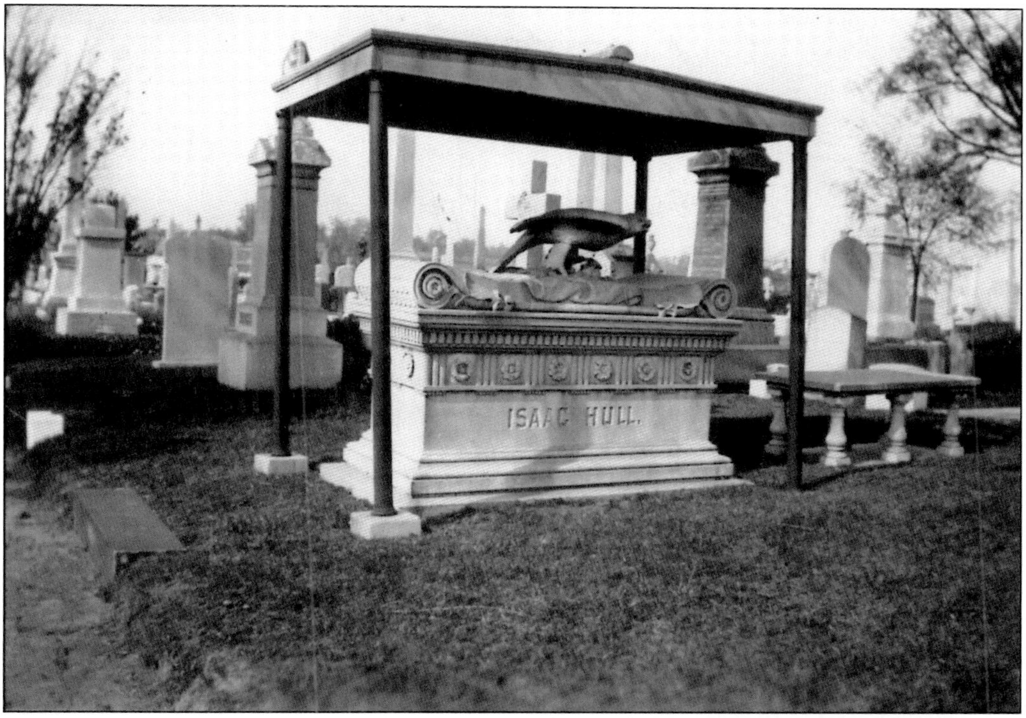

COMMODORE ISAAC HULL MEMORIAL (1921) AND PORTRAIT (C. 1813). One of the most distinctive monuments in North Laurel Hill belongs to Commodore Isaac Hull. Designed by William Strickland and executed by John Struthers, it shows an eagle perched on top of a sarcophagus. Born in 1773, Hull spent time at sea with his father, a Revolutionary War naval veteran. In 1798, he joined the US Navy and, during the War of 1812, earned fame as commander of the USS *Constitution*, or "Old Ironsides." (Right, LOC.)

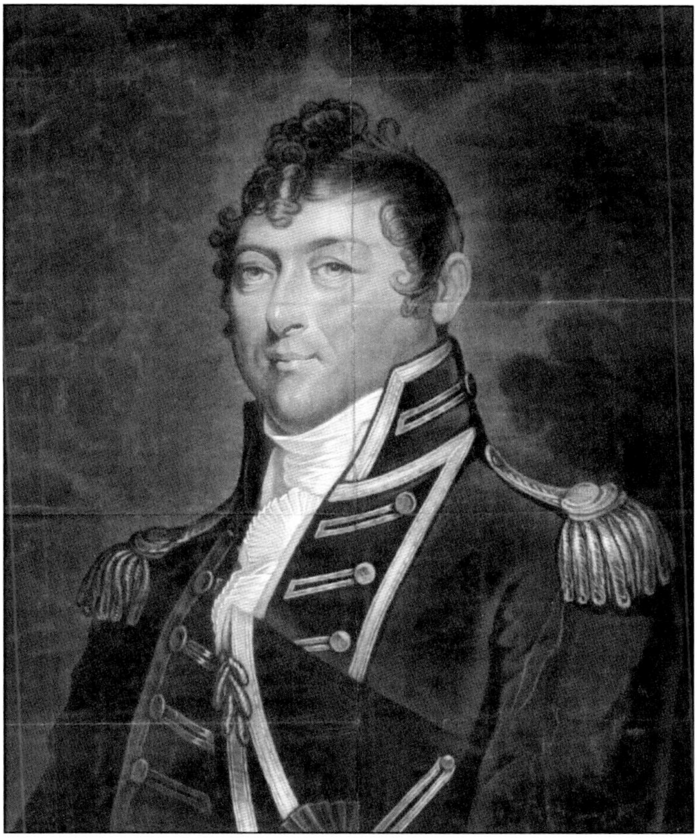

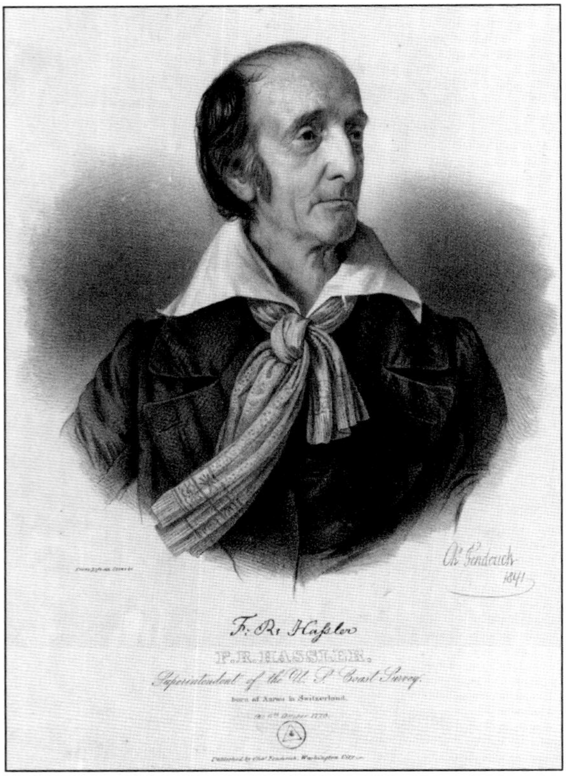

FERDINAND HASSLER PORTRAIT (1841) AND MONUMENT (1929). Born in Switzerland, Ferdinand Hassler came to the United States in 1805. In 1816, he was appointed first superintendent of the US Survey of the Coast, only to be removed from that position two years later. Under the direction of Pres. Andrew Jackson, Hassler became head of the Bureau of Weights and Measures, where he began the work of establishing the standards for weights and measures in the United States. In 1832, Hassler was again appointed superintendent of the survey, a post he held until his death in 1843. (Left, LOC).

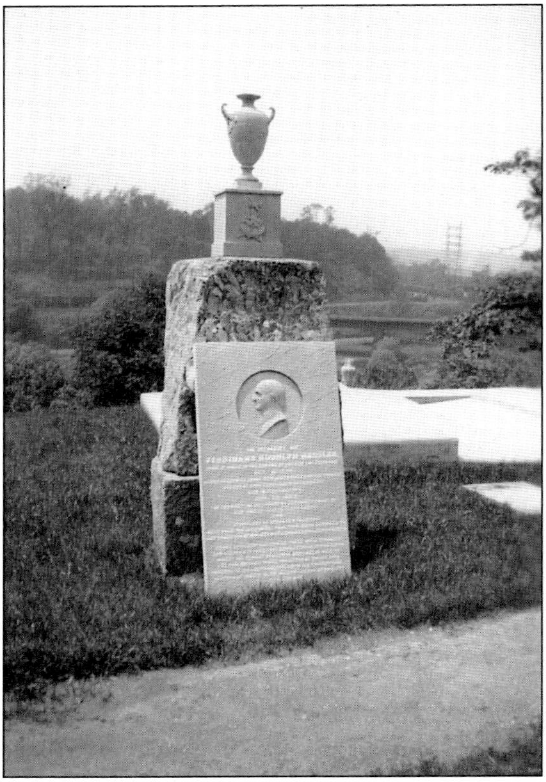

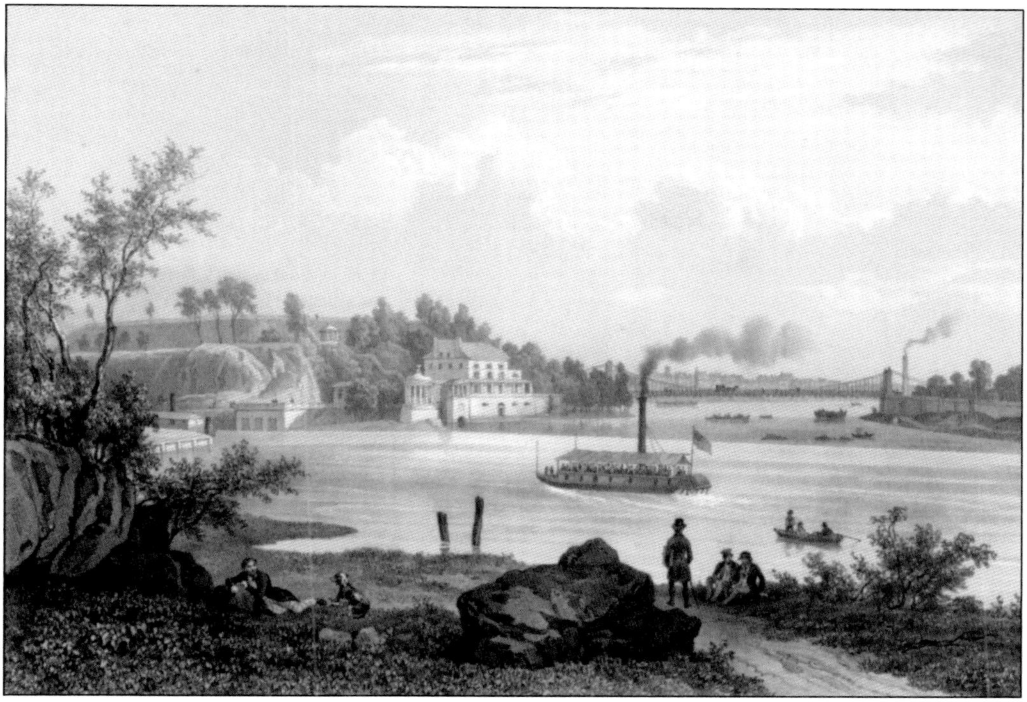

Fairmount Water Works and Monument to Frederick Graff. Two men buried in Laurel Hill played important roles in establishing Philadelphia's Fairmount Water Works: Joseph S. Lewis and Frederick Graff. With the city growing, there was a need for additional water pumping facilities. When the Fairmount Water Works opened in 1815, it was the most advanced municipal water system in the country. Joseph S. Lewis provided much of the financial support for the project. Frederick Graff was an engineer and architect who designed the Water Works' efficient hydraulic system and most of the buildings. He spent his entire career with the Water Works. (Above, LOC; below, NYPL.)

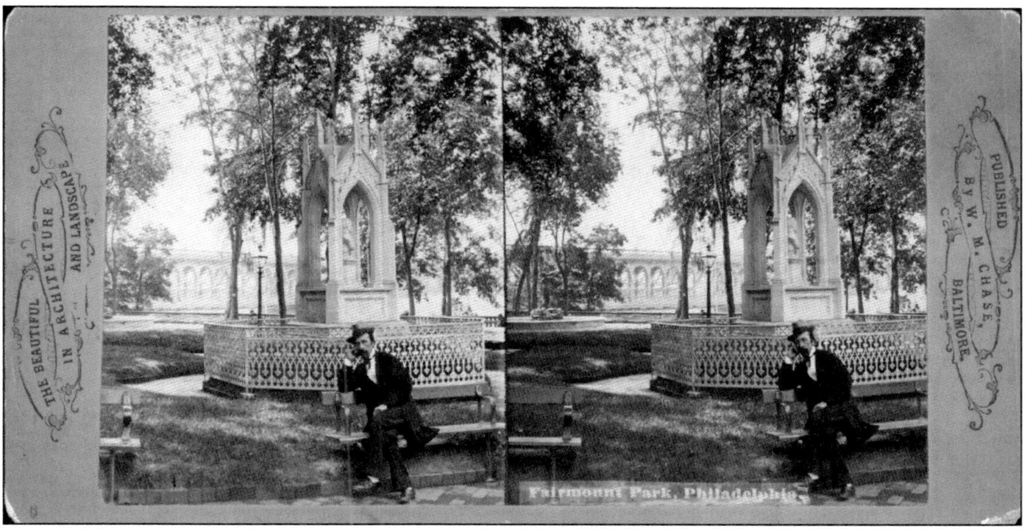

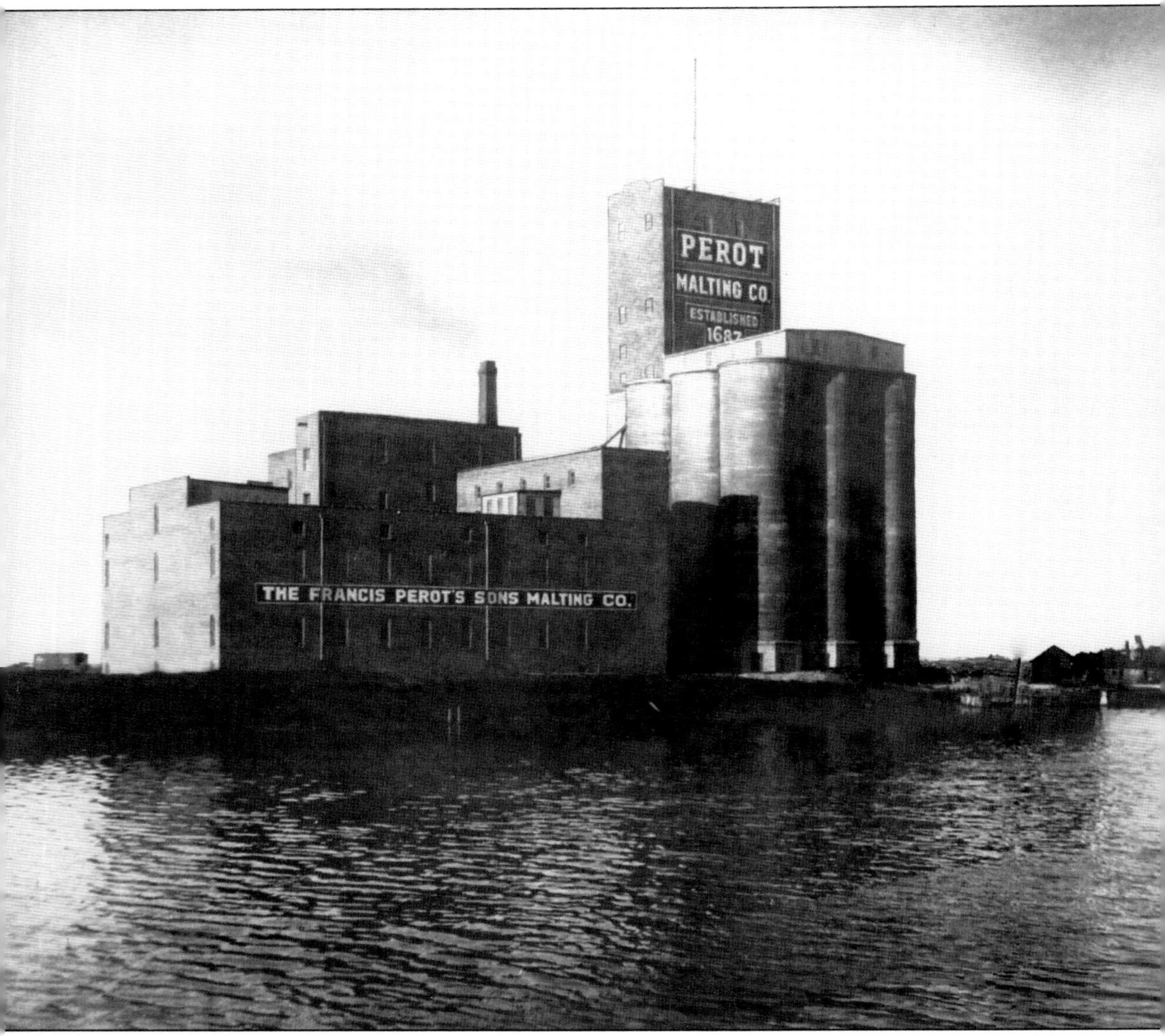

Francis Perot's Sons Malting Company. Born in Philadelphia in 1796, Francis Perot apprenticed to brewer Thomas Morris before opening his own brewing and malting plant in 1818. Perot married Elizabeth Morris in 1823, and his company later absorbed her father-in-law's brewery. Perot's sons joined the business, which existed until it was sold to E.P. Taylor, owner of Canadian Breweries Ltd., in 1963. (HSP.)

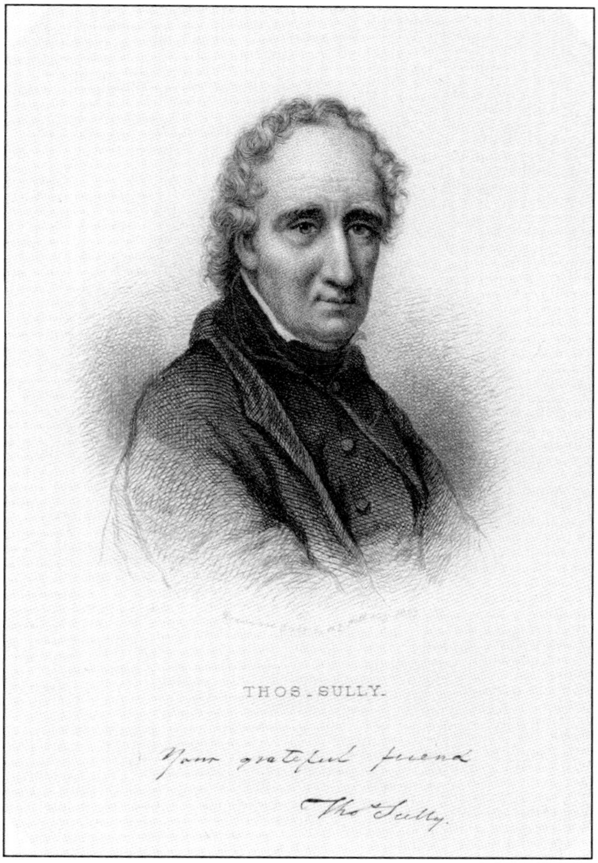

THOMAS SULLY PORTRAIT, 1869. Born in England but raised in South Carolina, Thomas Sully was a painter who created more than 2,000 works. Among these were landscapes and historical scenes, portraits of political figures, actors, musicians, and ordinary well-to-do citizens. After 1855, he struggled financially, so in 1867, the Pennsylvania Academy of the Fine Arts granted him a yearly stipend that continued until his death in 1872. (NYPL.)

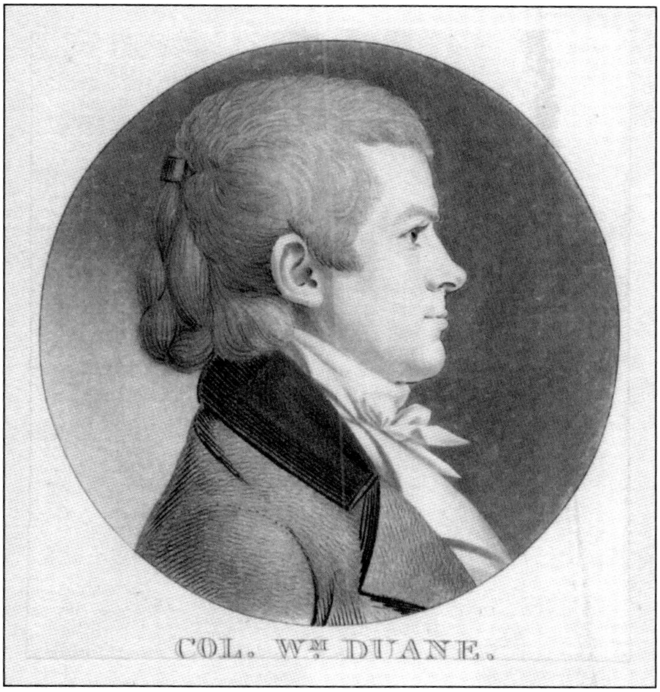

COLONEL WILLIAM DUANE PORTRAIT, 1802. Irishman William Duane was editor of the newspaper *Aurora*, one of the leading papers in the country. He was credited by Thomas Jefferson (and Jefferson's enemies) as being a major factor in Jefferson's election as president in 1801. Duane served as the Army's adjutant general in the War of 1812, and his son William John Duane served briefly as US treasury secretary. (NYPL.)

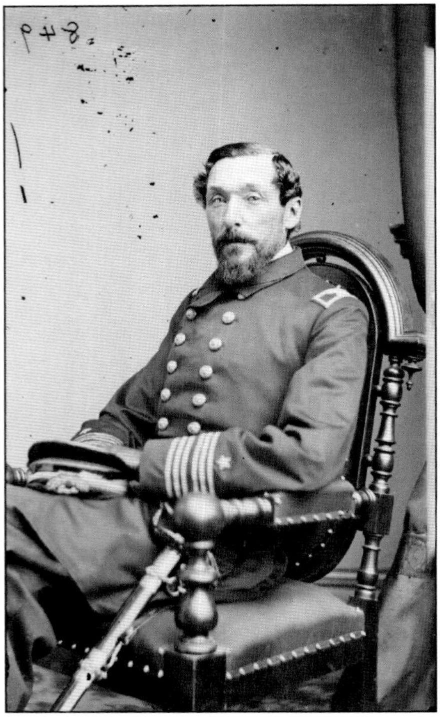

Portrait of Captain Percival Drayton, c. 1855–1865. Son of South Carolina congressman William Drayton, Percival Drayton entered the Navy in 1827. He served through the Civil War, eventually rising to the rank of captain. In the Battle of Port Royal, he fought against his brother, a commander of Confederate forces. Drayton survived the war, only to die in 1865 shortly after his appointment as chief of the Bureau of Navigation. (LOC.)

Nicola Monachesi Burial Permit, 1854. Born and educated in Italy, Nicola Monachesi was an artist whose frescoes were among the first in the United States. Among his projects were the frescoes in the Merchants' Exchange building. He also painted frescoes in the private homes of wealthy citizens and was in demand as a portrait painter. Today, his surviving works in Philadelphia can be seen inside St. Augustine Catholic Church.

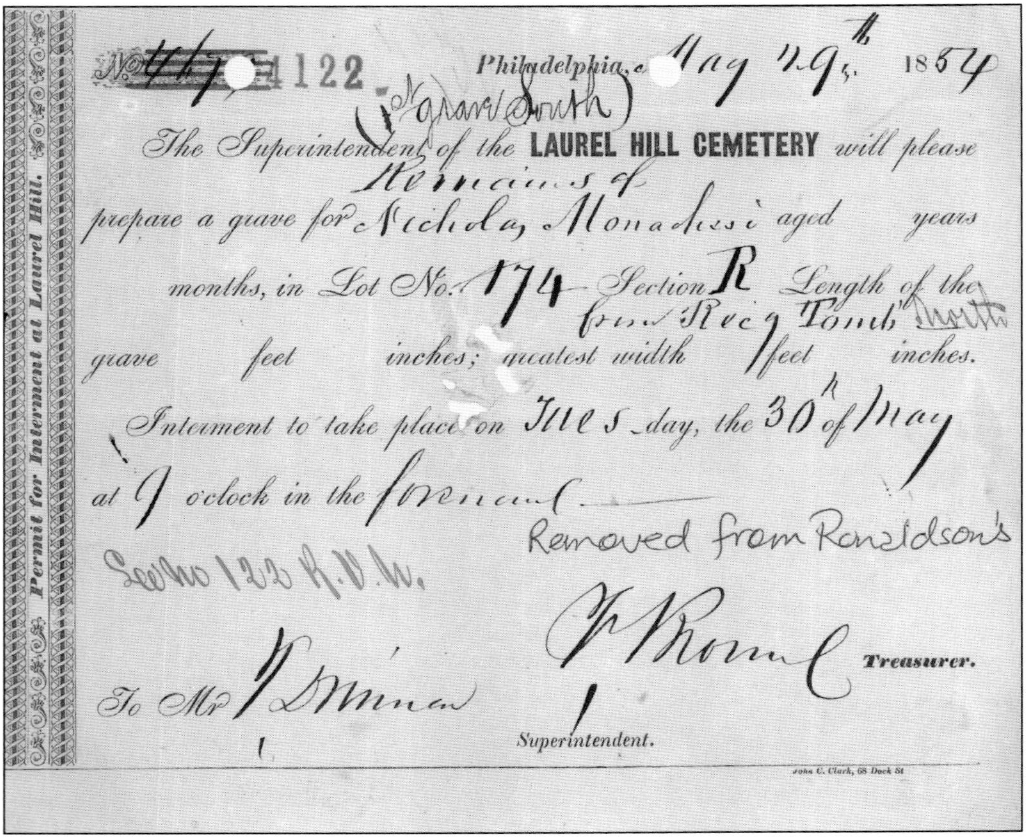

Permit for Interment at Laurel Hill.

No. 4122 Philadelphia, May 29th 1854

(1st grave South)

The Superintendent of the LAUREL HILL CEMETERY will please

Remains of

prepare a grave for Nichola Monachesi aged years months, in Lot No. 174 Section R Length of the

from Rec. Tomb North

grave feet inches; greatest width feet inches.

Interment to take place on Tues-day, the 30th of May at 9 o'clock in the forenoon.

Removed from Ronaldson's

See No 122 R.V.W.

Treasurer.

To Mr.

Superintendent.

John C. Clark, 68 Dock St

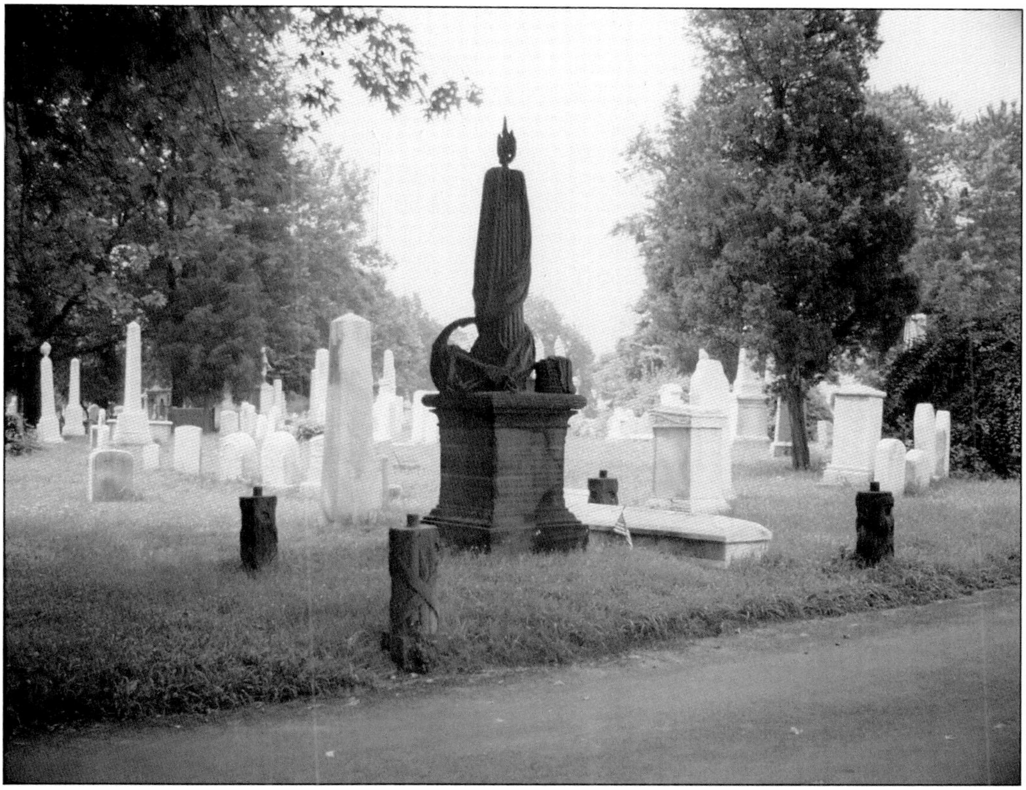

Levi Twiggs Memorial, 1979. Marine Levi Twiggs served through the War of 1812 and the Seminole Wars, obtaining the rank of major in 1840. In 1843, he assumed command of the Philadelphia Naval Yard before returning to active service in 1847. He was killed while leading his command at the storming of Chapultepec, now immortalized in the opening line of the "Marines' Hymn:" "From the halls of Montezuma . . ."

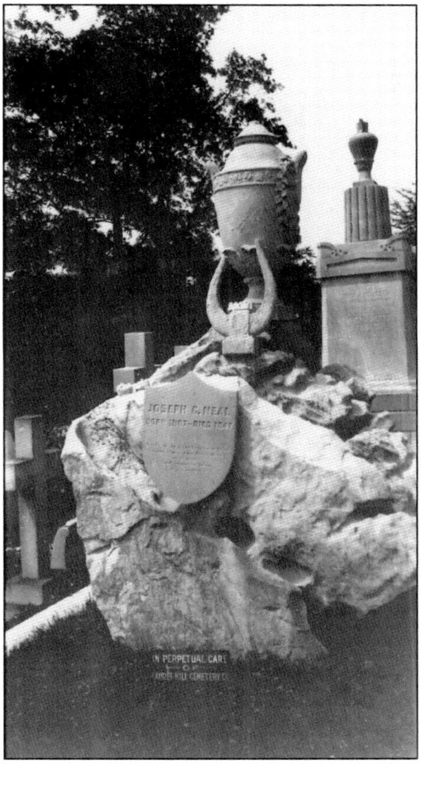

Joseph Clay Neal Monument, 1929. Known as a journalist and a humorist, Joseph Clay Neal was editor of the *Pennsylvanian*, a daily newspaper, and editor and part-owner of the *Saturday News and Literary Gazette*, a publication that eventually became a part of the *Saturday Evening Post*. In 1837, he published his book *Charcoal Sketches, or Scenes in a Metropolis*, a collection of stories first published in the *Saturday News*.

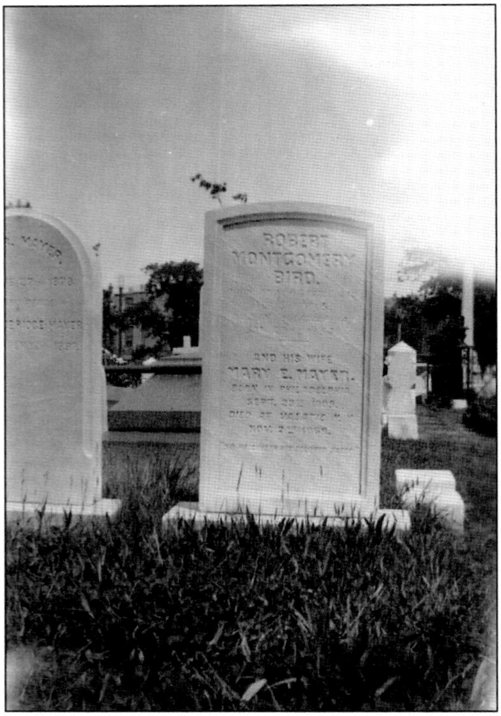

ROBERT MONTGOMERY BIRD HEADSTONE, 1929. Robert Montgomery Bird was born in Delaware in 1806. After graduating from medical school, he spent one year practicing medicine before deciding on a literary career. Bird's 1831 play, *The Gladiator*, written for Edwin Forrest, was a great success, but Bird was not generously paid. His frustration with Forrest turned him from a playwright into a novelist. He died in 1854.

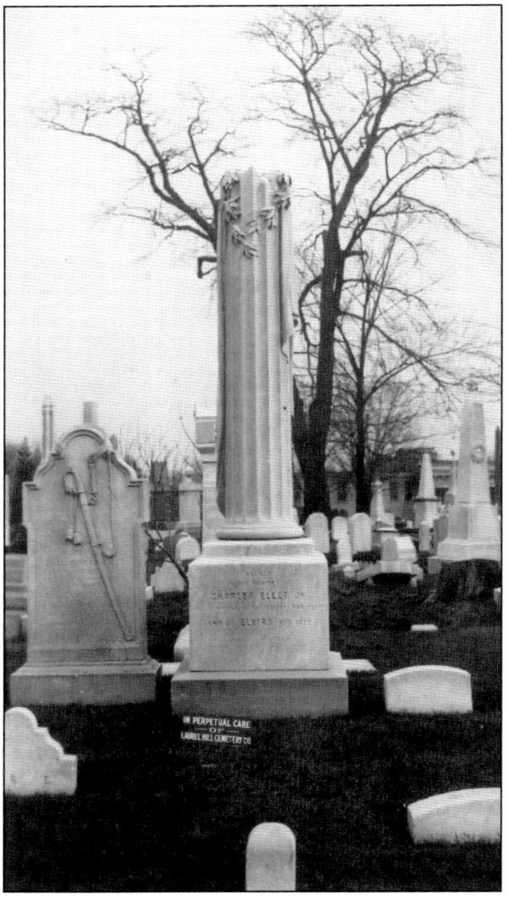

CHARLES ELLET JR. MEMORIAL. In 1842, Charles Ellet Jr. designed and built the first wire-suspension bridge in the United States. In 1848, he designed the Wheeling Suspension Bridge (which still stands) and a suspension footbridge at Niagara Falls. During the Civil War, Ellet was appointed colonel of engineers. He led his fleet in the Union victory at the Battle of Memphis but died from wounds received in battle.

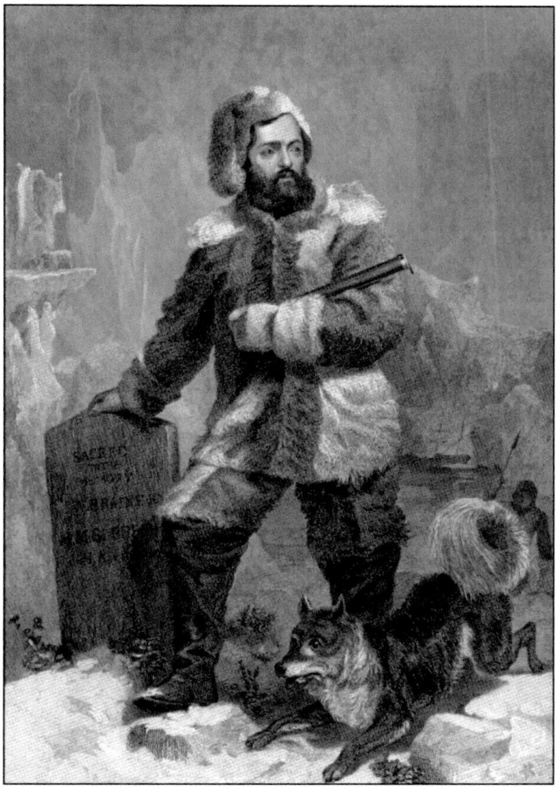

Elisha Kent Kane Portrait and Mausoleum. Born in Philadelphia in 1820, Elisha Kent Kane was educated in medicine at the University of Pennsylvania and earned a commission as a naval surgeon. His postings took him around the world, but his greatest fame came from expeditions to the Arctic. In 1850, he served as medical officer to an expedition searching for the lost expedition of Sir John Franklin. He organized a second expedition to the Arctic in 1853 and died in Cuba in 1857 while planning a third expedition. (Right, NYPL).

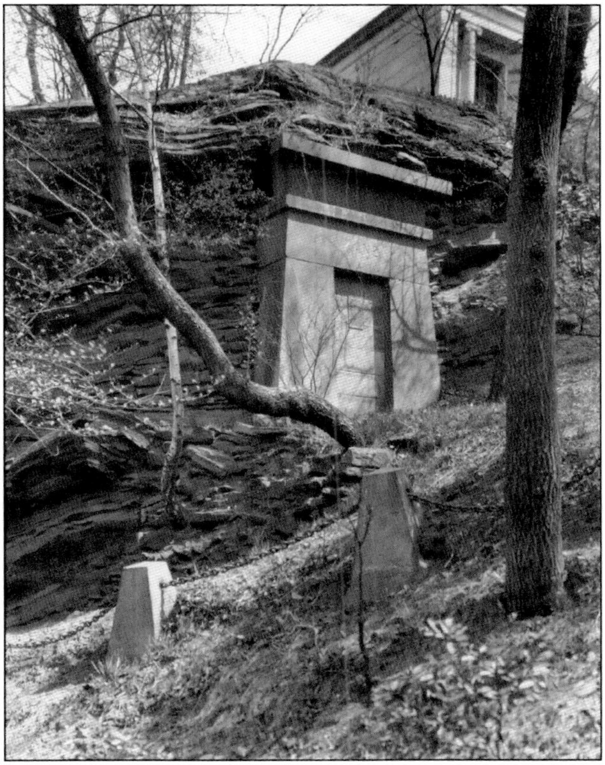

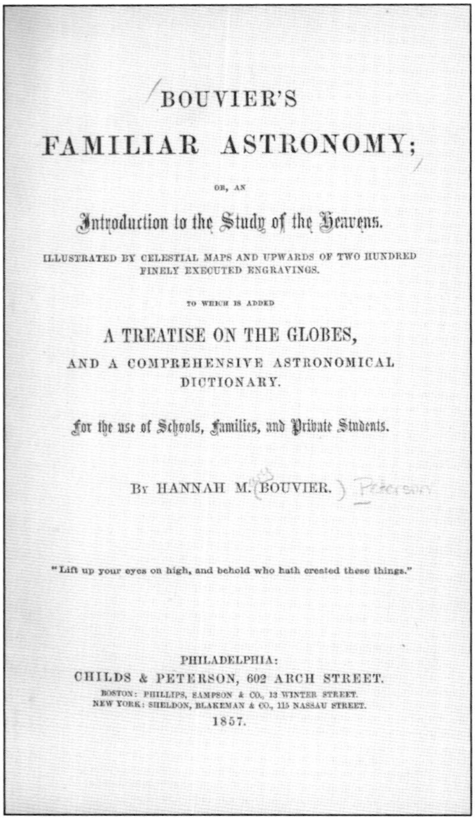
BOUVIER'S

FAMILIAR ASTRONOMY;

OR, AN

Introduction to the Study of the Heavens.

ILLUSTRATED BY CELESTIAL MAPS AND UPWARDS OF TWO HUNDRED FINELY EXECUTED ENGRAVINGS.

TO WHICH IS ADDED

A TREATISE ON THE GLOBES,

AND A COMPREHENSIVE ASTRONOMICAL DICTIONARY.

For the use of Schools, Families, and Private Students.

BY HANNAH M. BOUVIER.

"Lift up your eyes on high, and behold who hath created these things."

PHILADELPHIA:
CHILDS & PETERSON, 602 ARCH STREET.
BOSTON: PHILLIPS, SAMPSON & CO., 13 WINTER STREET.
NEW YORK: SHELDON, BLAKEMAN & CO., 115 NASSAU STREET.
1857.

BOUVIER'S *FAMILIAR ASTRONOMY* BY HANNAH M. BOUVIER, 1857. In 1855, Hannah M. Bouvier published *Bouvier's Familiar Astronomy*. It is written in a highly readable style, with information given as questions and answers. The book includes a history of astronomy, astronomical tables, an astronomical dictionary, and sky maps. Although she went on to publish other books, this was her only one about science.

JOHN NOTMAN MONUMENT, 1989. Overlooking the gatehouse he designed is the grave of architect John Notman. Born in Scotland in 1810, Notman was a recent immigrant to America with little experience when he won the design contract for Laurel Hill. This commission launched his career, and he spent the next 30 years designing buildings in Philadelphia and the mid-Atlantic region. (Photograph by Jack E. Boucher, HABS No. PA-1811-3, LOC.)

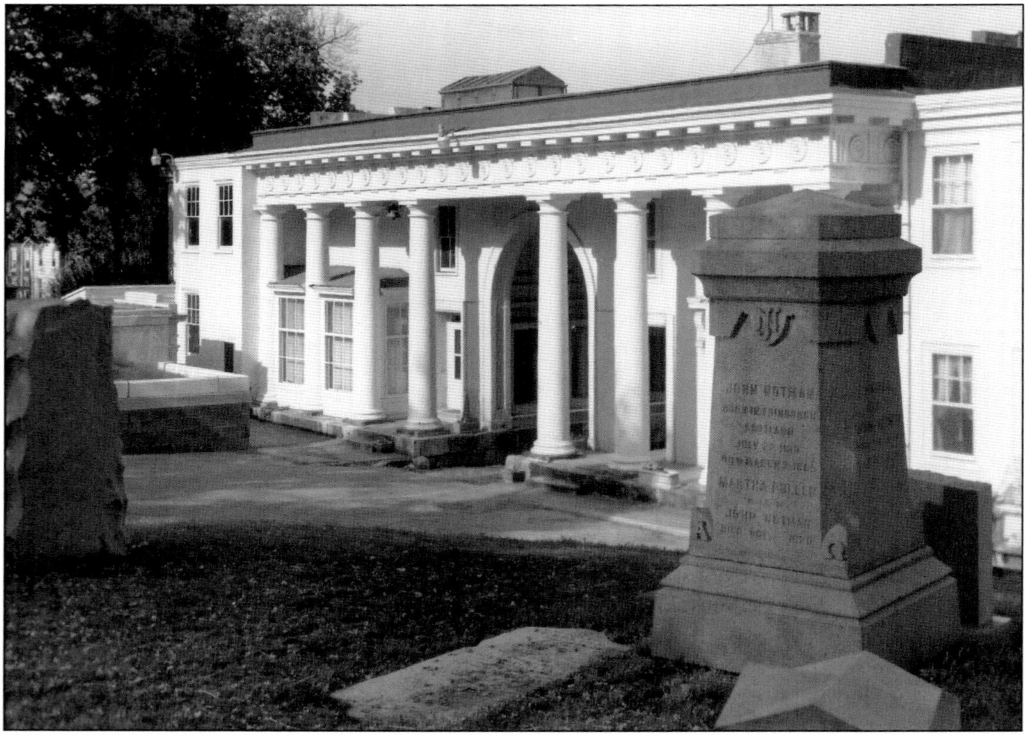

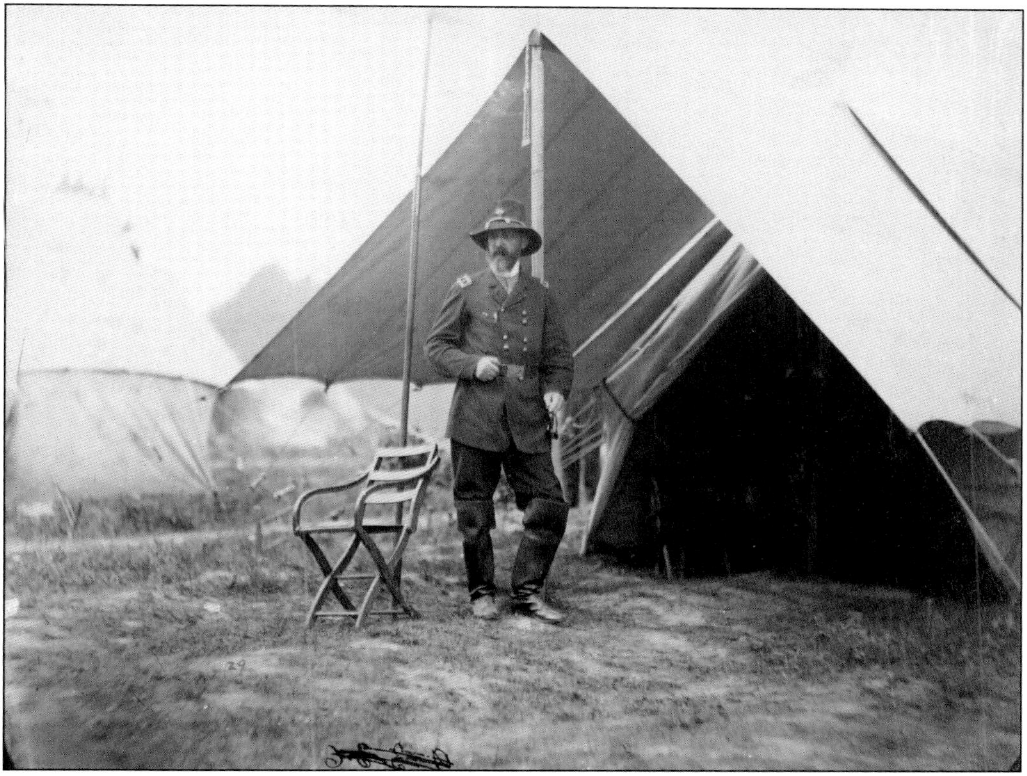

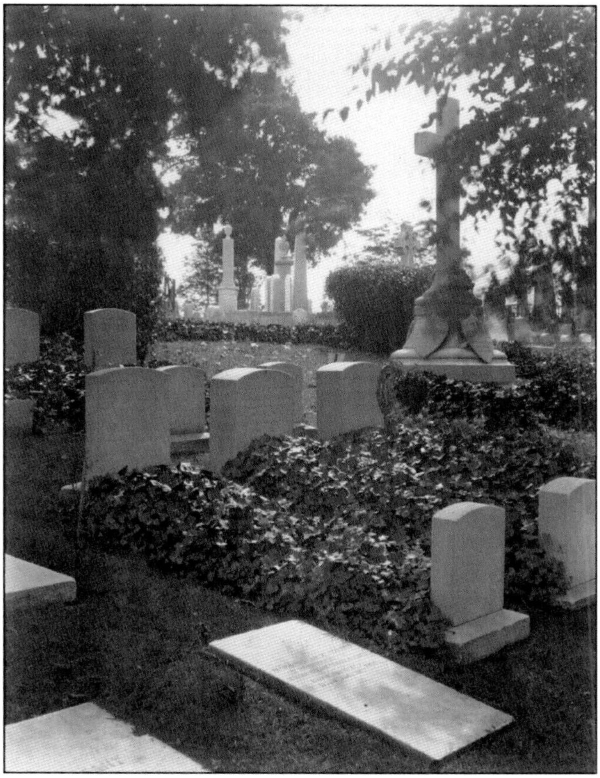

GEN. GEORGE G. MEADE PORTRAIT AND FAMILY LOT. George Meade graduated from the US Military Academy in 1835. After serving a year, he resigned his commission to become a civil engineer. He rejoined the Army in 1842 and was appointed second lieutenant in the Corps of Topographical Engineers. After serving in the Mexican-American War, he returned to engineering work with the Army. At the outbreak of the Civil War, Meade was given command of a brigade of Pennsylvania volunteers. He was promoted to commanding general of the Army of the Potomac three days before the Battle of Gettysburg erupted on July 1, 1863. His victory over the Confederate army marked a significant point in the war. Meade died in 1872 and was given a huge state funeral by the City of Philadelphia. (Above, LOC.)

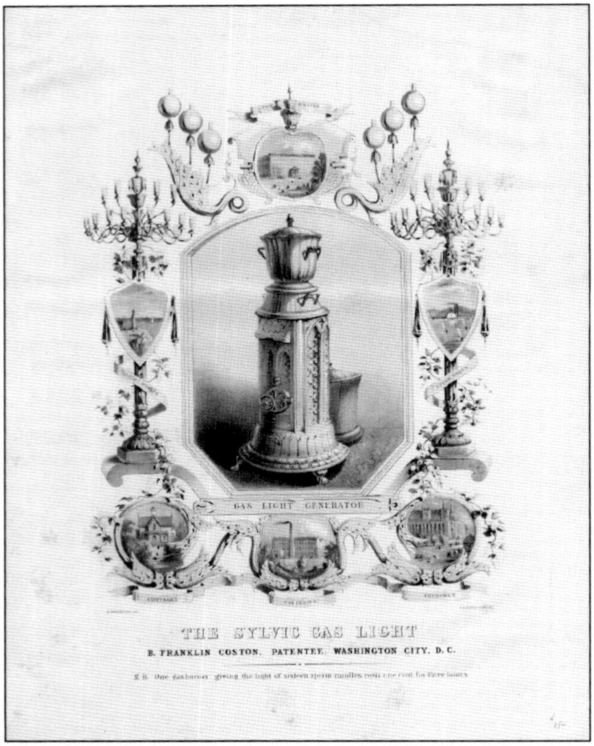

SYLVIC GAS LIGHT AND COSTON FAMILY LOT. Benjamin Franklin Coston was director of the US Navy's scientific laboratory before accepting the position of president of the Boston Gas Company. While in Boston, he received a patent for his Sylvic Gas Light. He died in 1848. After his death, his widow, Martha, developed a pyrotechnic night signal and code system. The signals, known as Coston signal flares, were used extensively by the Union during the Civil War, being particularly effective in capturing Confederate blockade runners during the Union's blockade of southern ports. After the war, her signals were supplied to every station of the US Life-Saving Service (now the US Coast Guard) and were instrumental in saving thousands of lives. (Left, LOC.)

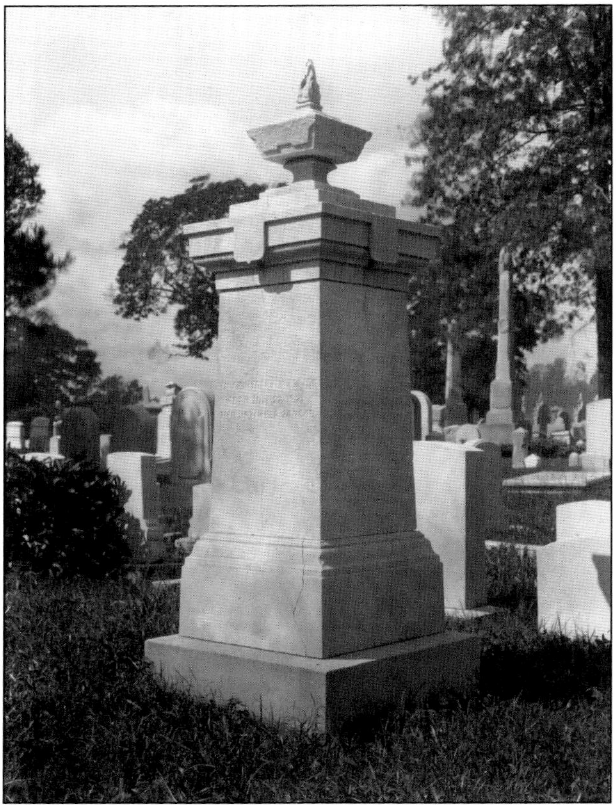

PORTRAIT OF GEORGE D. McCLELLAN, MD. Educated at Yale and the University of Pennsylvania, McClellan was offering private anatomy lectures to medical students when he decided to open a second medical school in Philadelphia. In 1824, Jefferson Medical College was founded, with McClellan as chair of surgery. (NLM.)

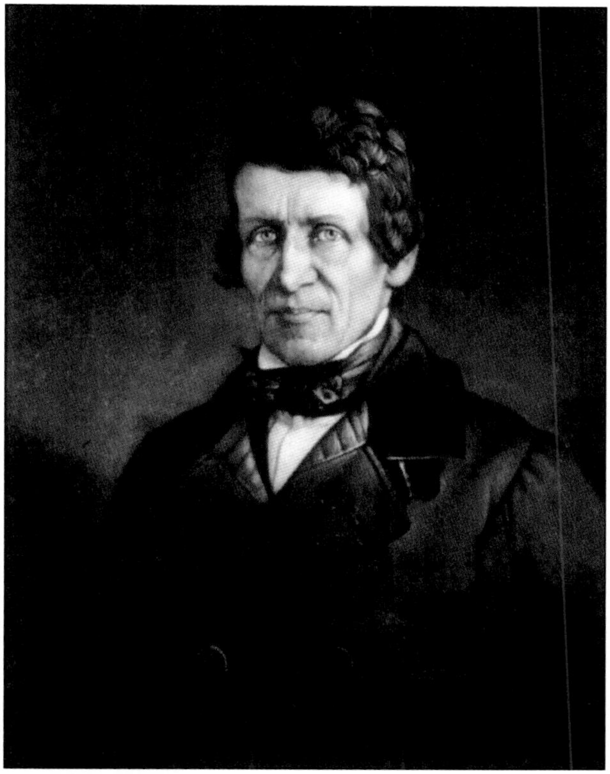

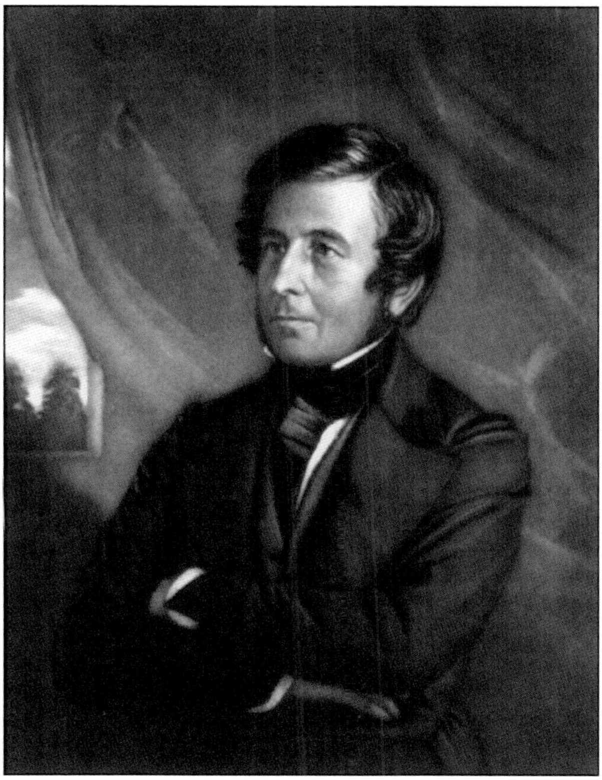

PORTRAIT OF JOSEPH PANCOAST, MD. A graduate of the University of Pennsylvania School of Medicine in 1828, Dr. Joseph Pancoast became a renowned American surgeon whose lectures and writings in anatomy and surgery educated countless physicians. In 1839, Pancoast succeeded George McClellan as Jefferson Medical College's second chair of surgery. (NLM.)

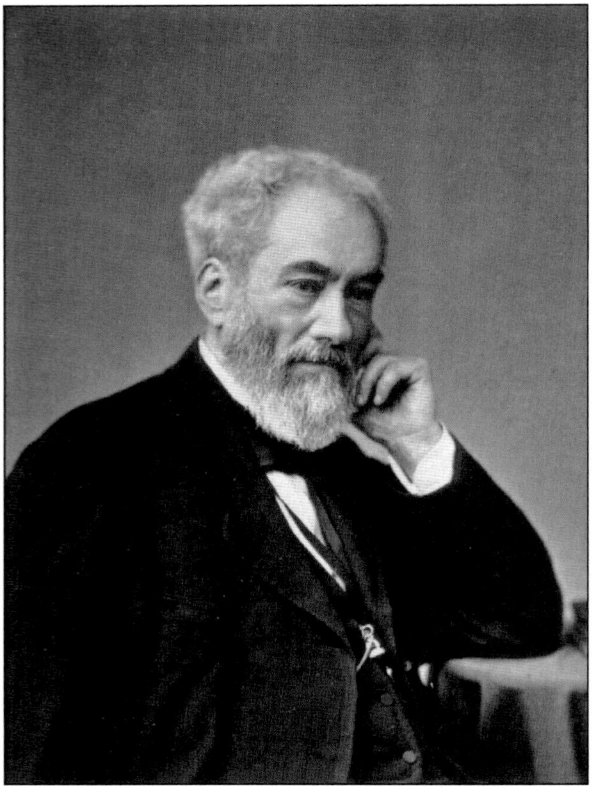

Portrait of Robley Dunglison, MD, c. 1865. Robley Dunglison was the first professor of anatomy and medicine at the University of Virginia. He was also personal physician to Thomas Jefferson, and treated presidents James Madison, James Monroe, and Andrew Jackson. In 1832, his most influential work was published, *Human Physiology*, and he is considered the "Father of American Physiology." Dunglison ended his career working at Jefferson Medical College. (NLM.)

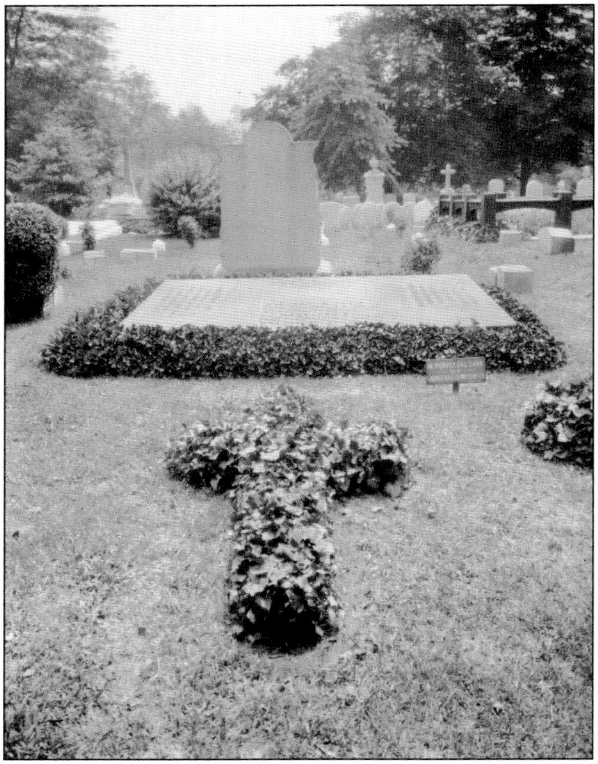

Gravesite of Francis West Lewis, MD, 1930. Inspired by London's Great Ormond Street Hospital for Children and the high infant and child mortality rates in the city of Philadelphia, Francis West Lewis recruited two other Philadelphia doctors to start a children's hospital. Founded in 1855, the Children's Hospital of Philadelphia was the first of its kind in America and dedicated solely to providing clinical care to sick children.

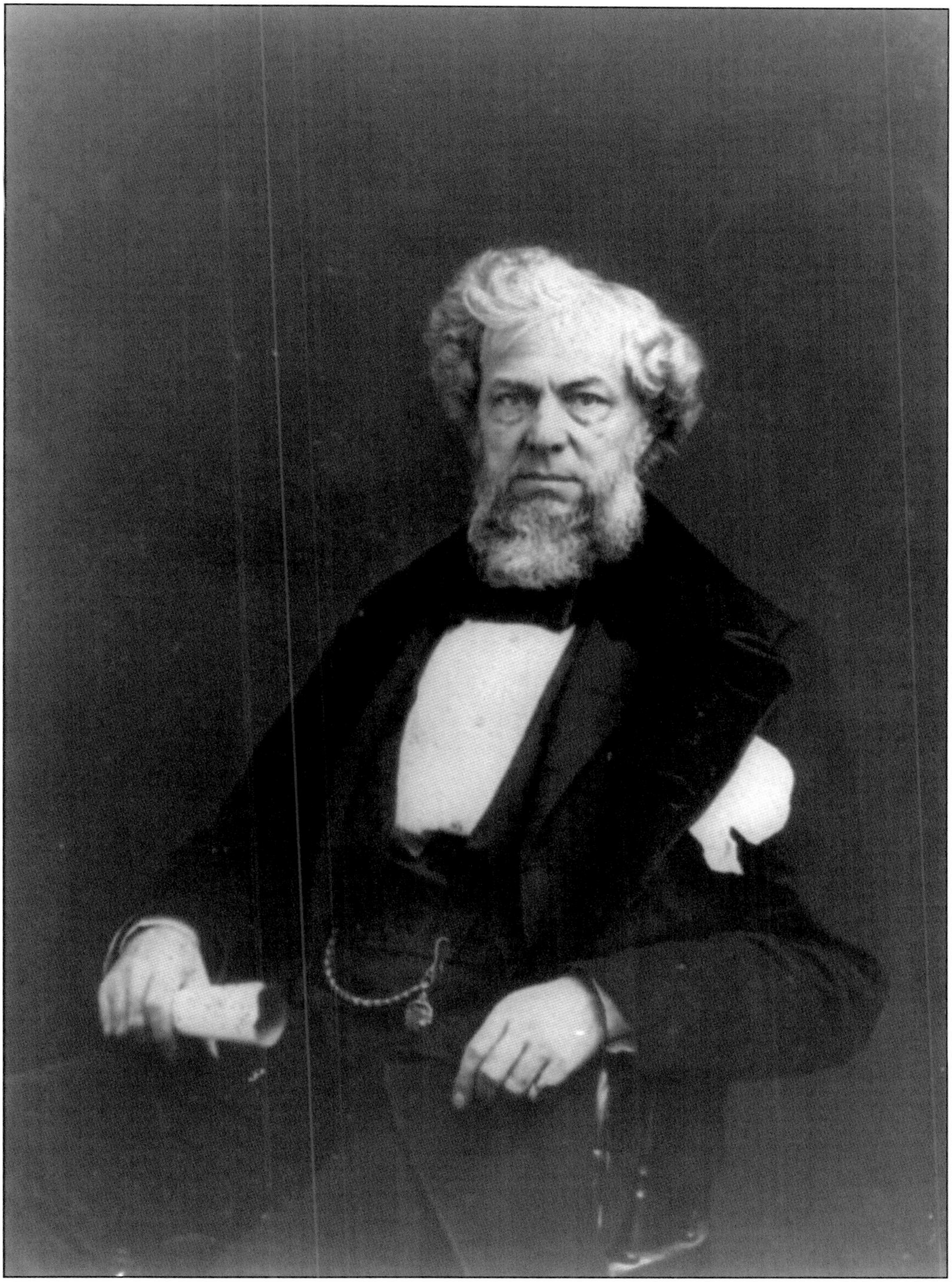

Portrait of Thomas Ustick Walter, c. 1859–1878. Trained in the offices of architect William Strickland, Thomas Ustick Walter first gained recognition with his design for Philadelphia's Moyamensing Prison. His design for the Girard College for Orphans established his national reputation. In 1850, his design for the dome and wings of the US Capitol made him a key figure in American architecture. In 1857, he was one of the 13 founders of the American Institute of Architects. (LOC.)

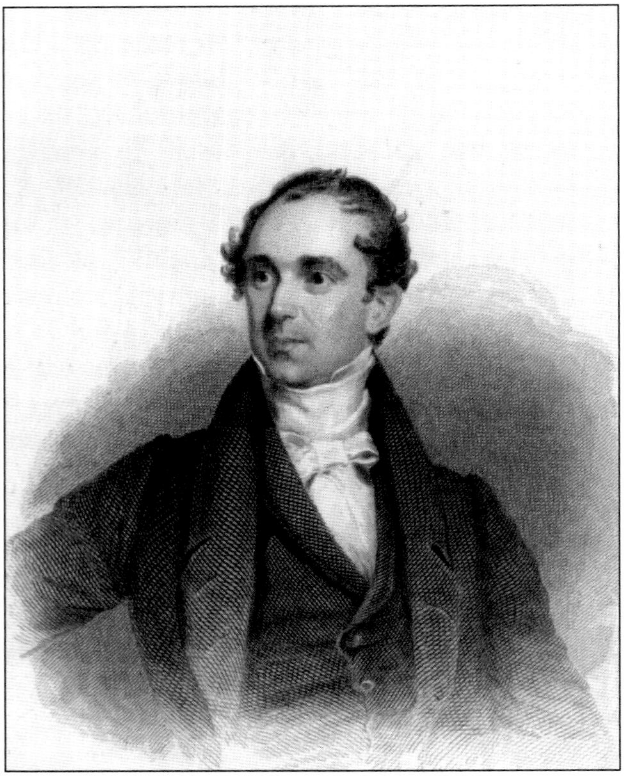

Portrait of Henry D. Gilpin. Henry D. Gilpin was a lawyer, politician, and writer. In 1840, Pres. Martin Van Buren appointed him attorney general, and in 1841, Gilpin presented the government's side in the *Amistad* case before the US Supreme Court. Gilpin was also a supporter of the arts, serving as president of the Pennsylvania Academy of Fine Arts from 1833 to 1835. (NYPL.)

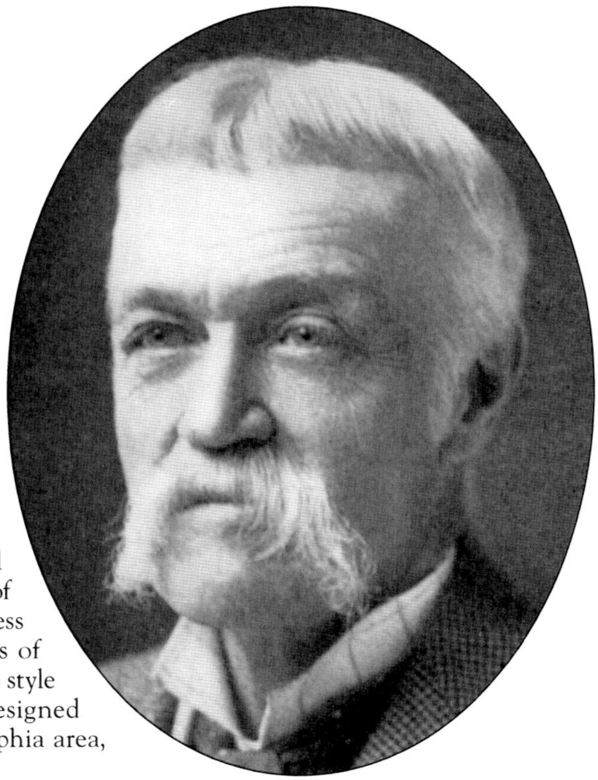

Portrait of Frank Furness. Frank Furness, born in 1839, was trained as an architect. Following the Civil War, he was awarded the Congressional Medal of Honor for actions during the Battle of Trevilian Station. After the war, Furness became one of the leading architects of his generation, although his distinctive style garnered much criticism. Furness designed hundreds of buildings in the Philadelphia area, some of which are still standing.

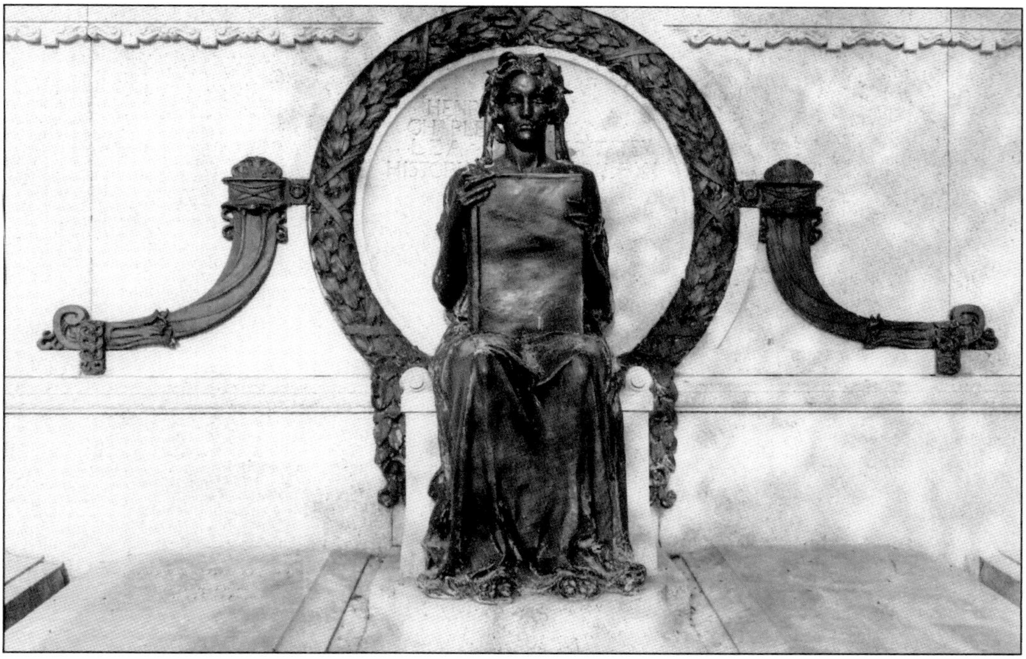

HENRY CHARLES LEA MEMORIAL BY ALEXANDER STIRLING CALDER, 1989. One of the most striking memorials in Laurel Hill belongs to that of publisher and historian Henry Charles Lea, an influential historian specializing in the middle ages. Upon his death, his library was given to the University of Pennsylvania. At the time of the bequest in 1925, it was one of the most complete collections of medieval and early modern European documents in the United States, consisting of around 7,000 volumes. His memorial, created by sculptor Alexander Stirling Calder, depicts the muse of history facing the Schuylkill River, seated, holding a large book. (Both photographs by Jack E. Boucher, LOC; above, HABS No. PA-1811-26; below, PA-1811-25.)

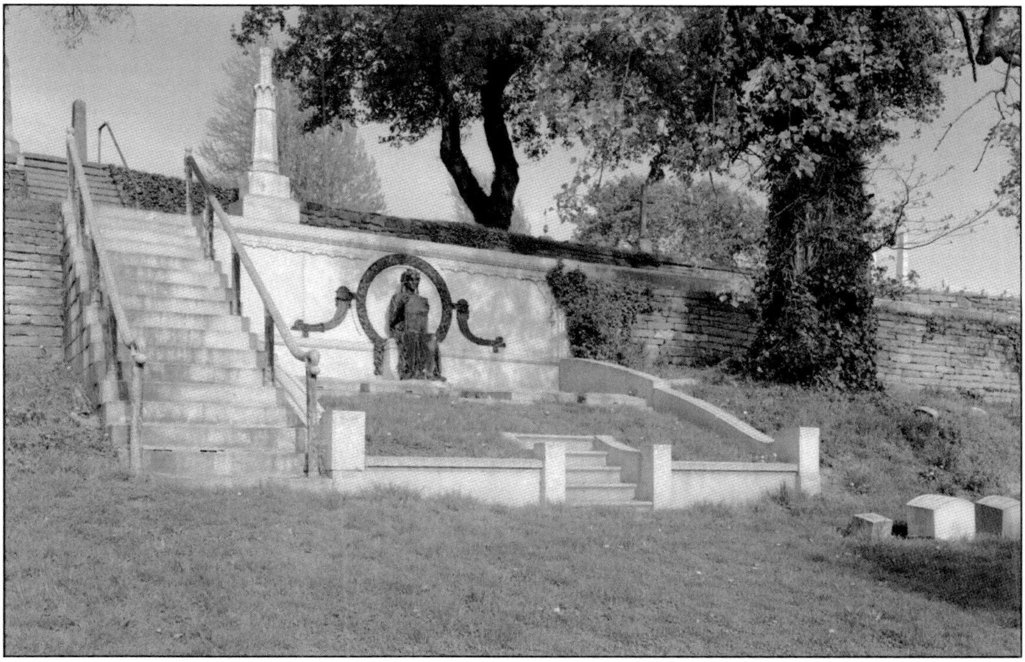

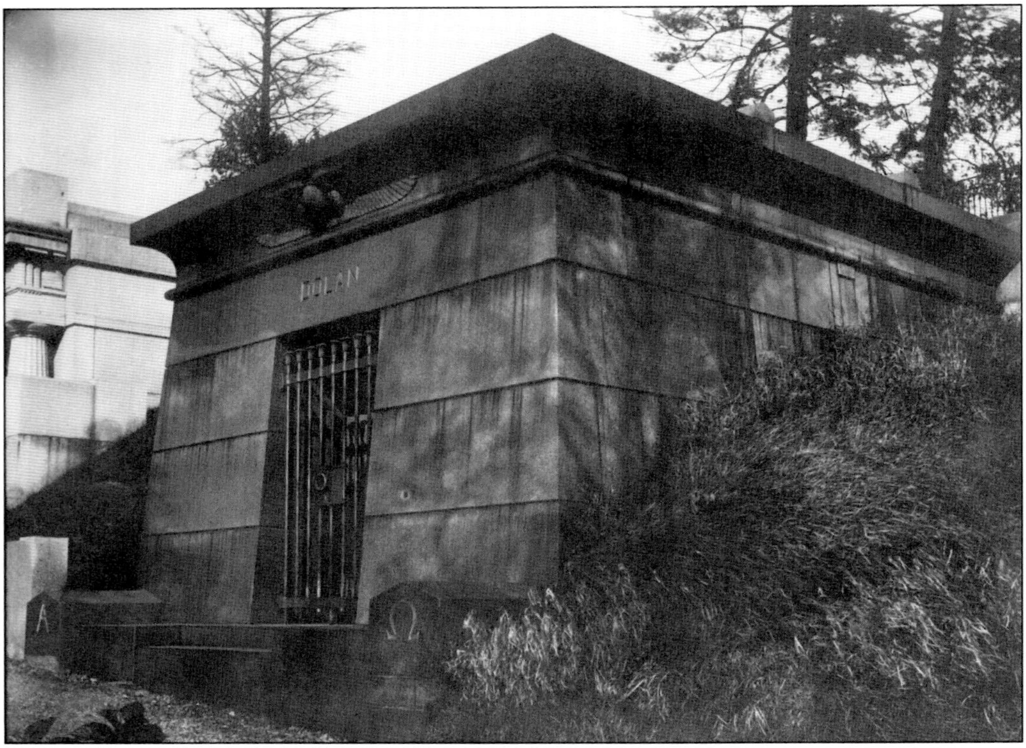

THOMAS DOLAN MAUSOLEUM, c. 1910. In 1905, as head of the United Gas Improvement Co. (UGI), Thomas Dolan offered to pay the city $25 million in exchange for a 75-year lease of the gas works. This would have resulted in a loss of rents for the city and profits for UGI equaling nearly $900 million. Calling it a "gas grab," public outcry against the deal was so great that UGI's offer was withdrawn.

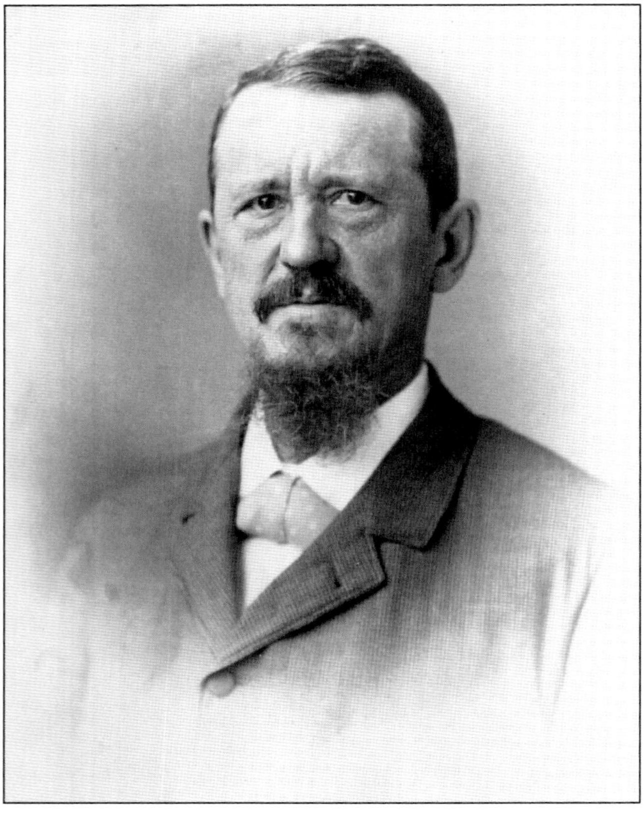

PORTRAIT OF JOSEPH WHARTON, c. 1890. Quaker Joseph Wharton was a businessman and industrialist who made his fortune as cofounder of the Bethlehem Steel Company. Wharton also cofounded Swarthmore College, and in 1881, he set aside $100,000 to endow a business school at the University of Pennsylvania—the Wharton School. (UPENN.)

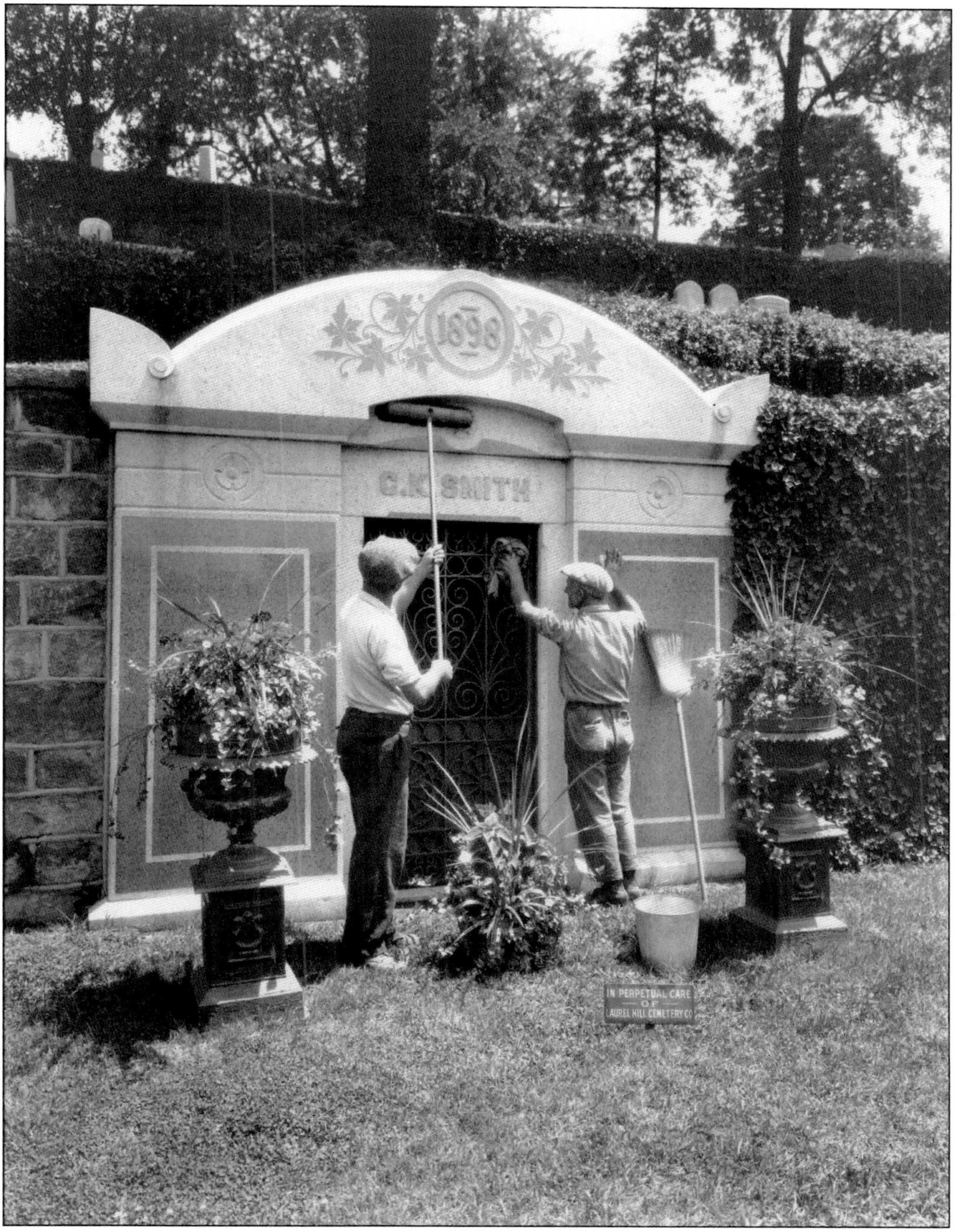

GEORGE K. SMITH MAUSOLEUM, 1930. The Philadelphia origins of the pharmaceutical giant now known as GlaxoSmithKline date to the 1830s, when druggist John K. Smith opened a store selling drugs, paints, and chemicals. In 1841, John's brother George joined him and the business grew, becoming a leading drug wholesaler. When John died, George continued in the business, employing advanced methods like catering directly to the precise requirements of physicians. He also focused on offering pure, quality products. In 1846, he began supplying medicine to the US Army. Smith died in 1864. He and several members of his company are buried in Laurel Hill Cemetery.

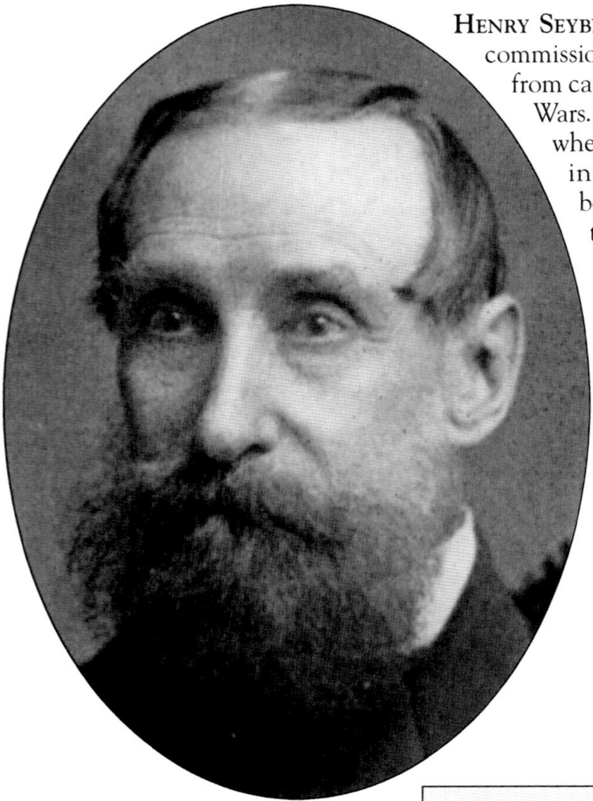

Henry Seybert Portrait. In 1873, Henry Seybert commissioned the casting of a bell made of metal from cannons from the Revolutionary and Civil Wars. The bell was placed in Independence Hall, where it remains today. An ardent believer in "modern spiritualism," Seybert left a bequest to the University of Pennsylvania to fund a study of spiritualism and endow a professorship in moral philosophy in honor of his late father.

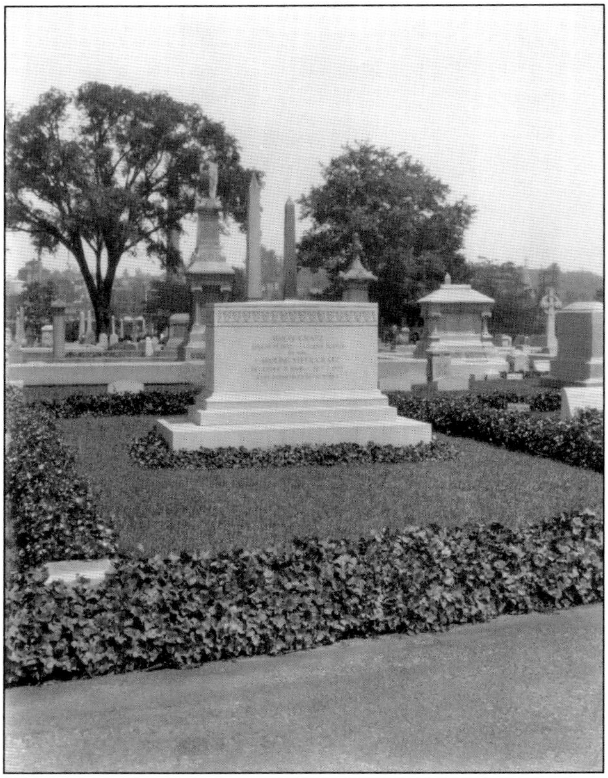

Simon Gratz Memorial. Simon Gratz is best remembered for his significant contributions to Philadelphia's Board of Education during his more than 50 years serving on the board. He was a lawyer and member of the Pennsylvania legislature in addition to serving as a member of the board of trustees of Jefferson Medical College and president of the Free Library of Philadelphia.

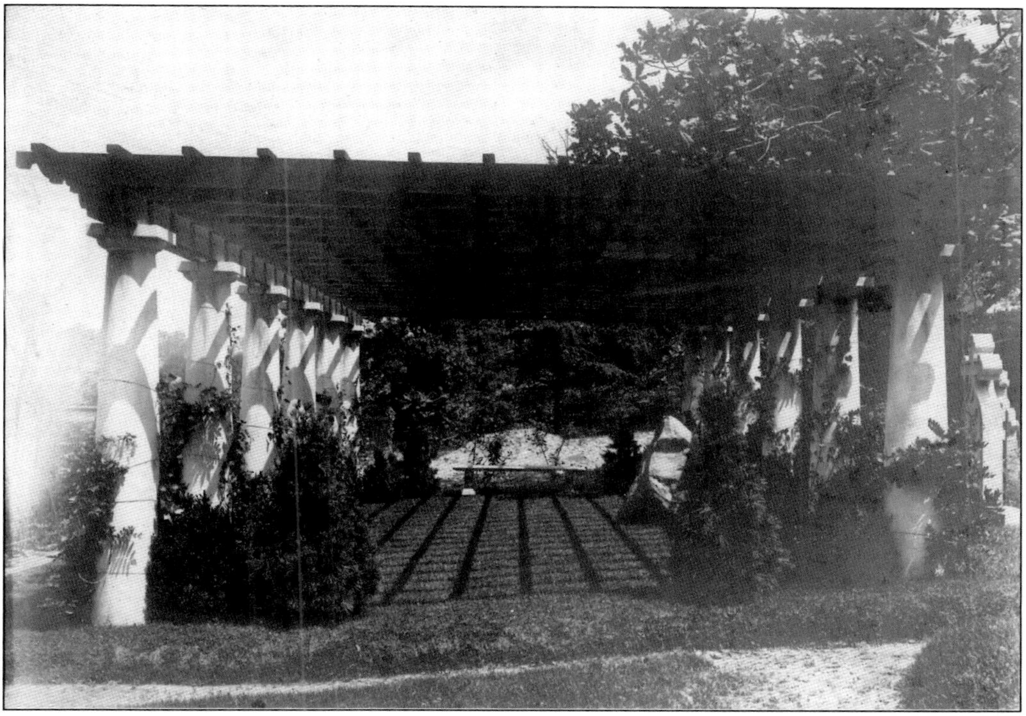

Louisa Knapp Curtis Lot, c. 1910. Louisa Knapp Curtis was the wife of publishing magnate Cyrus Curtis. She contributed a column to his magazine, *Tribune and Farmer*, which became so popular that an entirely new publication was created. In 1883, *Ladies Home Journal* was published, with Louisa serving as editor from 1883 to 1889.

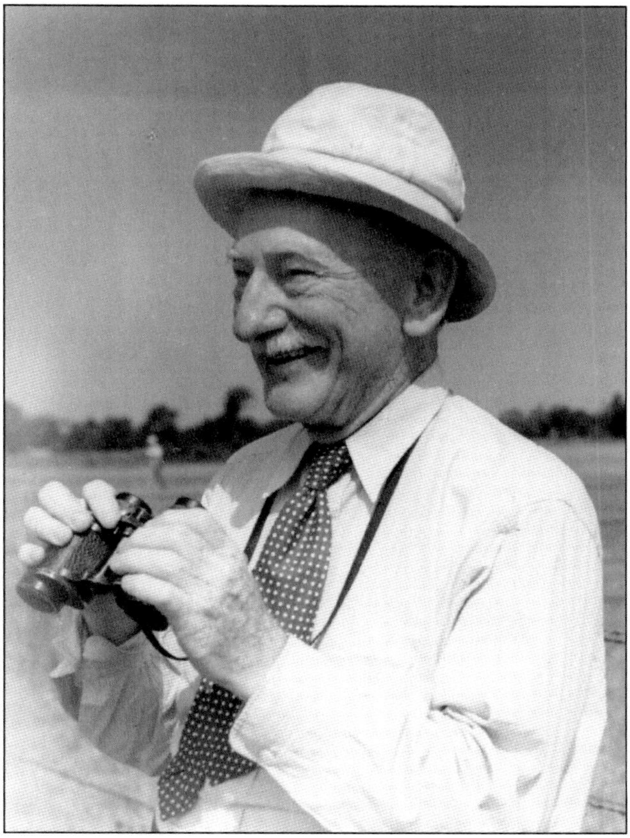

Portrait of Witmer Stone, c. 1930. Witmer Stone was a naturalist who studied botany, mammals, and reptiles, but his work as an ornithologist is the reason he is most remembered. Stone spent 50 years cataloguing and preserving the bird specimens at the Academy of Natural Sciences in Philadelphia. He authored hundreds of works on birds, including *Bird Studies at Old Cape May*, published shortly before his death in 1939. (UPENN.)

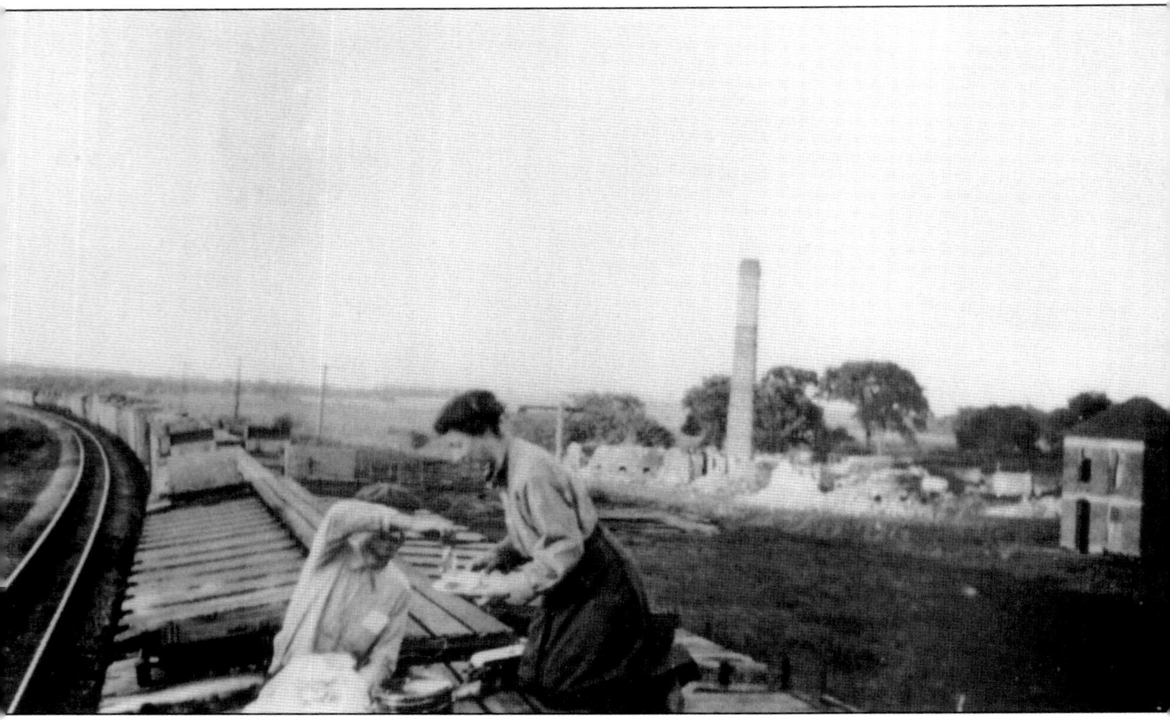

Mary Engle Pennington, c. 1910. Mary Engle Pennington is best remembered for perfecting refrigerated boxcars, which allowed fresh food to be shipped without spoiling, and inventing a shipping crate for eggs. Born in Nashville in 1872, she discovered her fascination for chemistry at a young age, but the girls' boarding school she attended would not allow instruction in science. Pennington was admitted to the University of Pennsylvania in 1890 and completed a major in chemistry, but upon graduation was awarded only a "certificate of proficiency," because the university did not grant bachelor's degrees to women. She remained at Penn and received her PhD in chemistry in 1895. Taking a job with the City of Philadelphia in 1904, Pennington persuaded the city's ice-cream vendors to regularly sterilize their equipment by boiling it, which drastically reduced the number of food poisoning cases in the city. She worked in the US Department of Agriculture as chief of its food research lab from 1906 to 1919 and opened her own consulting firm in 1922, which she ran until she died in 1952. (UPENN.)

Three

South Laurel Hill

By the early 1840s, North Laurel Hill was running out of available burial space. The managers looked for additional land, and in 1848, purchased the 27-acre Harleigh estate for $13,000. This parcel of land, once owned by Philadelphia jurist William Rawle, was located nearly a quarter of a mile south of North Laurel Hill and provided the same beautiful views of the river. The new cemetery property was laid out by civil engineer James C. Sidney, a cartographer whom John Jay Smith knew from the Library Company of Philadelphia. Sidney partnered with architect James P.W. Neff in 1850 to finish and refine the design. John McArthur Jr., the architect best remembered for the design of Philadelphia's City Hall, designed massive sandstone pillars that supported gates produced by the Robert Wood Iron Works for the cemetery's entrance off of Ridge Pike. McArthur also designed a cottage that stood directly behind the gates. Remnants of the Harleigh estate were likely used for the superintendent's accommodations and stables but were removed during the 1870s to make room for additional burials. The property, named South Laurel Hill, opened for burials in April 1849.

Since this new tract of land was not connected to the original part of Laurel Hill, it maintained its own records, superintendent, and office. South Laurel Hill was accessible by way of Nicetown Lane (which led to a ferry landing), or Ridge Avenue. The creation of this new area ushered in a trend of religious organizations purchasing entire blocks of the cemetery to be resold to members of their congregations. Also, more space was allotted for single-grave burials. Later, in 1913, a receiving tomb was added just inside the entrance to South Laurel Hill.

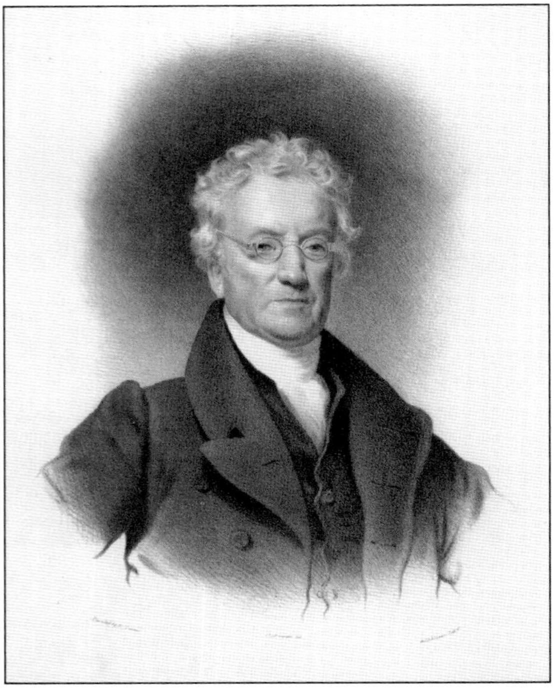

William Rawle, 1832. South Laurel Hill was developed from the former country seat of jurist William Rawle. Rawle named the estate Harleigh and was forced to sell in 1816 due to financial difficulties. The property passed through four other owners before the managers of Laurel Hill acquired it in 1848. (NYPL.)

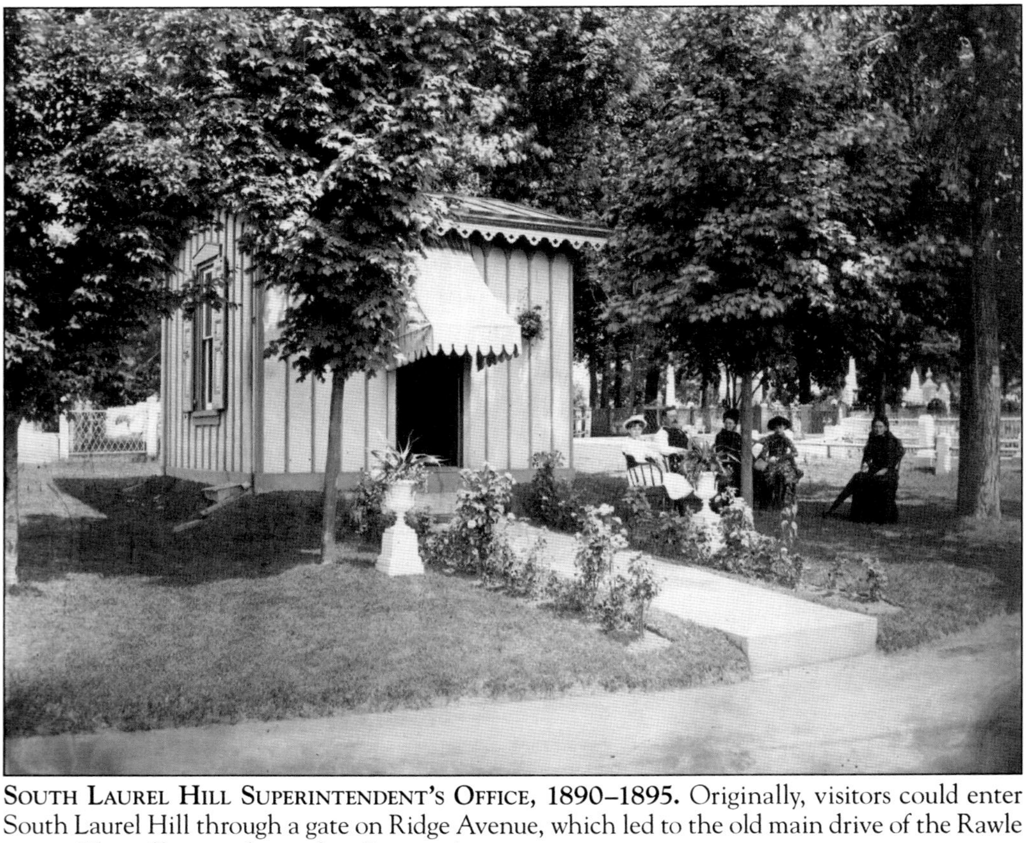

South Laurel Hill Superintendent's Office, 1890–1895. Originally, visitors could enter South Laurel Hill through a gate on Ridge Avenue, which led to the old main drive of the Rawle estate. This office was located in Section 4.

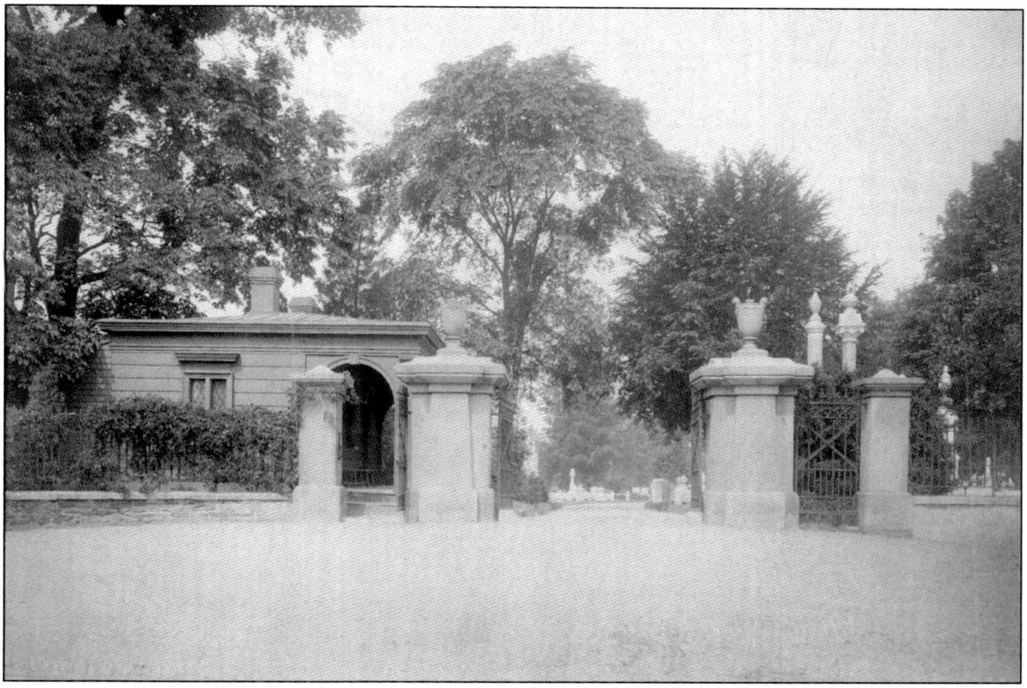

SOUTH LAUREL HILL ENTRANCES, C. 1890 (ABOVE) AND C. 1909 (BELOW). These two photographs show the South Laurel Hill entrance on Ridge Avenue. This office and sandstone posts were designed by John McArthur Jr. (later the designer of Philadelphia's City Hall). Completed in 1854, it was demolished sometime after 1920.

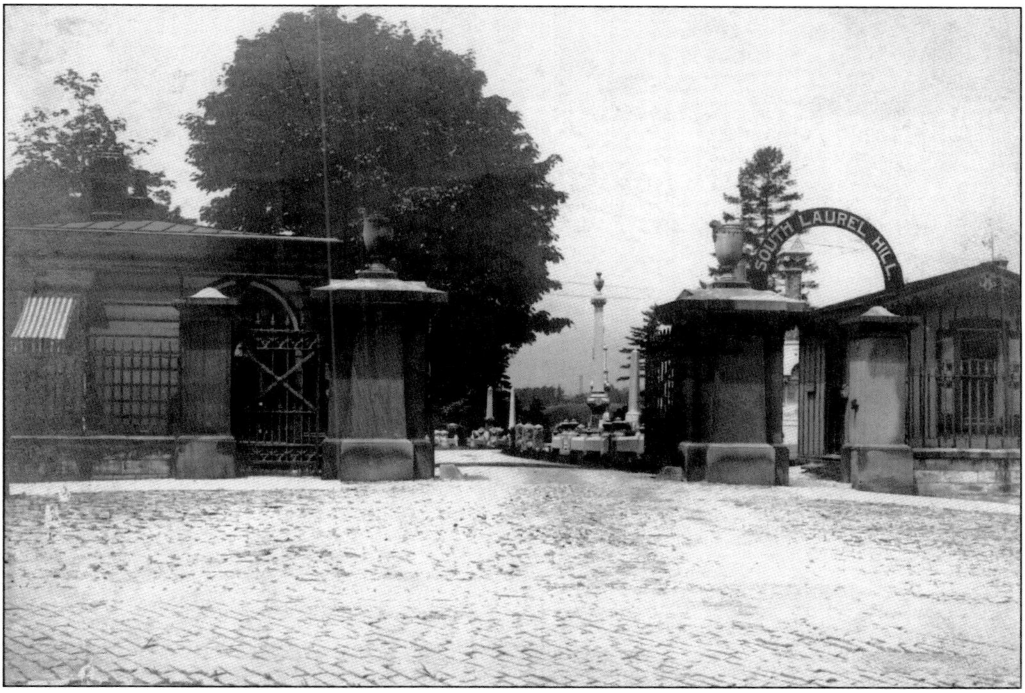

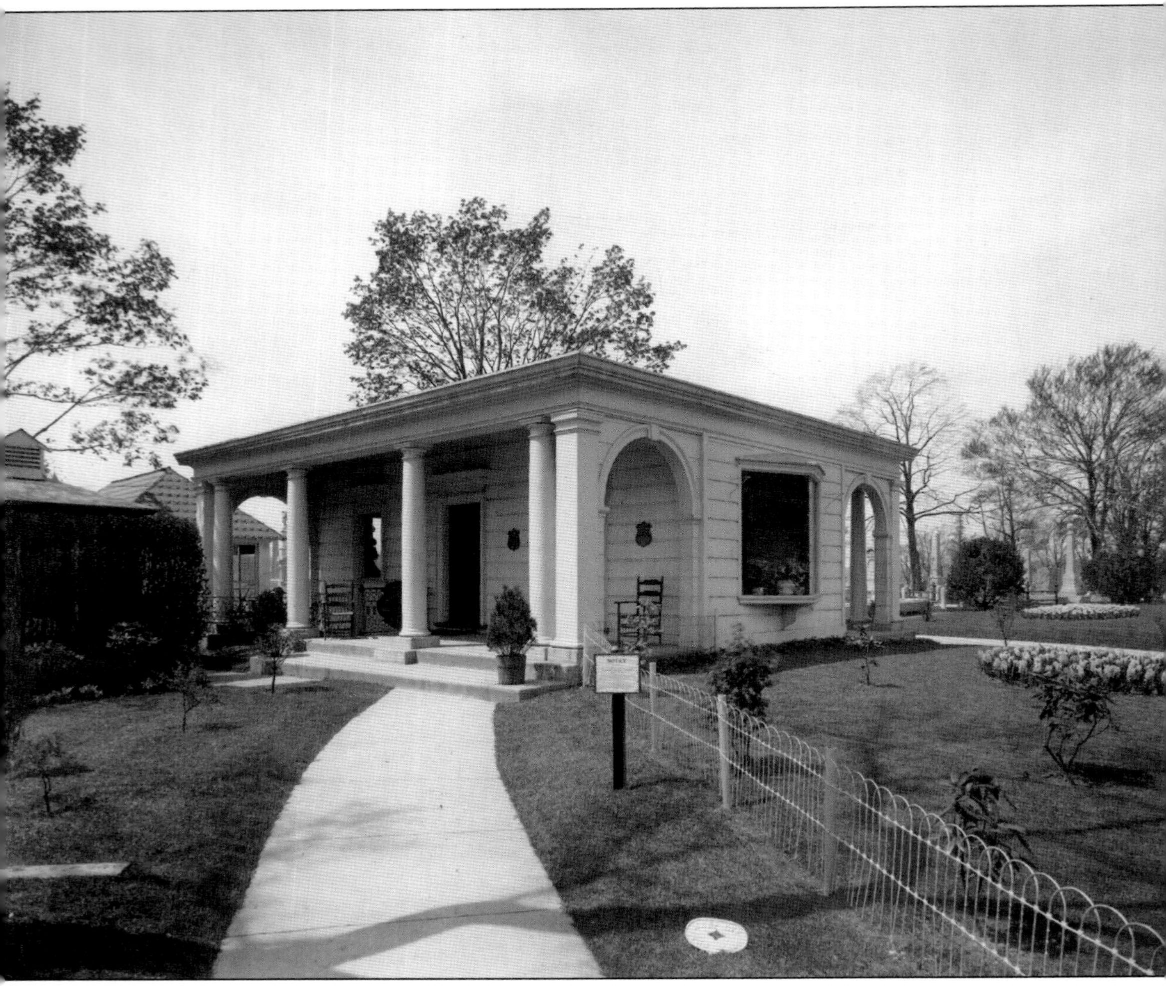

SOUTH LAUREL HILL OFFICE, 1918. Due to the physical gap between North Laurel Hill and South Laurel Hill, each functioned as its own distinct cemetery, with separate entrances, superintendents, offices, and records. The two also maintained their own crews of workers, stables, and maintenance buildings as well.

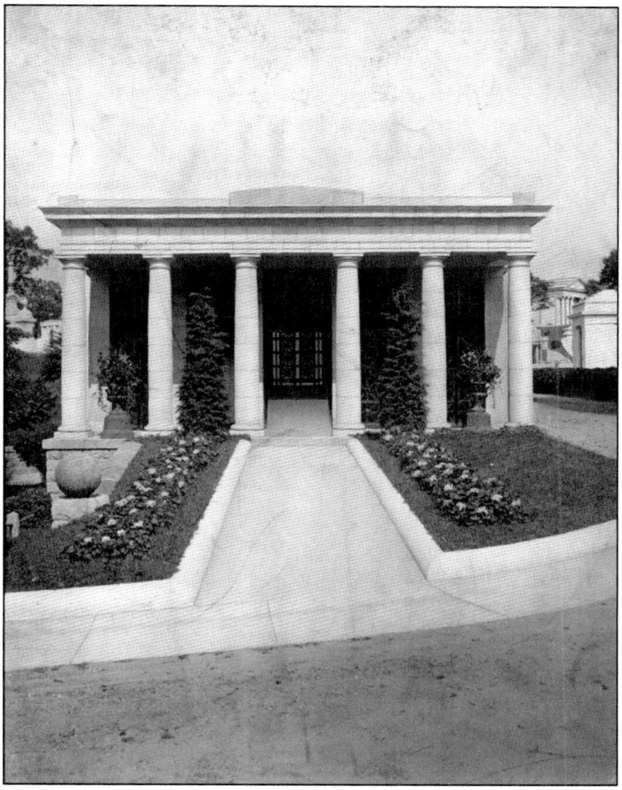

Receiving Vault, c. 1916–1918. A receiving vault was an important part of a 19th-century cemetery. In an era before mechanized digging and refrigeration for keeping bodies at a controlled temperature, the deceased were kept in temporary storage until a final resting place was completed. The first receiving vault was in North Laurel Hill, adjacent to the chapel. Various spaces throughout the cemetery were also used to temporarily house bodies until, in 1913, the Conkling Armstrong Terra Cotta Company built this receiving vault in South Laurel Hill. Although no longer in use, the structure still stands today.

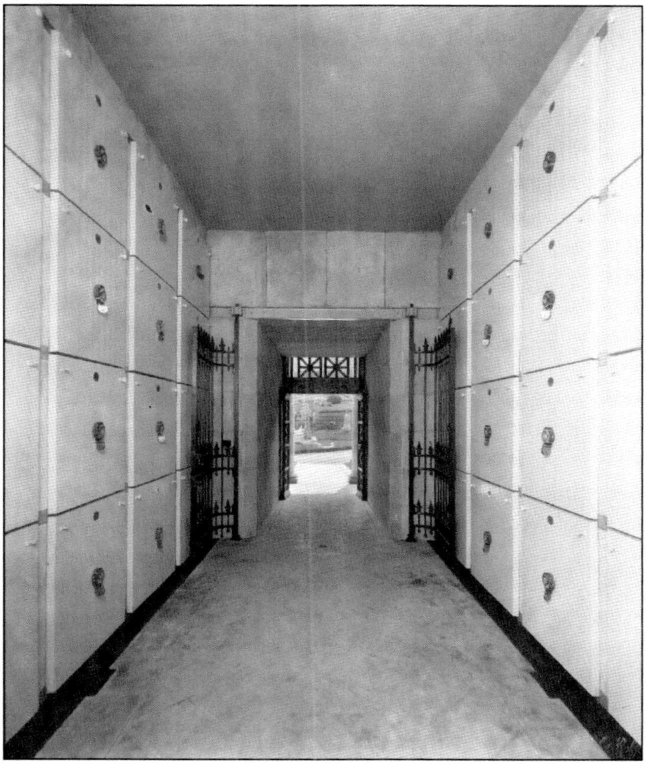

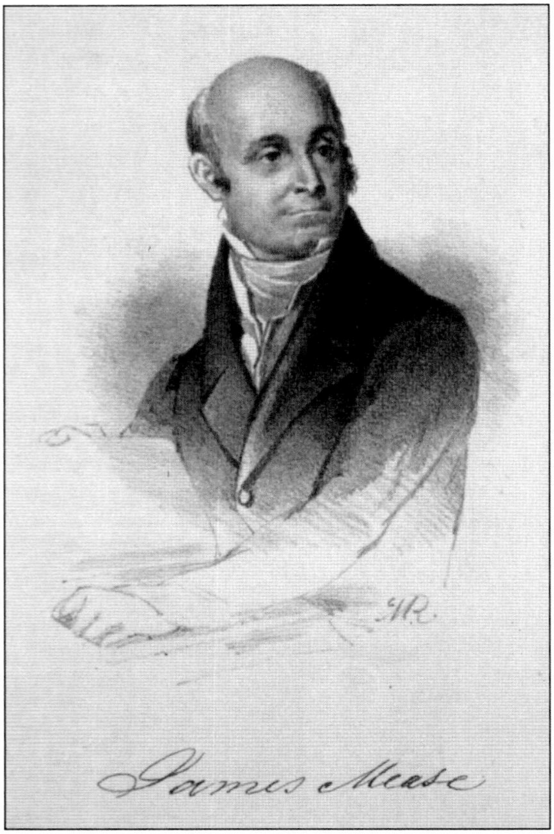

Dr. James Mease and Mease Family Monument. John Mease was one of the founders of Philadelphia's First City Troop and served with them from 1774 to 1775. From 1775 to 1777, he served with the Continental Army. John Mease's son Dr. James Mease was a scientist and medical doctor who served as a hospital surgeon during the War of 1812. After the war, he went on to become the first vice president of the Athenaeum of Philadelphia. He was also the author of the first published tomato ketchup recipe. The Mease family was moved to Laurel Hill in 1904. (Left, NLM).

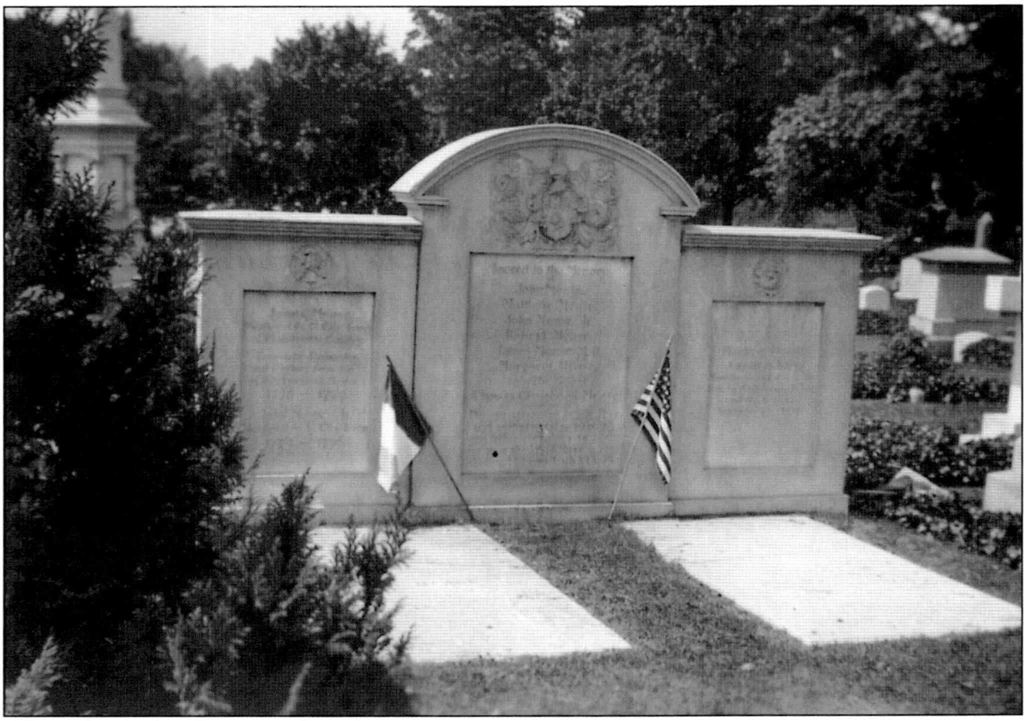

Stereoview of Robert Taylor Conrad Memorial. Robert Conrad was born in Philadelphia in 1810. He worked as a writer and editor for *Graham's Magazine*, where he edited the works of Edgar Allen Poe and others. He later served a short term as mayor of Philadelphia from 1854 to 1856. Conrad's lot, located in Section 14, was donated by cemetery managers.

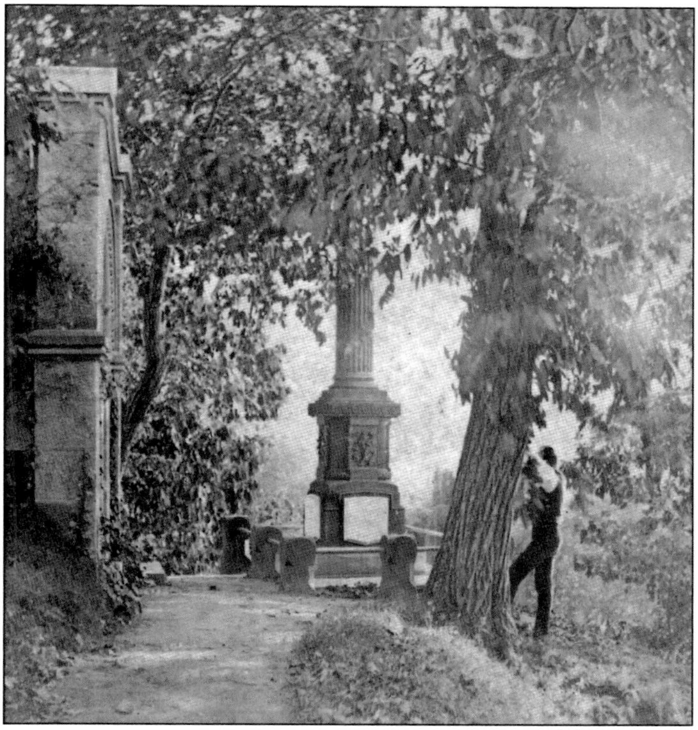

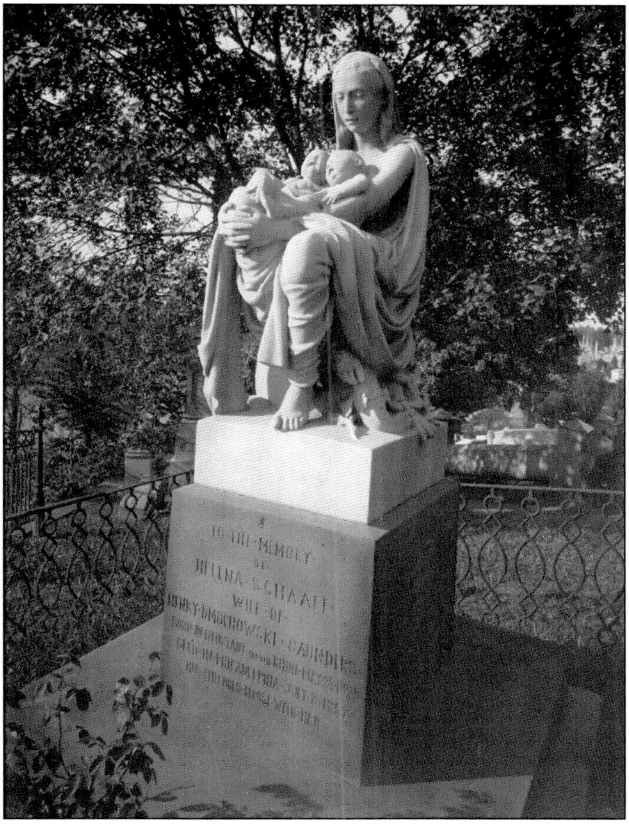

Henry Dmochowski Saunders, "Mother and Twins" Memorial. Born in Wilno, or Vilnius (capital of modern-day Lithuania), in 1810, sculptor Henry Dmochowski Saunders created this memorial to his wife, pianist and composer Helena Schaaff, and their two children. Dmochowski, who added the name Saunders when he came to America, was well regarded for his sculptures of Thaddeus Kosciusko and Casimir Pulaski, which are still on display in the US Capitol.

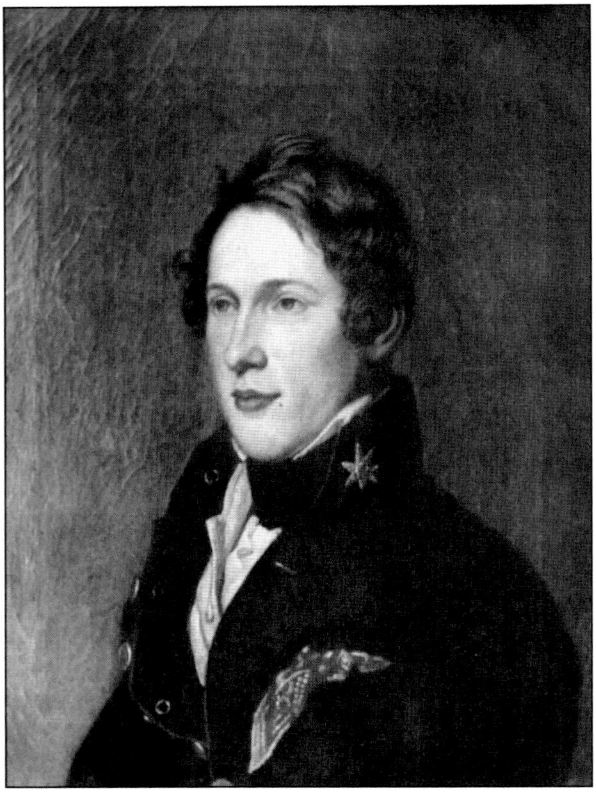

Titian Ramsay Peale, 1819. The youngest son of American naturalist Charles Wilson Peale, Titian Peale worked as a scientific illustrator and joined expeditions to document flora and fauna in the United States and around the world. He also worked in the US Patent Office and developed a love for photography. (LOC.)

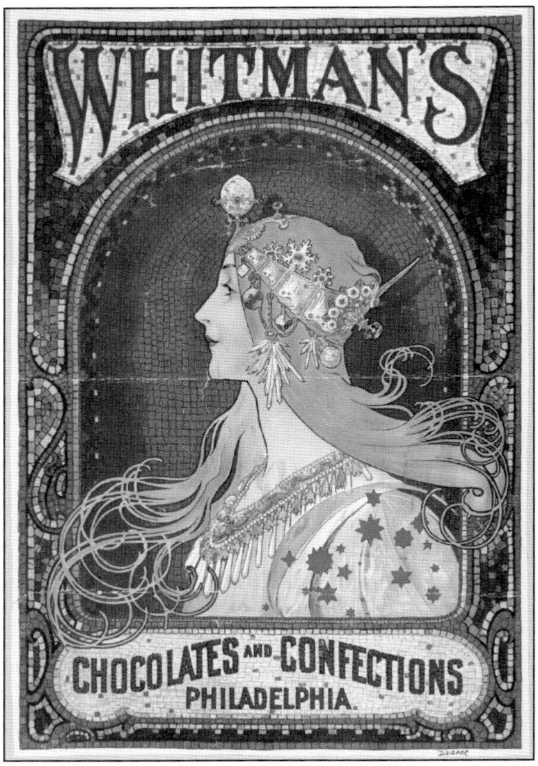

Whitman's Chocolates Advertisement. As a young man in 1842, Stephen Whitman opened a small confectionery shop in Philadelphia near the waterfront. Inspired by the sailors who frequented his shop, Whitman worked to create boxed chocolates of high quality to rival European imports. He began advertising in newspapers, and his business grew and expanded. Today, Whitman's is one of the oldest brands of chocolates in the country. (NYPL.)

Richard Alexander Fullerton "R.A.F." Penrose, MD. A graduate of Dickinson College and the University of Pennsylvania Medical School, R.A.F. Penrose was one of the founders of the Children's Hospital of Philadelphia. Penrose was a surgeon during the Civil War and became professor of obstetrics and the diseases of women and children at the University of Pennsylvania in 1863. (NLM.)

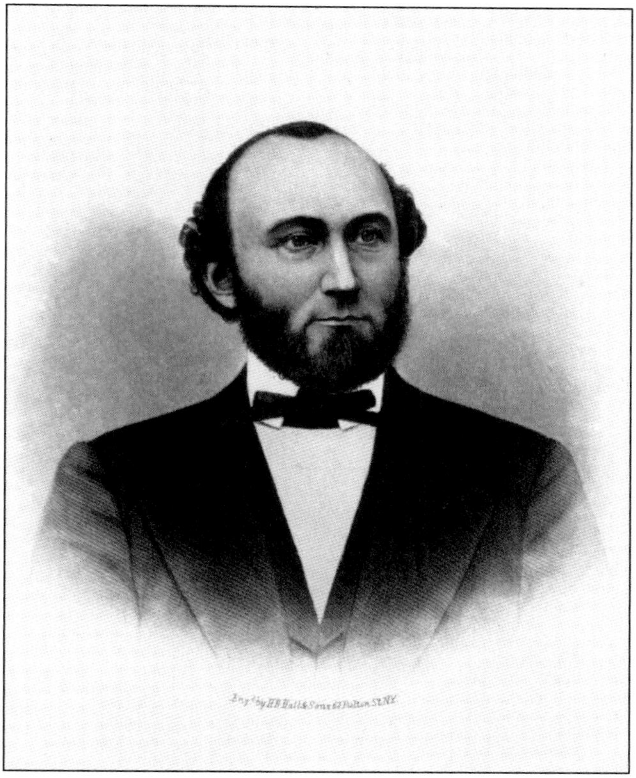

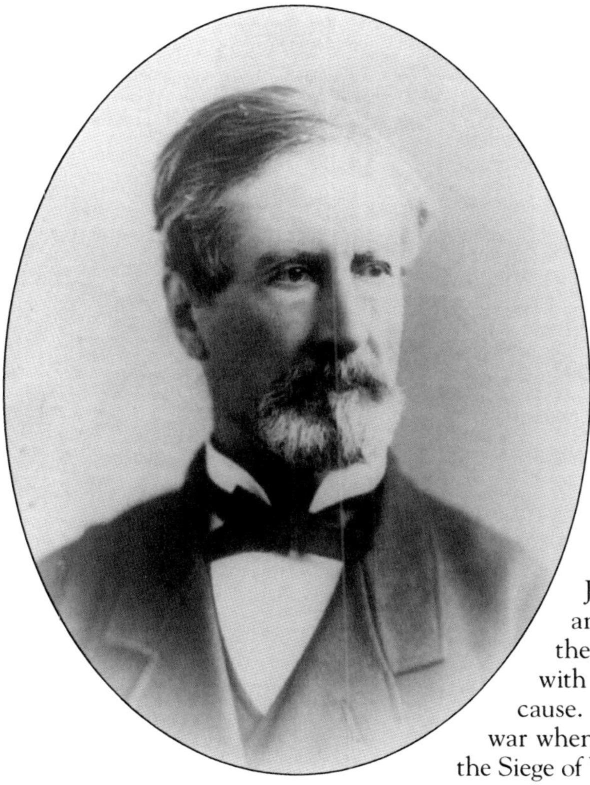

Gen. John C. Pemberton. A graduate of the US Military Academy at West Point, John C. Pemberton served in the Mexican and Seminole Wars. At the beginning of the Civil War, he resigned his commission with the US Army and joined the Confederate cause. Pemberton played a critical role in the war when he surrendered to Ulysses S. Grant at the Siege of Vicksburg. (LOC.)

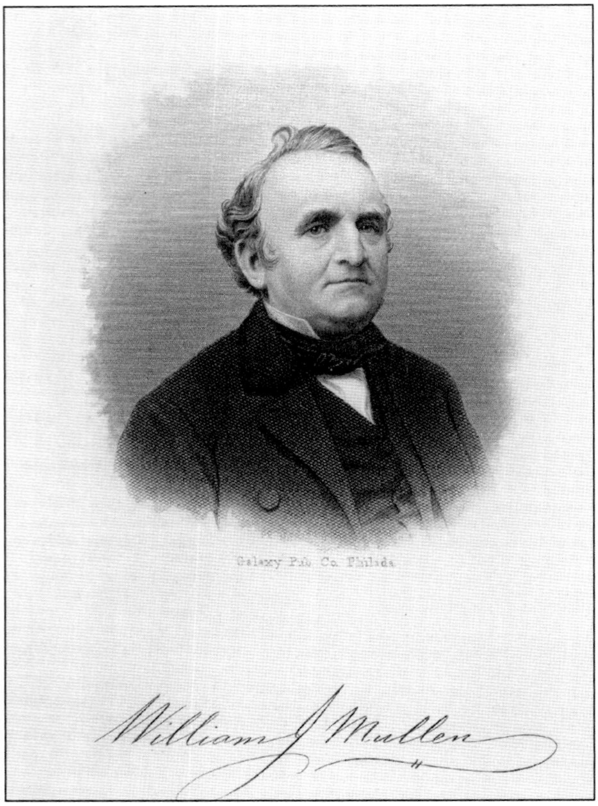

William J. Mullen Portrait and Monument (c. 1910). One of the most distinctive memorials in South Laurel Hill was erected by philanthropist and prison agent William J. Mullen, the "Prisoners' Friend." The memorial, first shown at the Centennial Exposition in Philadelphia in 1876, was both admired and ridiculed. A marble door, made to look like the entrance to Moyamensing Prison, is partially open. A weeping woman sits just outside the door. William J. Mullen stands on a pedestal. A bat, an owl, a bulldog, a set of open handcuffs and a weeping woman clinging to a cross were all originally part of this complicated sculpture. While some of the details of the memorial have been lost over time, it still inspires both positive and negative reactions from visitors.

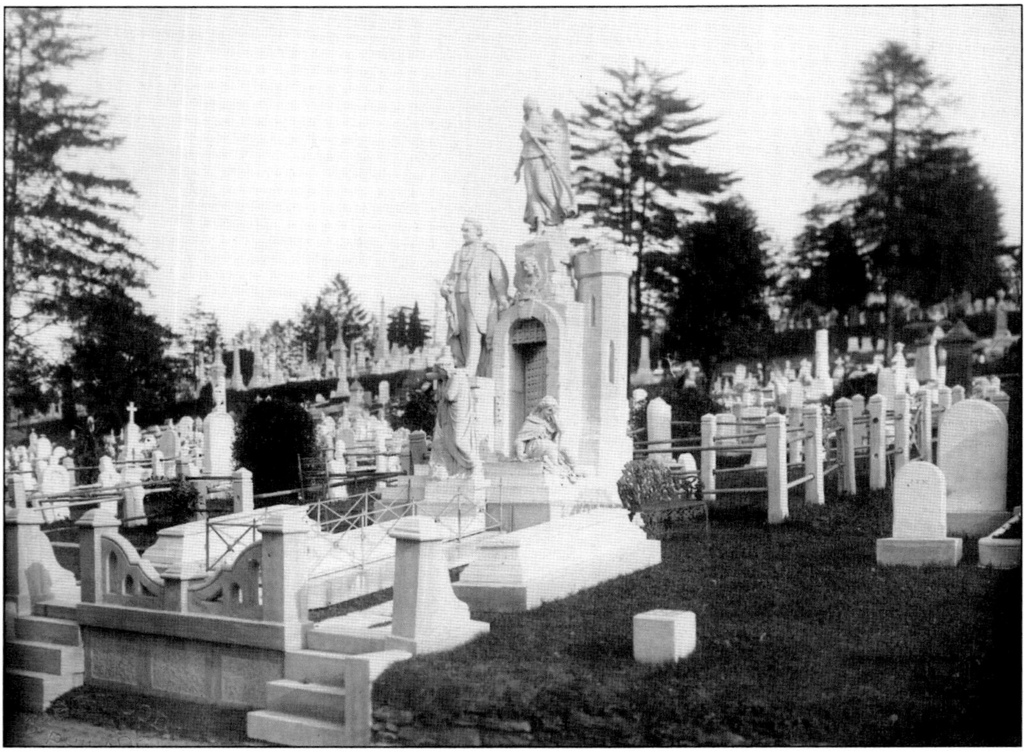

THOMAS STORY KIRKBRIDE, MD. In 1844, Thomas Story Kirkbride became superintendent of the Pennsylvania Hospital for the Insane. During his tenure, Kirkbride influenced the treatment of the mentally ill in the United States. He advocated humane and "moral treatment" for the insane, and his Kirkbride Plan was adopted by asylums across the United States. He was a founder of the Medical Superintendents of American Institutions for the Insane, today's American Psychiatric Association. (NLM.)

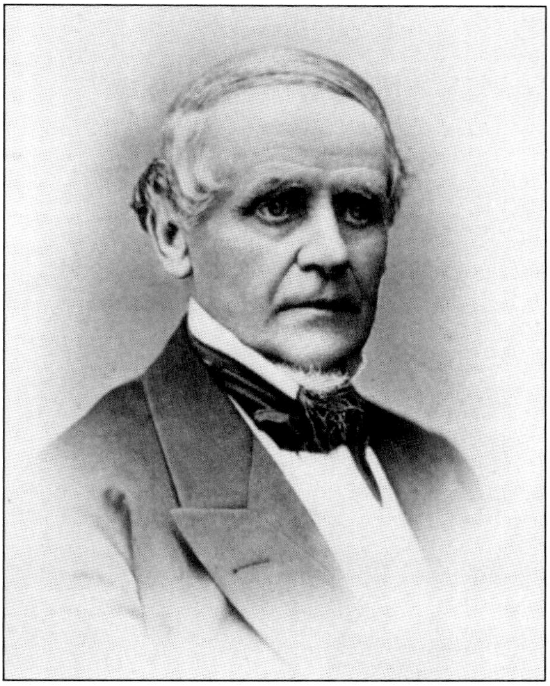

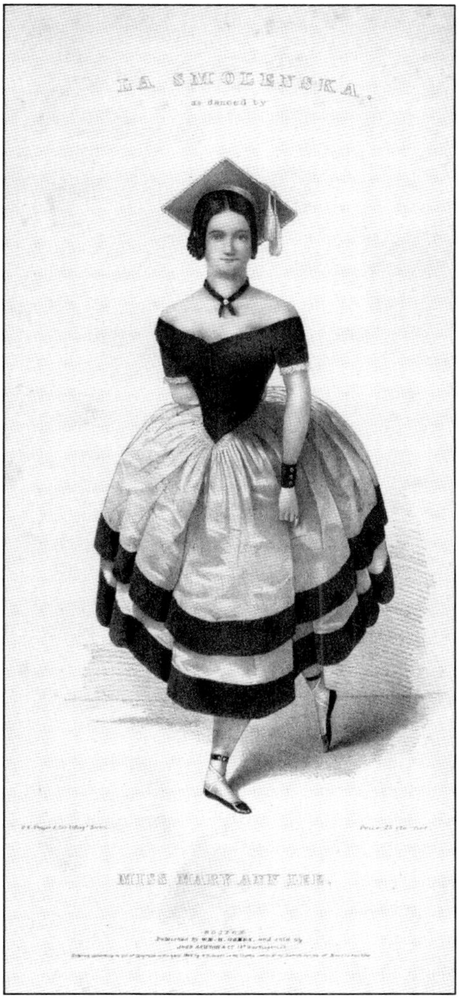

MARY ANN LEE, 1842. Mary Ann Lee was one of the first American ballerinas. She performed not just in ballet, but in melodramas, pantomimes, farces, and burlesque comedies. Lee toured the country and became an established favorite with the American public. In 1846, she danced *Giselle,* the first time this ballet was performed in the United States. Lee retired from the stage in 1847. (NYPL.)

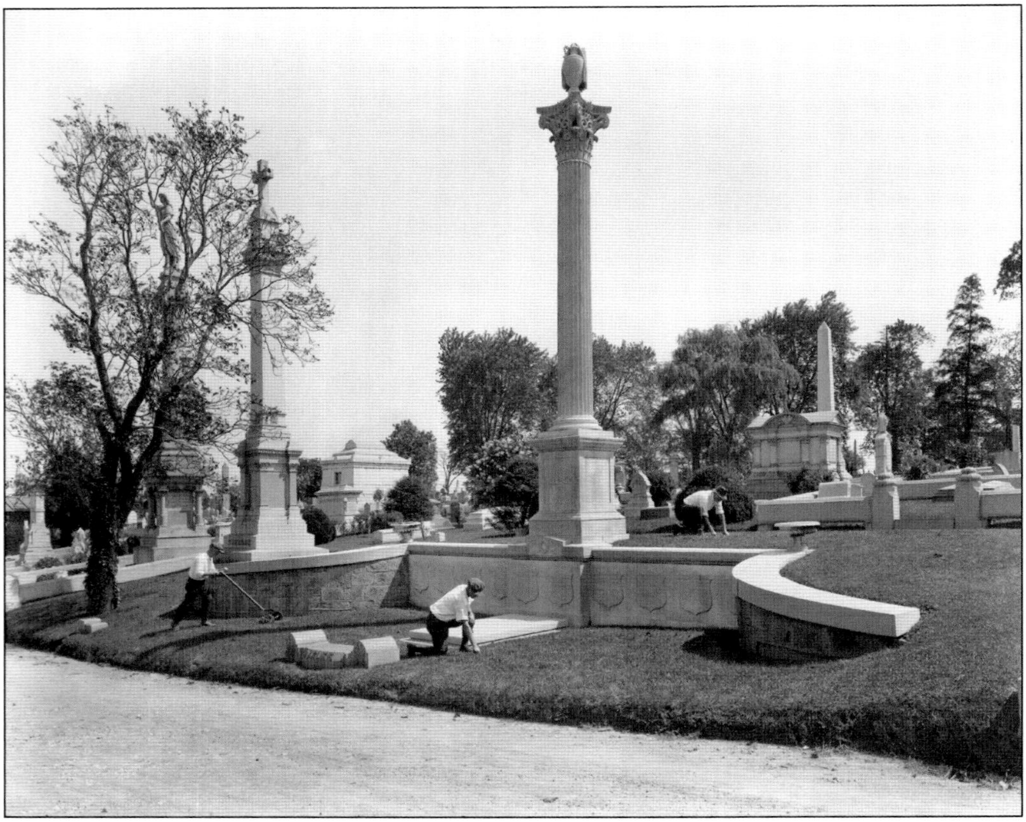

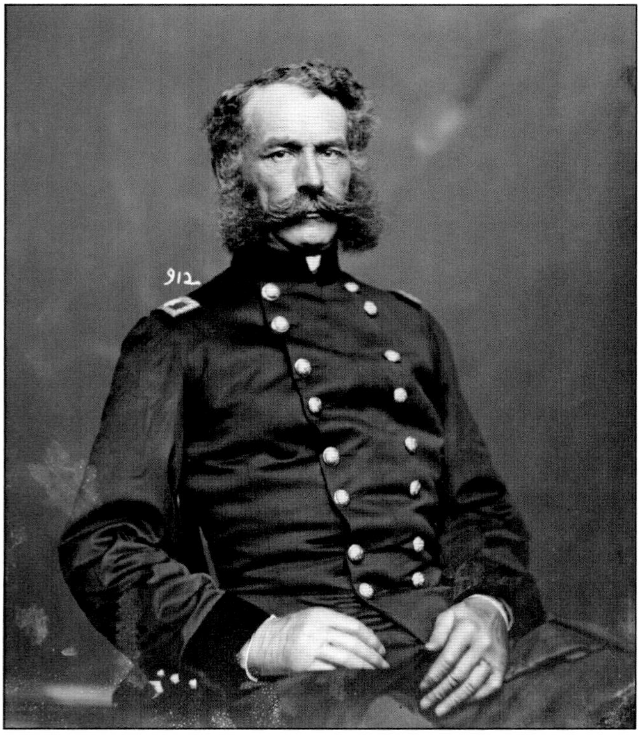

Brig. Gen. Henry Morris Naglee Monument (1917) and Portrait (c. 1860–1865). Born in Philadelphia in 1815, Naglee graduated from West Point in 1835. Shortly after graduation, he resigned his commission and began a career as a civil engineer. He later served in the Mexican War, then with a California militia unit in San Francisco. Remaining for a time in California, he gained a positive reputation as a vintner and the title "Father of California's Brandy Industry." During the Civil War, he served with the Army of the Potomac and was shot four times during the Battle of Fair Oaks. Following the war, he studied winemaking in Europe before returning to Santa Clara, California. (Left, LOC.)

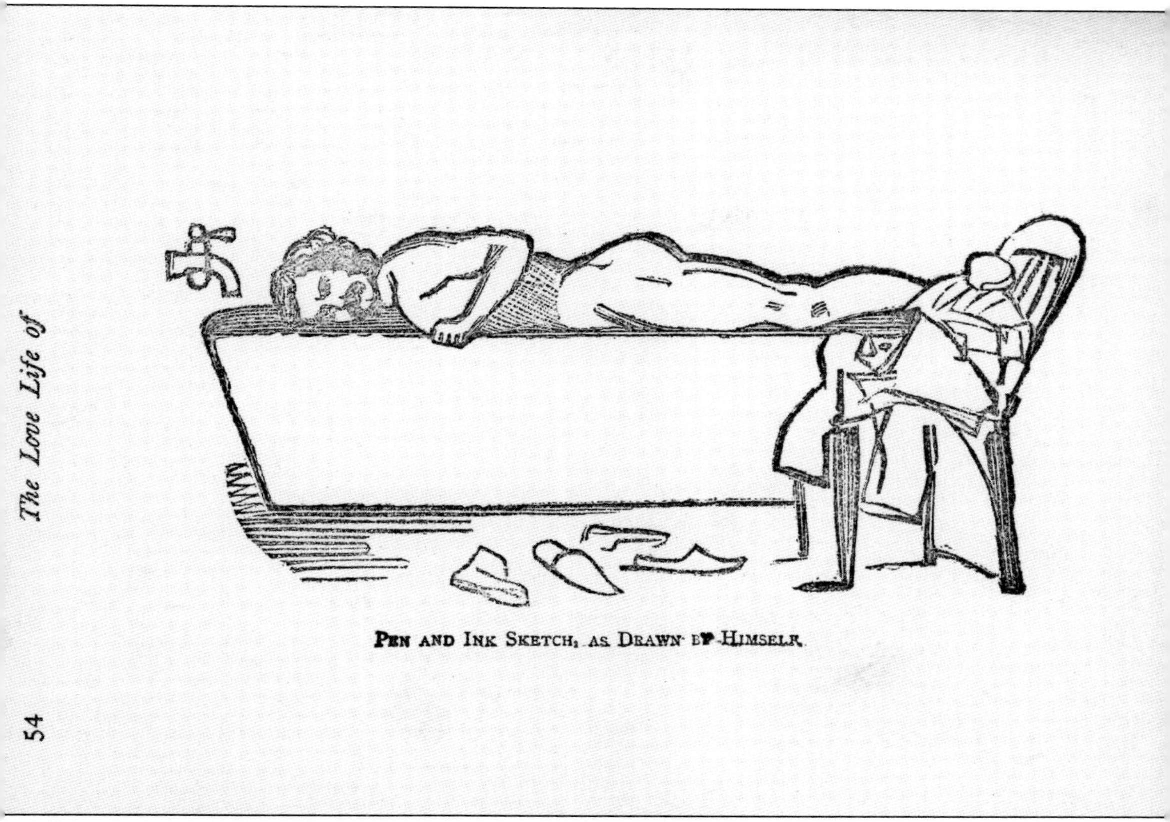

SKETCH FROM *THE LOVE LIFE OF GENERAL HENRY M. NAGLEE*, 1867. Naglee's life was not without controversy. In 1865, Mary Schell, a San Francisco woman he spent six years sending torrid love letters to, published those letters after Naglee rejected her. Among the more humorous elements of the book was a sketch of Naglee doing naked pushups on his bathtub, which he claimed built up his arm strength. Some years later, he was taken to trial by the nursemaid he employed following his wife's death for a breach of promise suit, in which the woman claimed Naglee promised marriage, seduced her, and then rejected her.

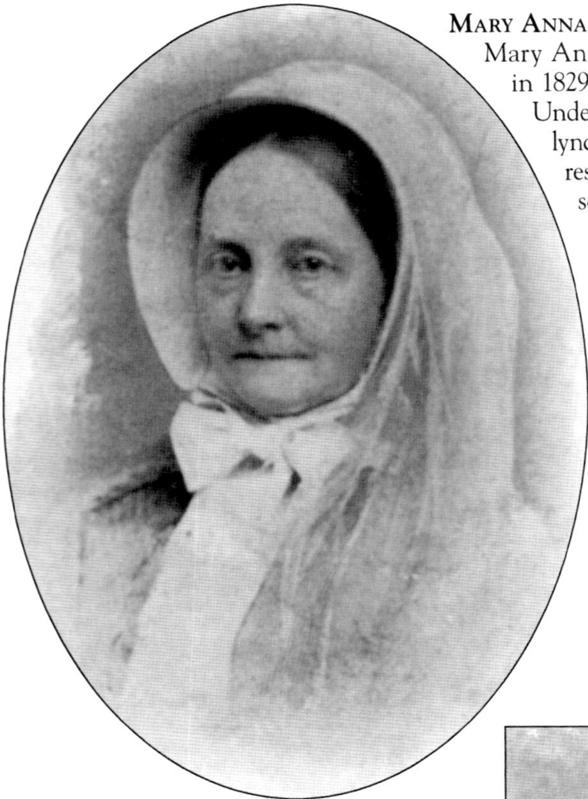

Mary Anna Longstreth. Educator and abolitionist Mary Anna Longstreth started a school for girls in 1829. In the 1850s, due to her work with the Underground Railroad, she was kidnapped by a lynch mob that attempted to hang her, but was rescued by a group of fellow abolitionists. Her school continued through the Civil War. She supported the Hampton Institute in Virginia, a normal and industrial school for freedmen. (HSP.)

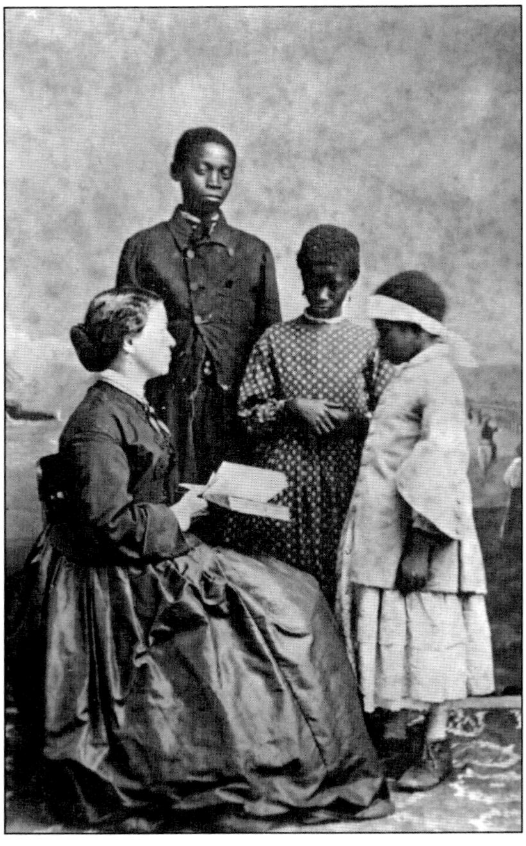

Laura Matilda Towne, with Students Dick, Maria, and Amoretta, 1866. When Union forces liberated slaves in South Carolina's Beaufort County, abolitionist and educator Laura Matilda Towne journeyed south to provide medical care and education for the former slaves. Along with Ellen Murray, she opened the Penn School, the first school for freedmen. They made a life in South Carolina, educating former slaves and their descendants for the next 40 years. (NYPL.)

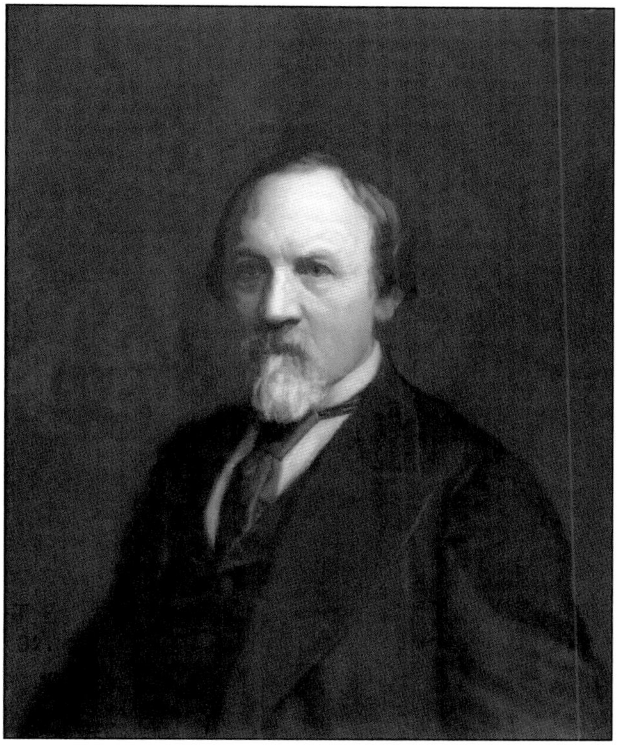

JOSHUA BALLINGER LIPPINCOTT PORTRAIT, 1892. This painting by Thomas Eakens depicts the founder of publishing house J.B. Lippincott & Co. Lippincott began by publishing religious works, but the company saw its greatest success with the printing of trade books. (Philadelphia Museum of Art, partial gift of Mrs. Bertha Coles in memory of Mrs. Stricker Coles, 1967-37-1.)

H.N. BURROUGHS MAUSOLEUM, 1926. The brownstone Burroughs mausoleum sits at the top of South Laurel Hill. The soft stone has not held up well over the past century, but its color and cast-iron door make it a standout in a line of mausoleums.

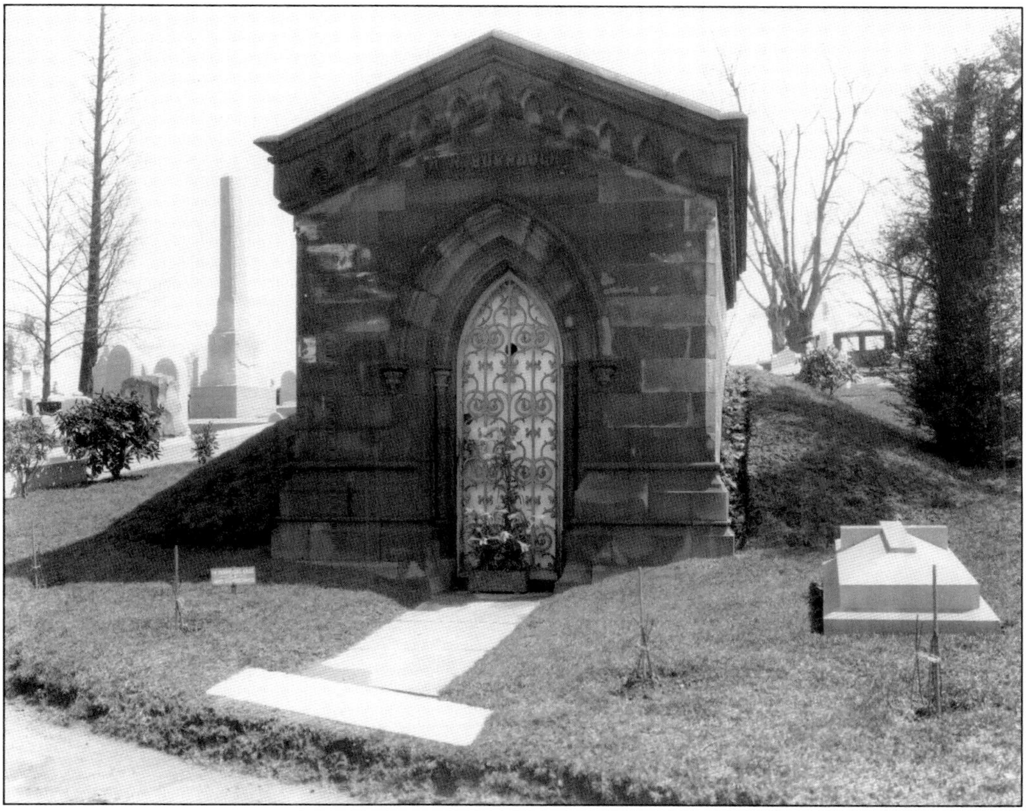

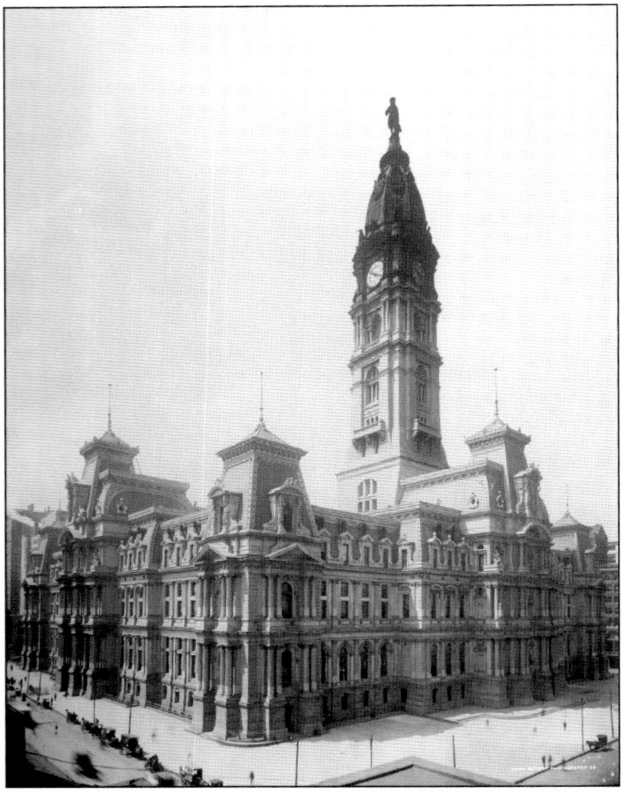

Philadelphia City Hall, c. 1905. Scottish architect John McArthur Jr. is best remembered for designing Philadelphia's City Hall, even though he did not live to see its completion. McArthur received commissions for residences and commercial buildings prior to the Civil War; during the war, he constructed temporary hospitals. After the war, he supervised the construction of federal buildings in Philadelphia. (LOC.)

William Stokley Mausoleum, 1909. William Stokley served as Philadelphia's mayor from 1872 to 1881, during the time of City Hall's construction. Due to the political machine, deals, and corruption, City Hall took 30 years to build, and Stokley likely directly benefitted from some of the deals made.

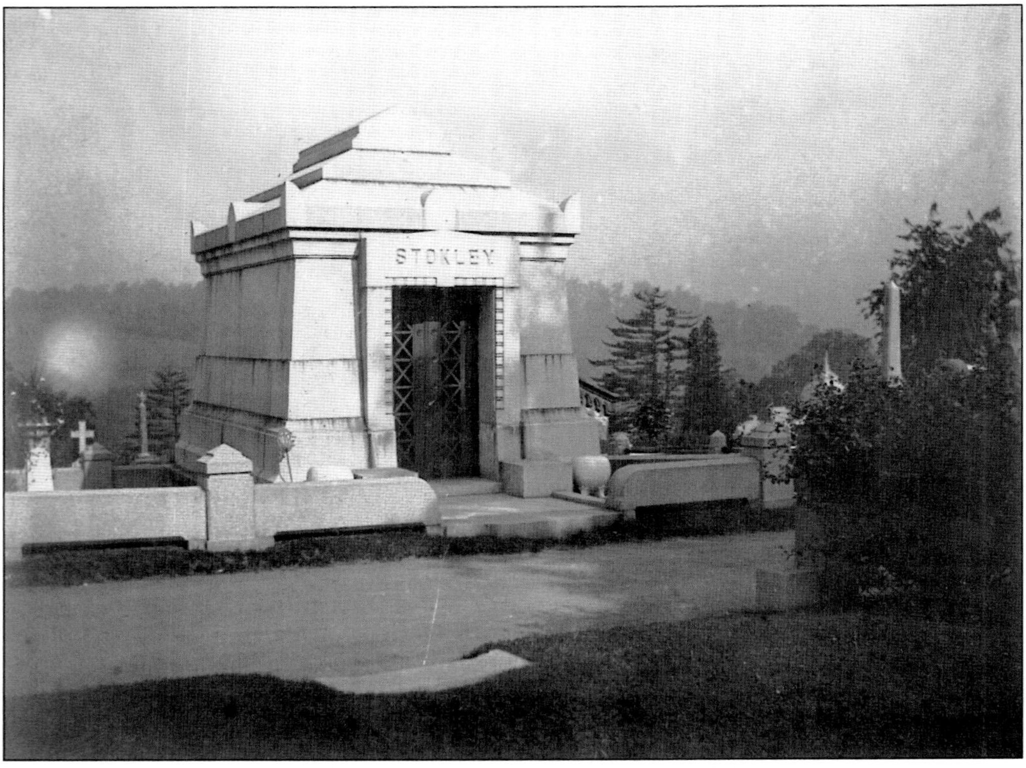

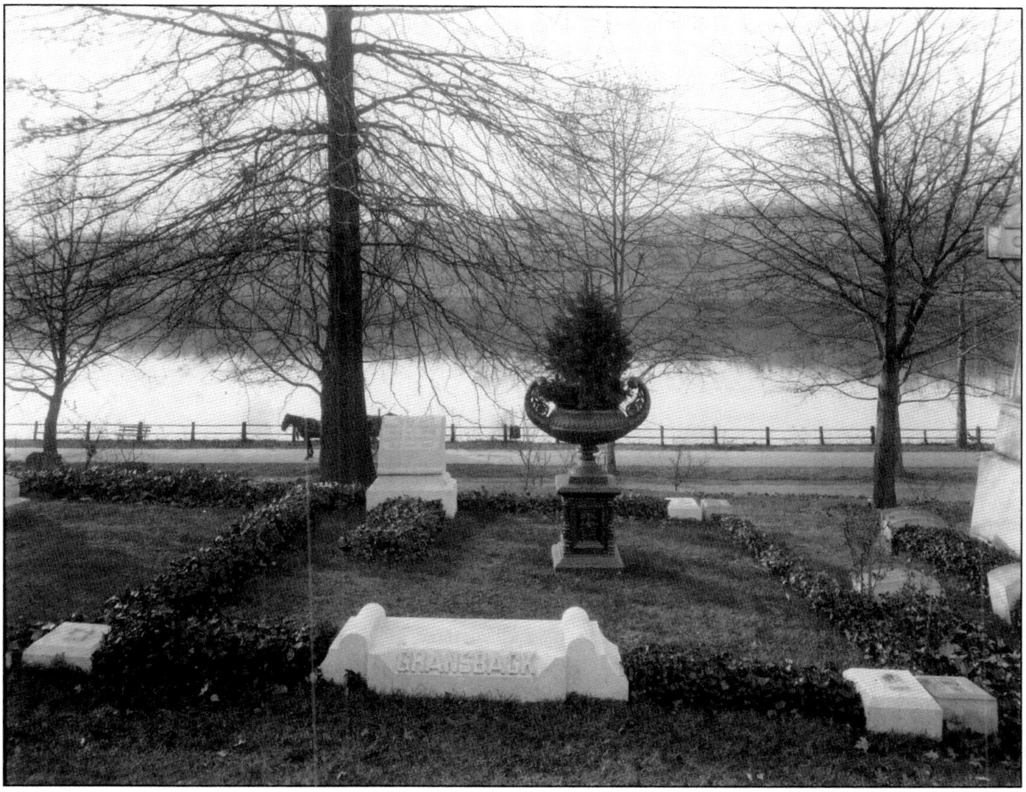

Gransback Lot, 1925. Henry Gransback was born in Philadelphia in 1836. A veteran of the Civil War, he was a public servant, working as a lifelong Republican in the Pennsylvania General Assembly. The Gransback lot features a view of the Schuylkill River in its otherwise simple ornamentation.

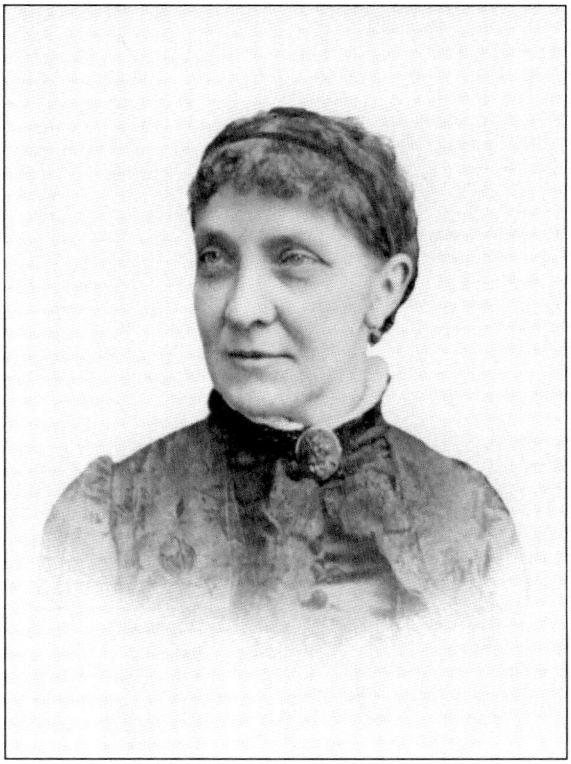

Rachel Holloway Lloyd, PhD. Rachel Lloyd supported herself by working as a science teacher before moving to Switzerland in 1884. She enrolled at the University of Zurich and received her PhD in chemistry in 1887, making her the first American woman to earn a doctorate in chemistry. After returning to the United States, she accepted the position of assistant professor of analytical chemistry at the University of Nebraska, where she remained until her retirement in 1894. (University Archives and Special Collections, University of Nebraska–Lincoln Libraries.)

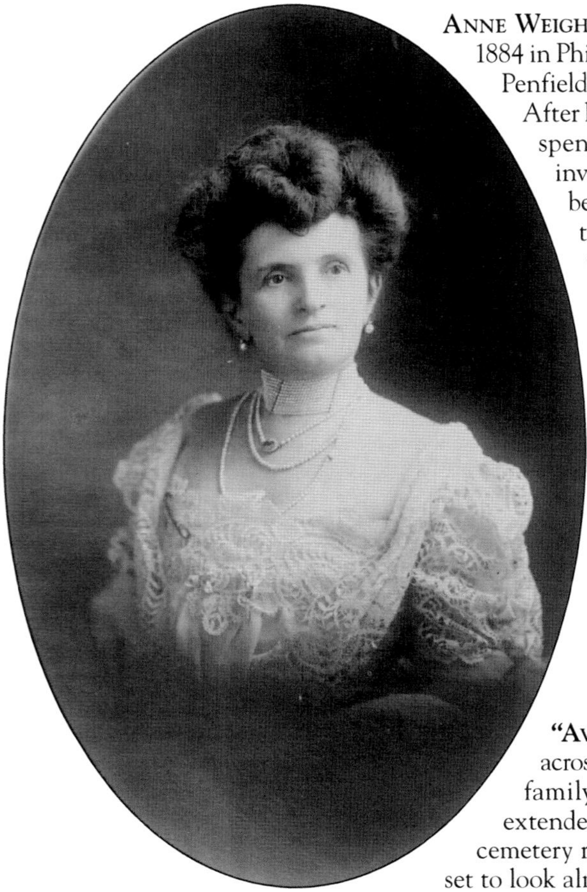

Anne Weightman Walker Penfield, 1913. Born in 1884 in Philadelphia, multiple inheritances left Anne Penfield one of the richest women in the world. After her second husband died in 1922, Penfield spent years traveling Europe. A disastrous investment in a stage production marked the beginning of her financial losses, and by the time she died in 1932, her fortune amounted to less than $4 million. (LOC.)

"Avenue of the Angels," c. 1910. Directly across from Anne Weightman Walker Penfield's family lot lies a group of lots owned by one extended family. The edge of the lots along the cemetery road is delineated by a line of tall angels, set to look almost like guardians.

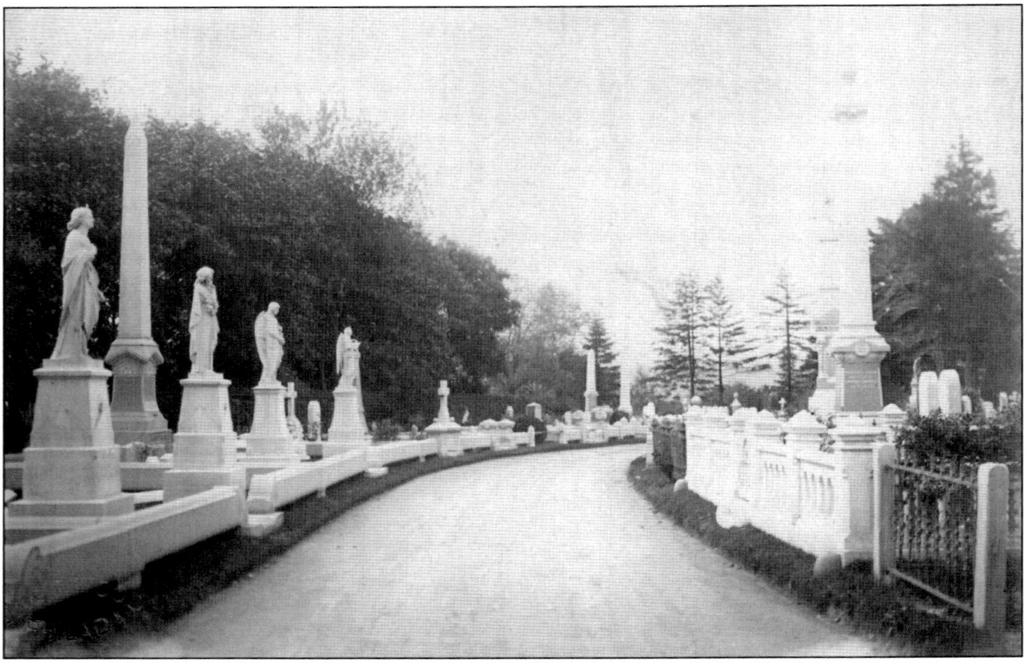

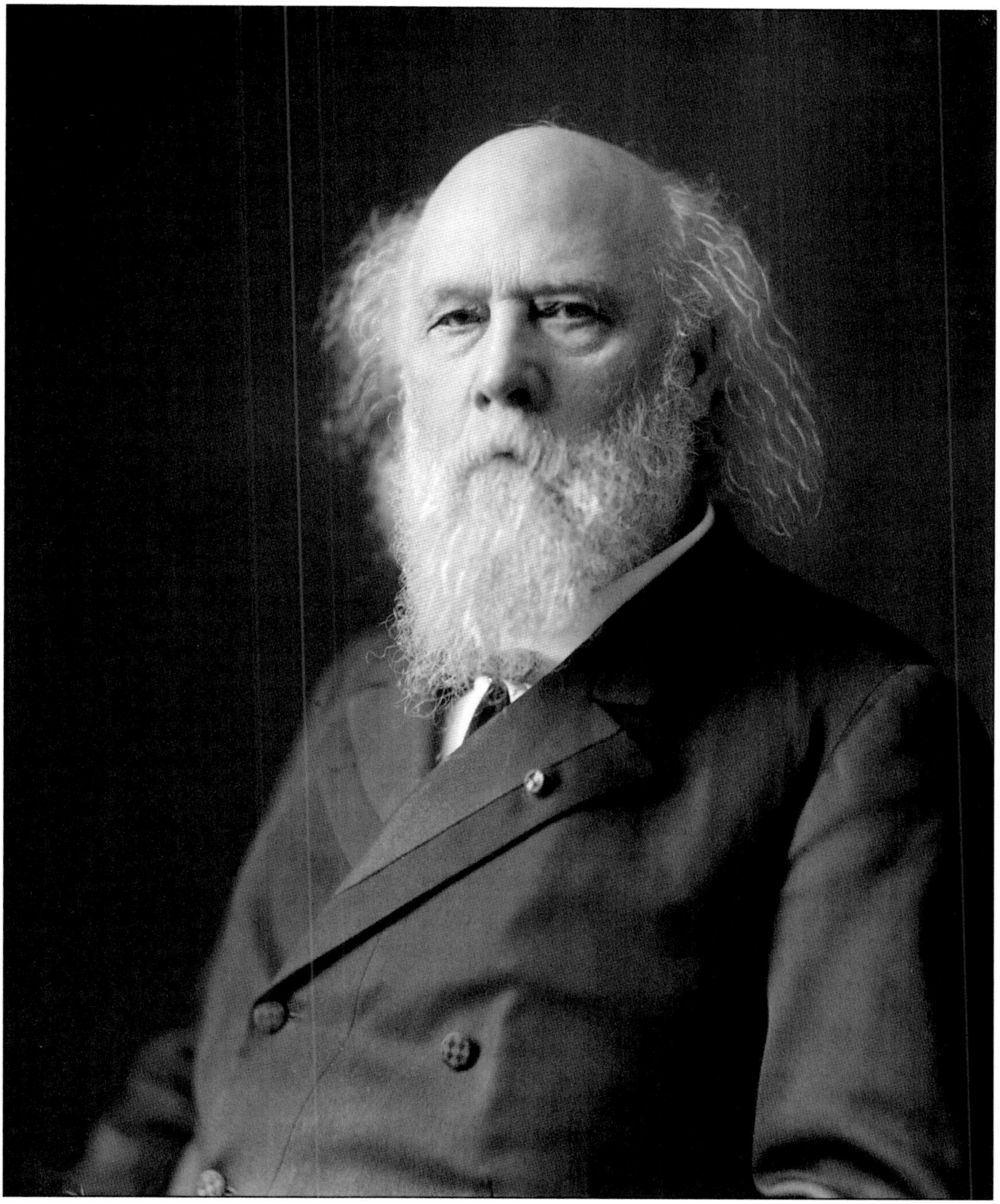

ADM. GEORGE WALLACE MELVILLE, C. 1910. Born in New York City, George Melville entered the US Navy in 1861 and became an officer of the Engineer Corps. In 1873, he volunteered for the first of his expeditions to the Arctic, and in 1879, served aboard the USS *Jeannette* during the search for a quick way to the North Pole by way of the Bering Strait. The ship became icebound and sank in June 1881, leaving the crew on ice floes mid-ocean with only three small boats and few provisions. Melville was the only commander to rescue his men. He also retrieved all records of the expedition. To reward his efforts, the US Congress advanced him 15 numbers on the promotion list and awarded him the Congressional Gold Medal. In 1888, he was one of the 33 founders of the National Geographic Society. Melville was promoted to rear engineer-in-chief of the Navy in 1900. In this position, he established the Engineering Experiment Station in Annapolis. He retired from active duty in 1903 and died in 1912. (LOC.)

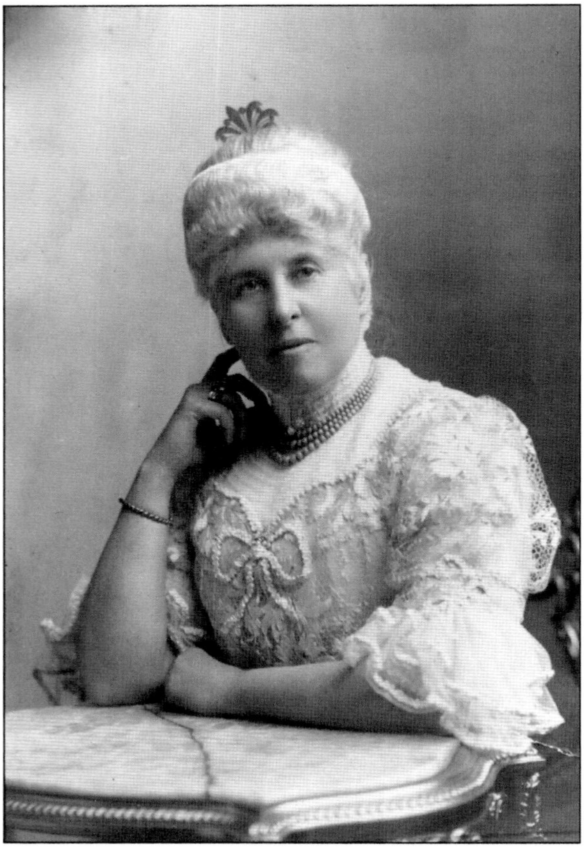

Lydia Thompson Morris. Lydia and John Morris inherited their fortune from their father's iron-manufacturing firm. Their estate, Compton, held extensive and varied gardens filled with specimens from their travels. Upon her death, Lydia Morris left the property in trust to the University of Pennsylvania. The estate became the Morris Arboretum and is now listed in the National Register of Historic Places. (Morris Arboretum of the University of Pennsylvania.)

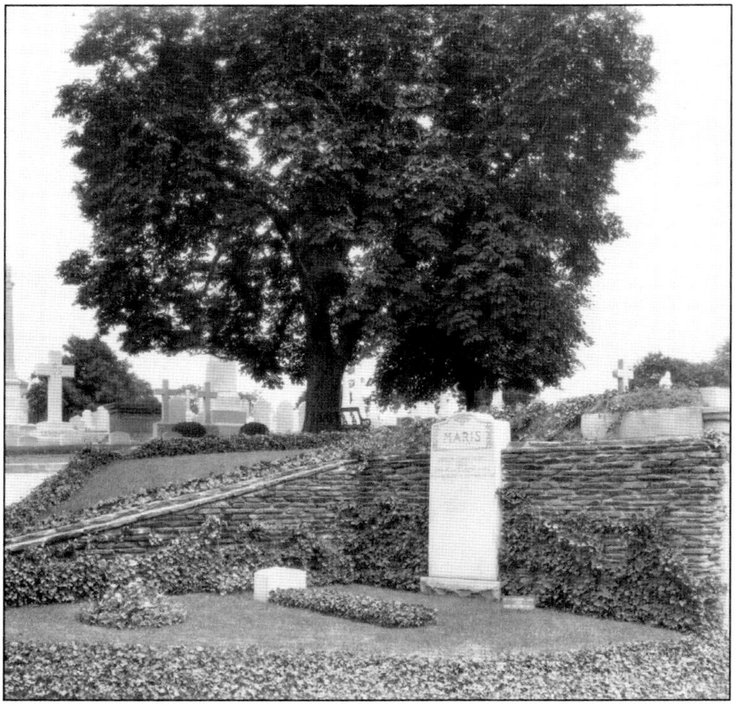

Maris Lot, 1931. Set into a terraced wall in Section 7 is the Maris lot. While little is known about the Maris family, the lot is distinctive due to its well-manicured appearance and monument set into the terrace wall.

Gen. Jacob Zeilin Lot. Brig. Gen. Jacob Zeilin was the seventh commandant of the US Marine Corps, serving from 1864 to 1876. Commissioned in 1831, he served in the Mexican-American and Civil Wars. In 1868, he approved the Marines' modern insignia of the eagle, globe, and anchor. On November 10 of every year, a group of Marines comes to Laurel Hill to honor Zeilin on the corps' birthday. (Emma Stern.)

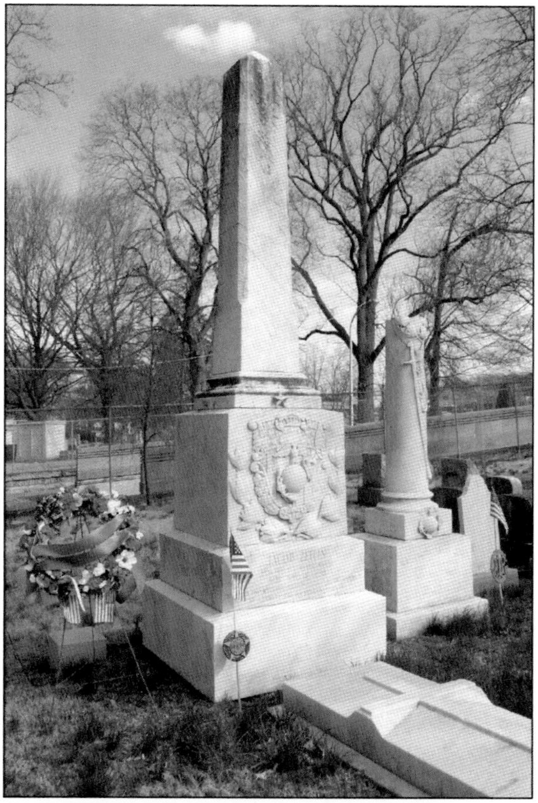

Harrison Newhall Funeral, January 15, 1918. Floral decorations were often an elaborate part of a graveside scene. Lilies, palms, and other greens sometimes completely covered the gravesite of the deceased. This image is from the funeral for Civil War veteran Harrison Newhall.

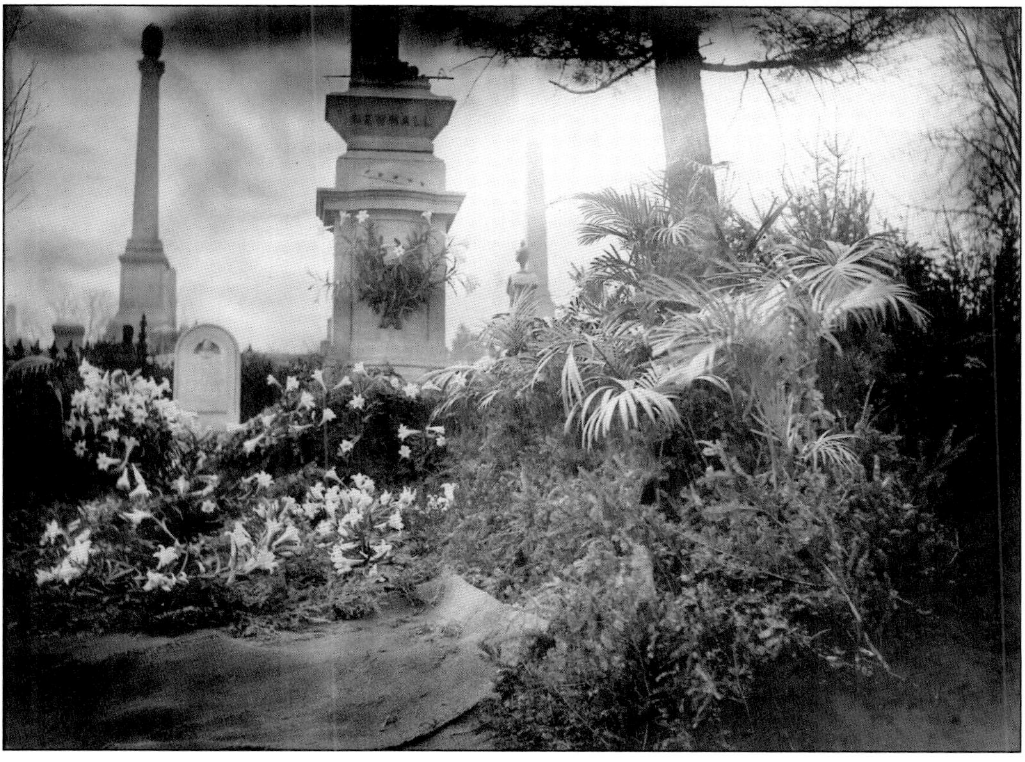

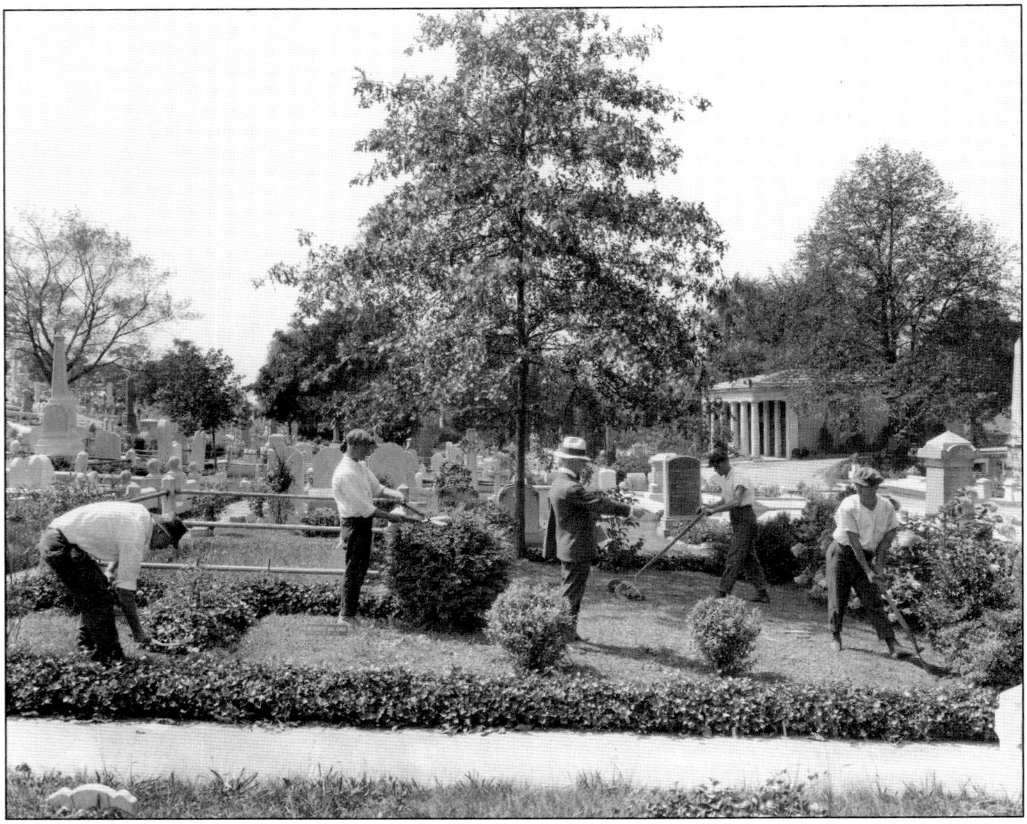

WORKERS IN SOUTH LAUREL HILL. In this photograph, a foreman supervises work in South Laurel Hill. A small sign indicates the lot is "In Perpetual Care," which likely means the lot holders paid an extra sum for the pruning and care of the lot.

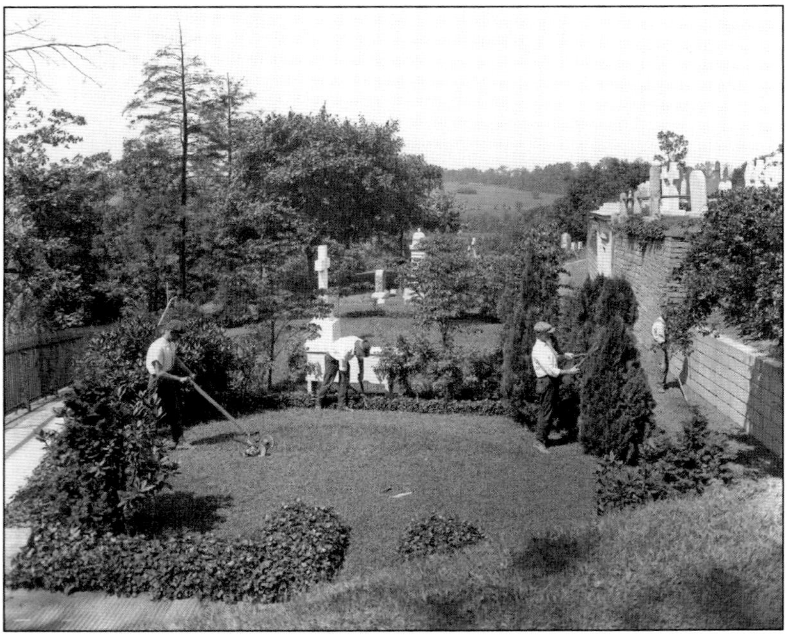

WORKERS IN SECTION 7, 1917. Maintaining a lot in Laurel Hill involved more than just cutting the grass. Workers were responsible for pruning shrubs and plantings, which could be very labor intensive. In this photograph, four men are at work in a lot in Section 7.

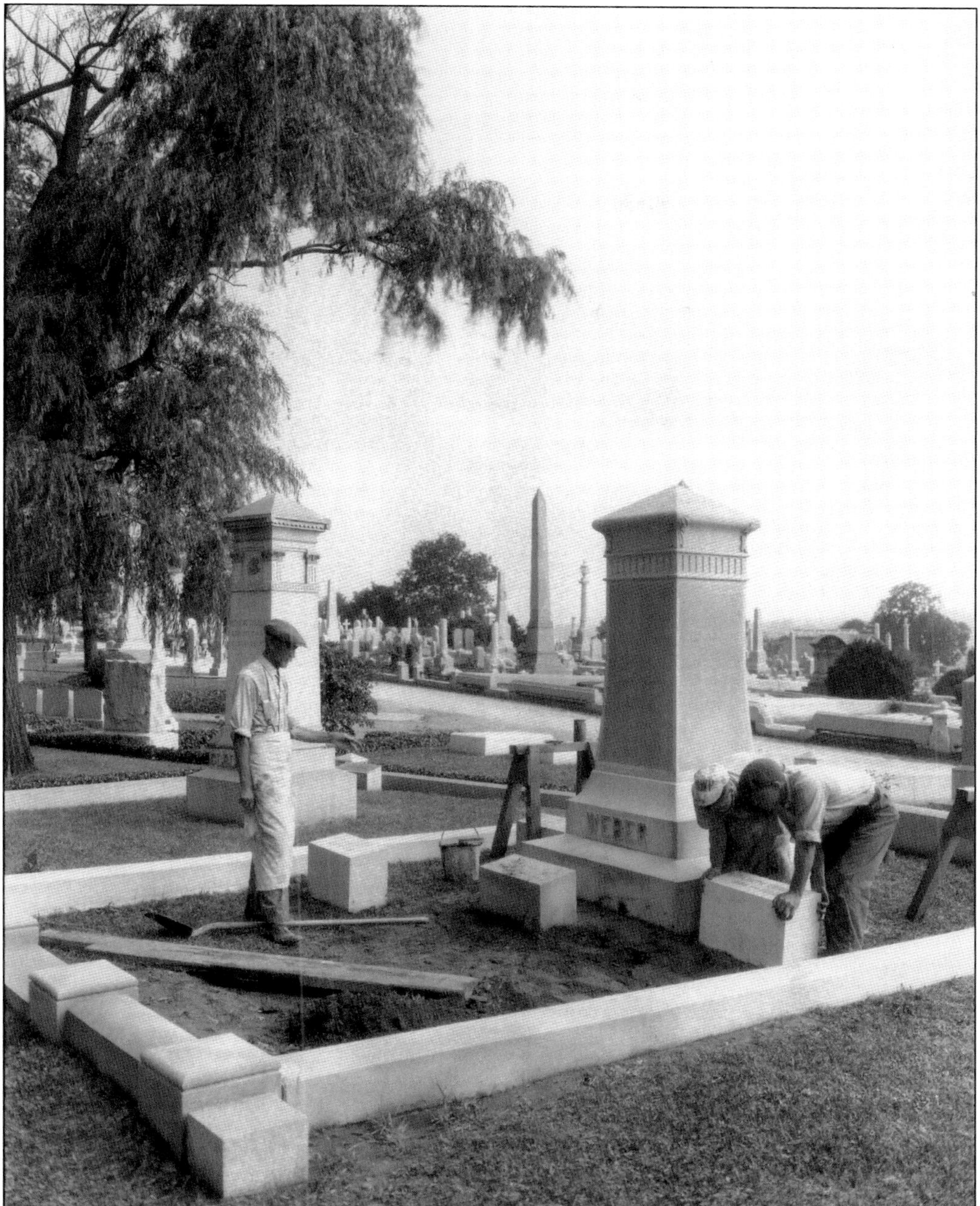

MASONS INSTALL STONE, 1930. It was not until the late 20th century that Laurel Hill began selling its own monuments. Until that time, property owners purchased their monuments from outside dealers. This photograph shows masons installing a monument in the Weber lot in Section 4.

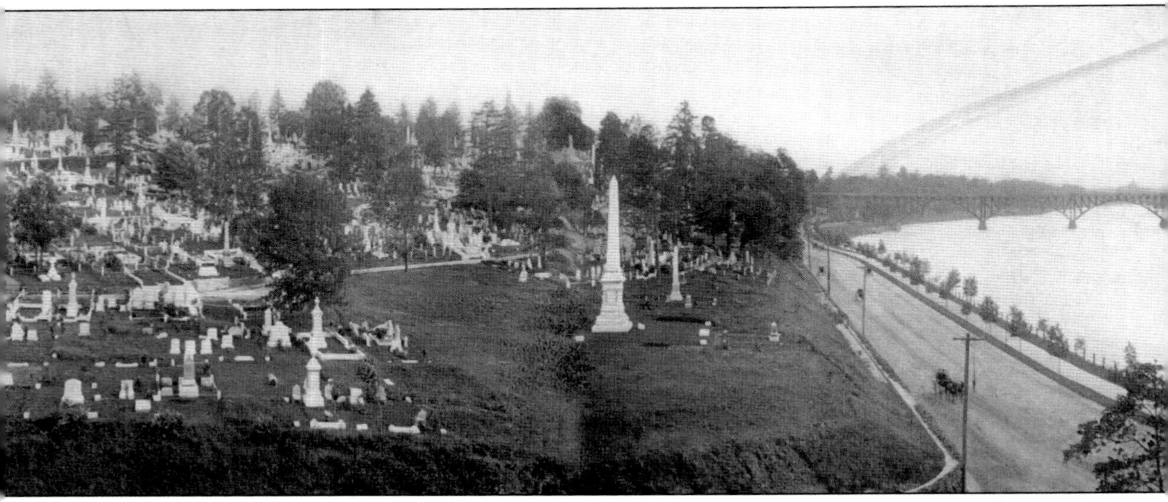

SOUTH ALONG EAST RIVER DRIVE. East River Drive (renamed Kelly Drive in 1985), separated Laurel Hill from the Schuylkill River. This view shows traffic along the major thoroughfare, with Center City Philadelphia in the background.

Four

STOEVER TRACT

In 1855, the cemetery had the opportunity to expand again through the purchase of an additional 10 acres of land from Frederick Stoever. This tract, located between North Laurel Hill and the Philadelphia and Reading Railroad, was small enough and similar enough to its neighbor that the cemetery managers decided not to establish a new design plan. Instead, they treated the Stoever tract more as an annex to North Laurel Hill. They extended existing drives and surveyed the area into lots. Lots were sold in Section W and X first, working back from the road between the sections. The first burial there occurred on November 7, 1855. The body of Samuel Gillespie had been held in the receiving vault for over a month before his lot in Section W was ready for burial.

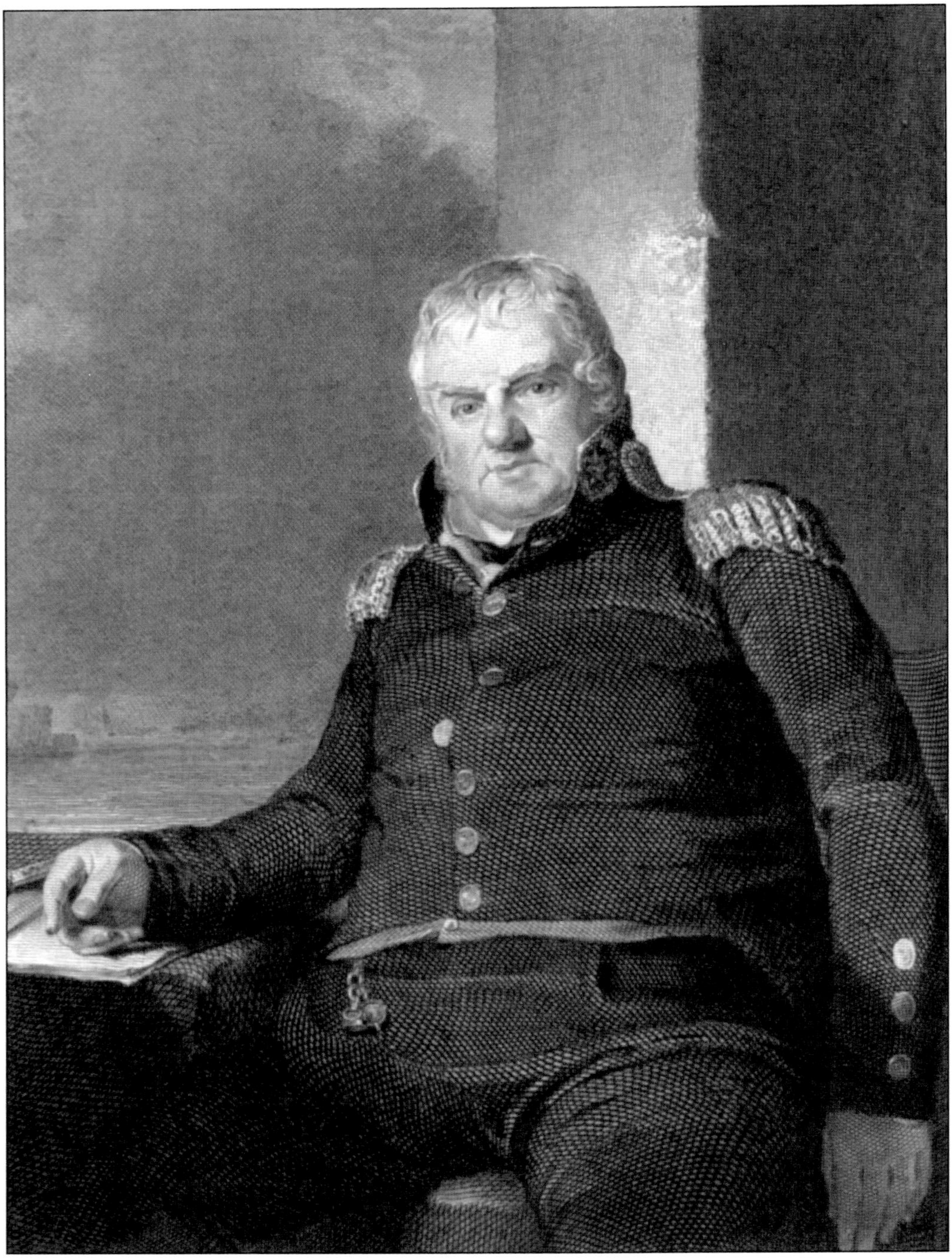

GEN. JONATHAN WILLIAMS PORTRAIT. Jonathan Williams had a distinguished and varied career, both as a military leader and as a scientist. His work on military fortifications brought him to the attention of Thomas Jefferson, who made him inspector of fortifications for the Army. He later became the commander of the post at West Point and the first superintendent of the US Military Academy there. Williams also surveyed the area of Brooklyn known as Williamsburg in 1802. (NYPL.)

YELLOW FEVER MEMORIAL. In July 1855, when an epidemic of yellow fever erupted in Virginia, a group of Philadelphia's most prominent citizens sent 60 volunteers—doctors, nurses, medical students, druggists, and cuppers and bleeders—to aid the sick and dying. By the time the epidemic ended that October, 15 of those volunteers had died of the disease and were buried in Virginia. In 1856, the same group of prominent citizens purchased a lot in Laurel Hill with the intention of bringing the remains of the deceased volunteers back to Philadelphia. They ordered a Roman Doric column of Italian marble, 25 feet high, with an engraved pedestal base, from John Baird, a local marble dealer. On January 18, 1859, the remains of the volunteers were placed in a vault underneath the monument.

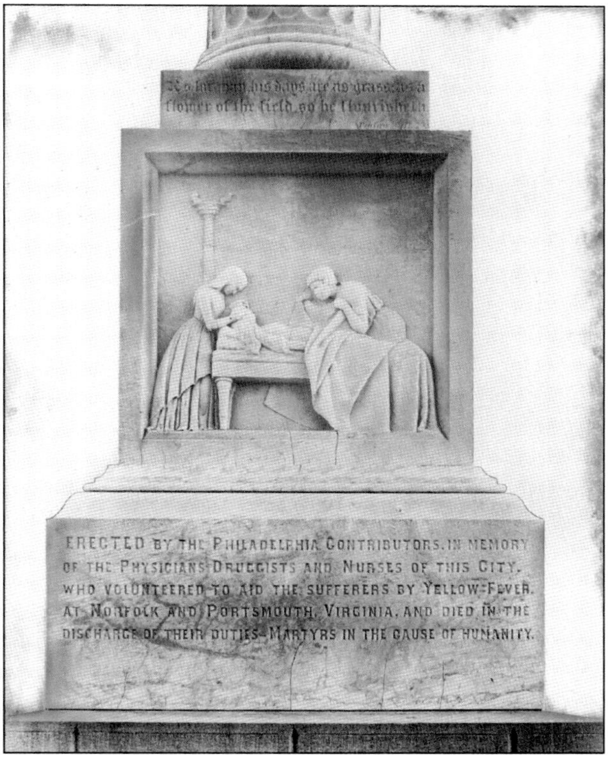

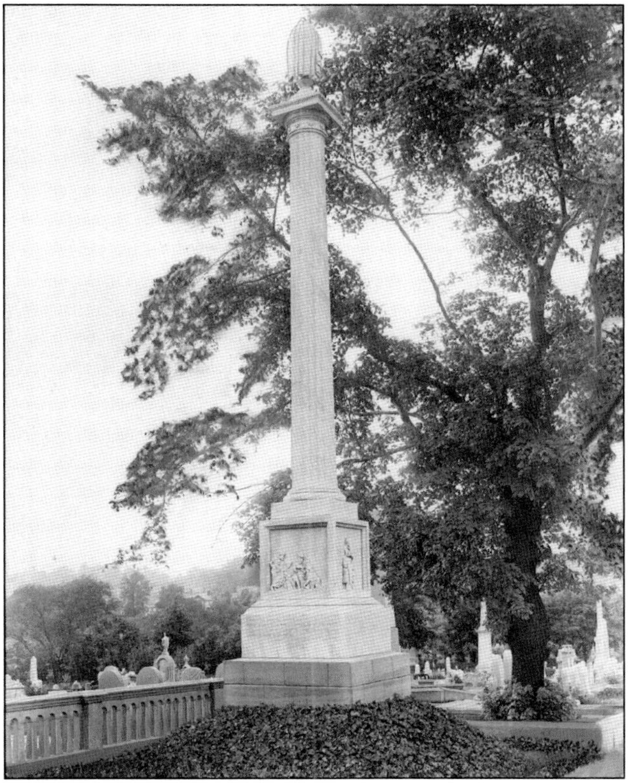

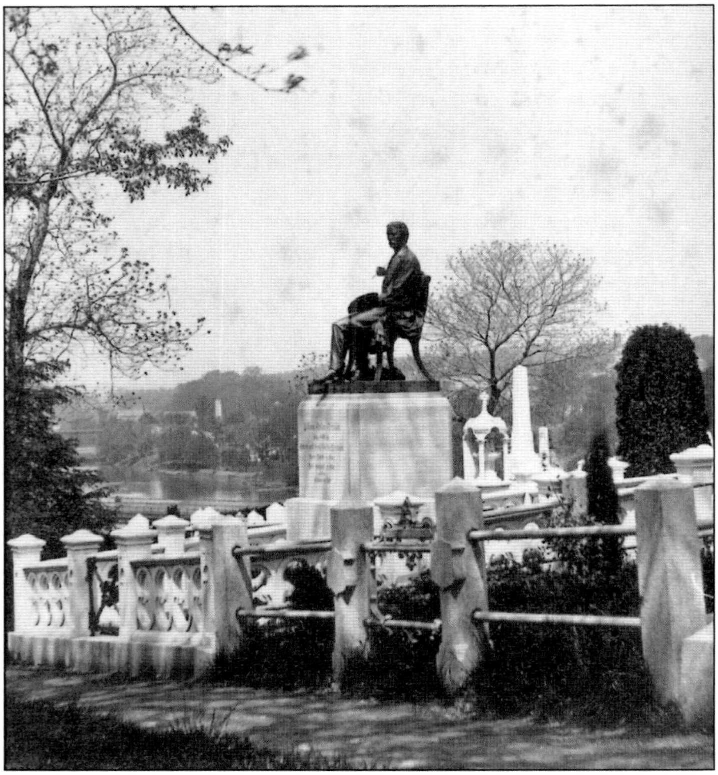

William Emlen Cresson Monument. Perhaps the most notable monument in the Stoever tract is the memorial to William Emlen Cresson. A lover of art, Cresson died at a young age. Upon his death, his parents established the Cresson Prize at the Pennsylvania Academy of Fine Arts, which is still awarded today. The bronze memorial was the work of sculptor Joseph A. Bailly.

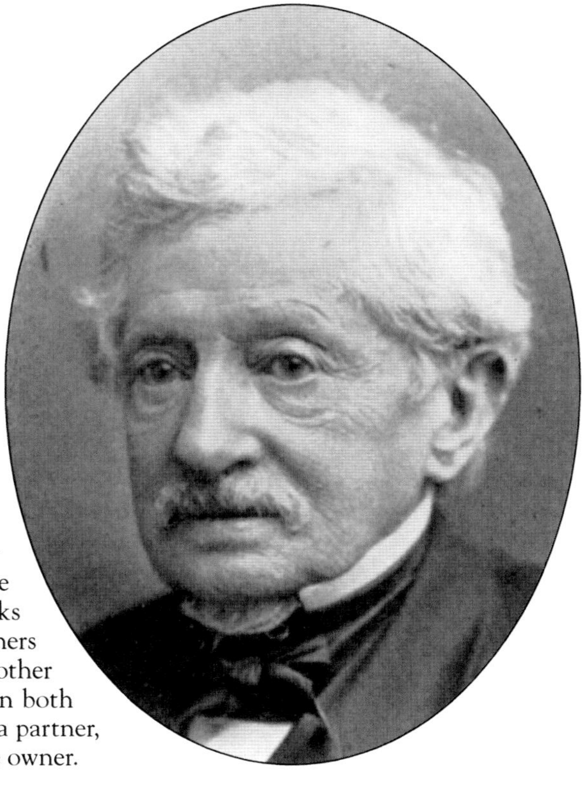

George D. Rosengarten Portrait. George Rosengarten was born in Germany in 1801 and came to America at the age of 18. He was hired by a chemical works to mediate discussions between two partners because one spoke only French and the other only German. Rosengarten was fluent in both languages and in English. He was made a partner, and within a year was the company's sole owner.

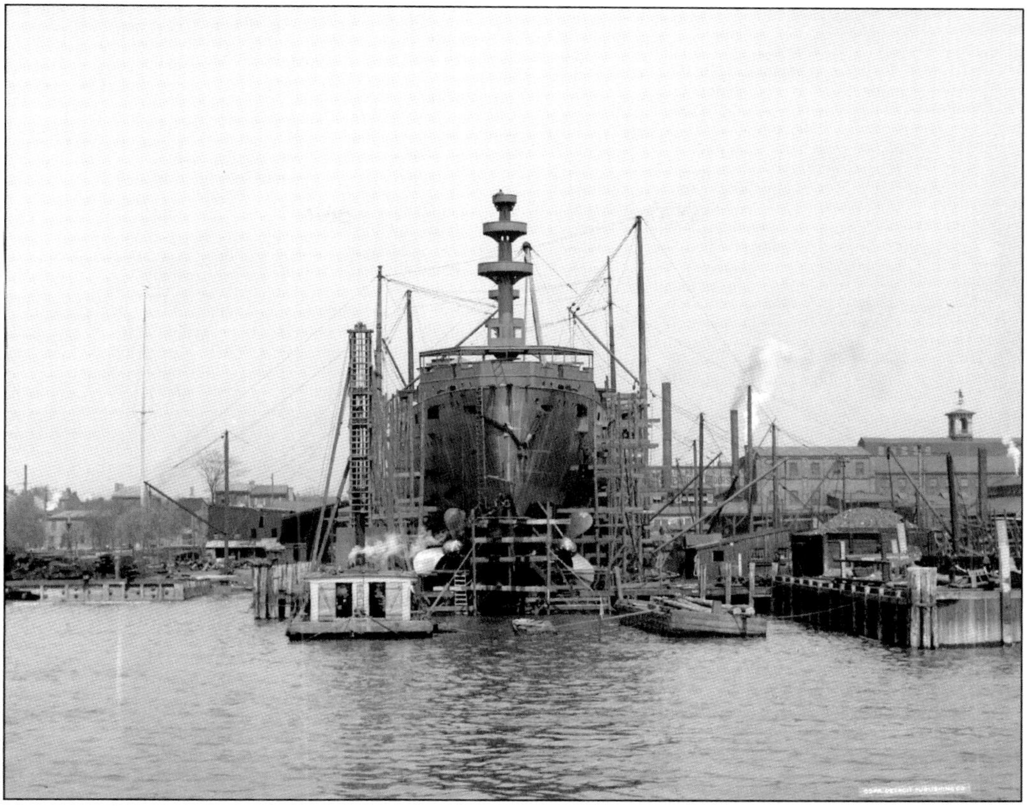

WILLIAM CRAMP & SONS SHIP AND ENGINE BUILDING COMPANY, C. 1905. Founded in 1830, William Cramp & Sons became the most important iron shipbuilding firm in Philadelphia and, for a time, one of the world's leading shipbuilders. Cramp was known for adopting new technology; the company progressed from building wooden ships to iron and then eventually steel. During the Civil War, the firm constructed ships for the US Navy. (LOC.)

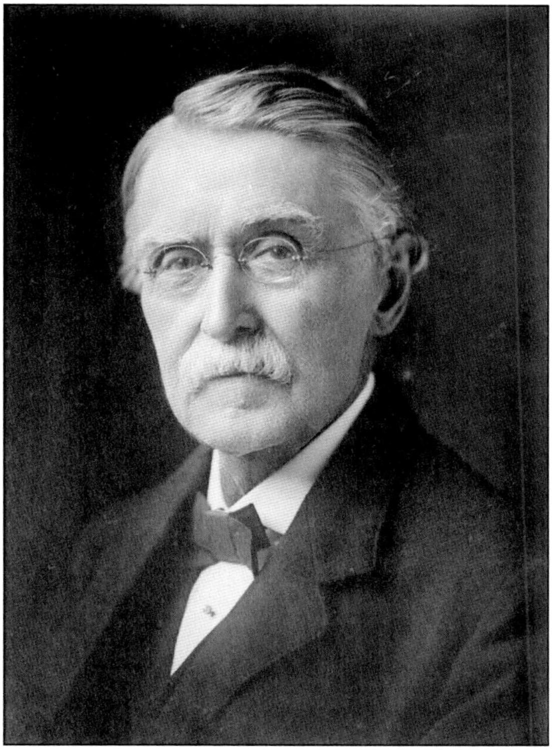

FREDERICK GUTEKUNST PORTRAIT. Frederick Gutekunst opened his first photographic studio in 1856. His business grew until he was one of the best-known photographers of his day. He photographed many of the leaders and wealthy individuals of his time, including Ulysses S. Grant, whose portrait was very well received. He was also a photographer for the Pennsylvania Railroad. Laurel Hill used Gutekunst to photograph its grounds. (LOC.)

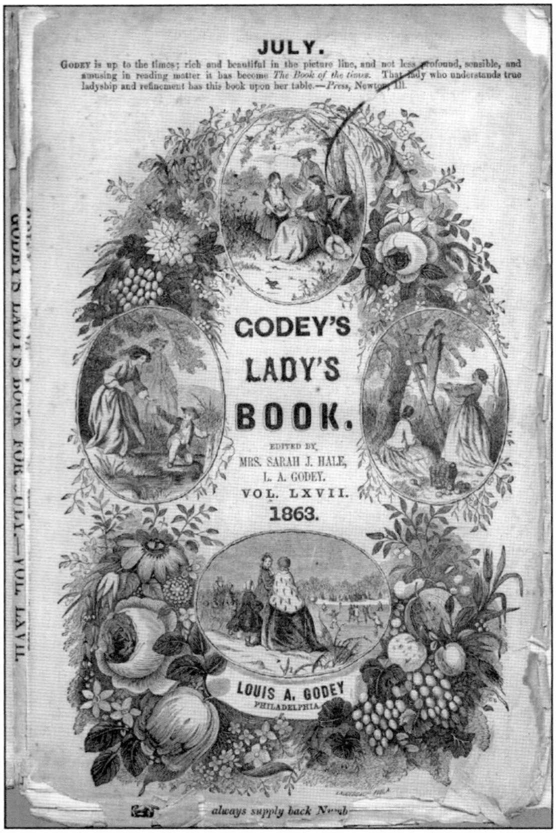

GODEY'S LADY'S BOOK COVER, 1863. Published between 1830 and 1878, *Godey's Lady's Book* featured poems, music, and hand-colored plates showing the latest fashions for women. The magazine also featured works by important 19th-century American writers like Harriet Beecher Stowe, Nathaniel Hawthorne, and Edgar Allen Poe.

LOUIS A. GODEY MAUSOLEUM, C. 1910. *Godey's Lady's Book* was the most widely circulated magazine in the United States prior to the Civil War. Louis Godey was born in New York in 1804, the son of French immigrants. Working in the newspaper industry, he established *Godey's Lady's Book* in 1830.

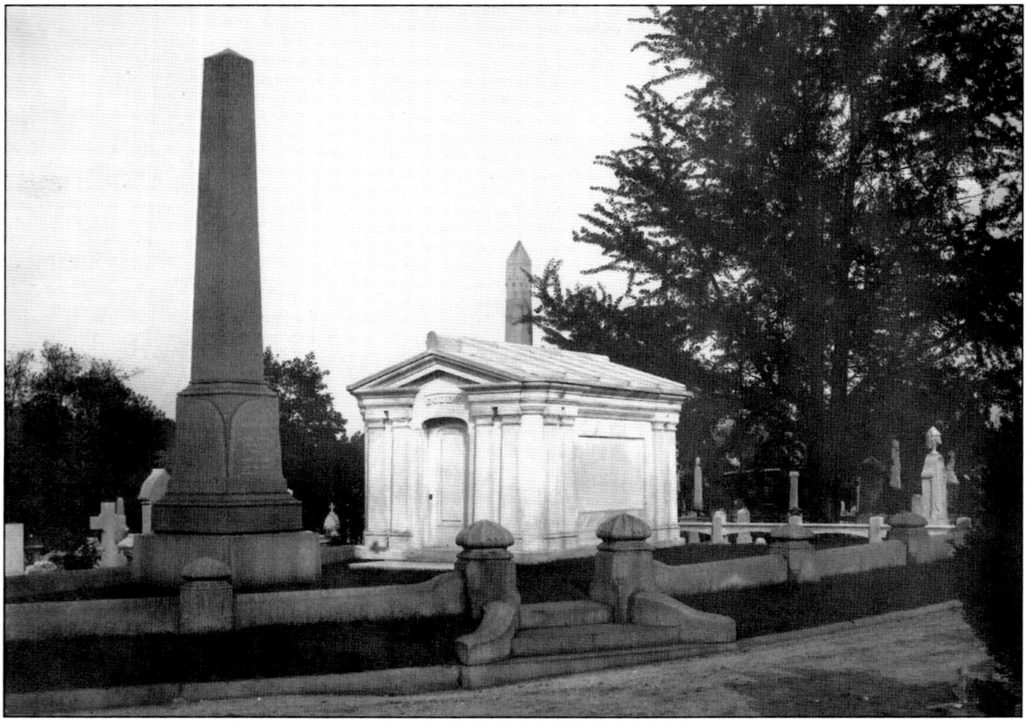

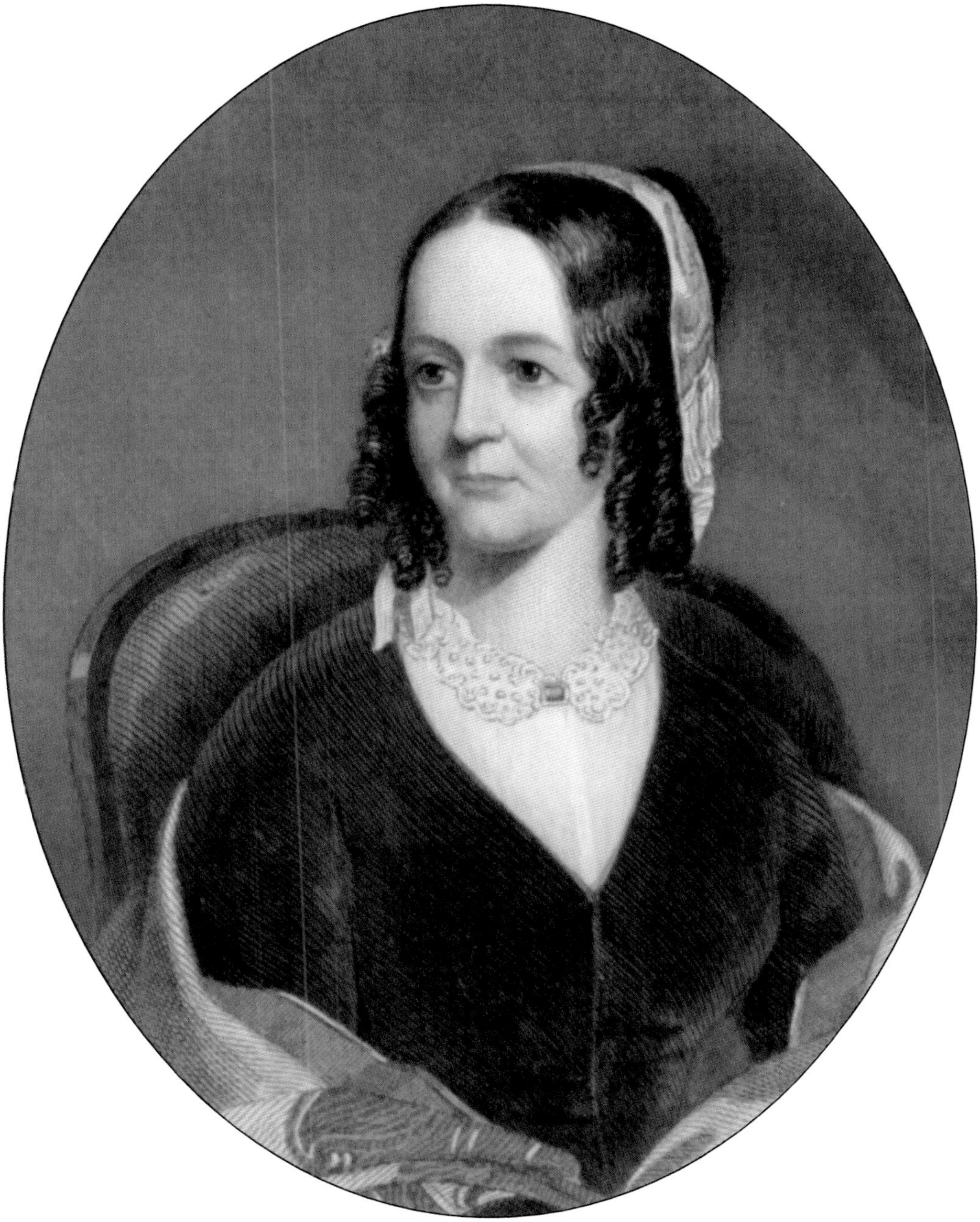

SARAH JOSEPHA HALE, C. 1850. Sarah Josepha Hale edited *Godey's Lady's Book* from 1837 to 1877, but she is best remembered today as the writer of "Mary Had a Little Lamb," and as the "Mother of Thanksgiving" for her efforts to make the holiday a national celebration. Hale was also a forceful proponent for girls' education and actively supported the newly opened Vassar College. (LCP.)

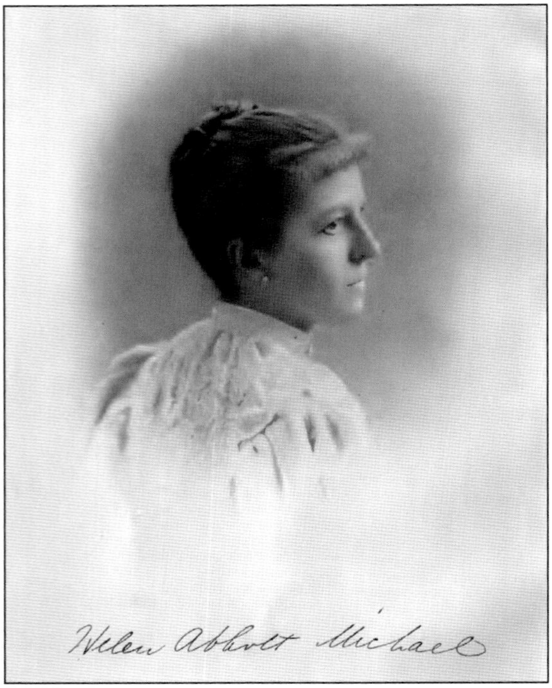

Helen Abbott Michael, c. 1907. Helen Abbott Michael was one of the first to study the chemical properties of plants. She attended the Women's Medical College in Philadelphia and eventually earned her medical degree from Tufts University. Her work was innovative and pioneering.

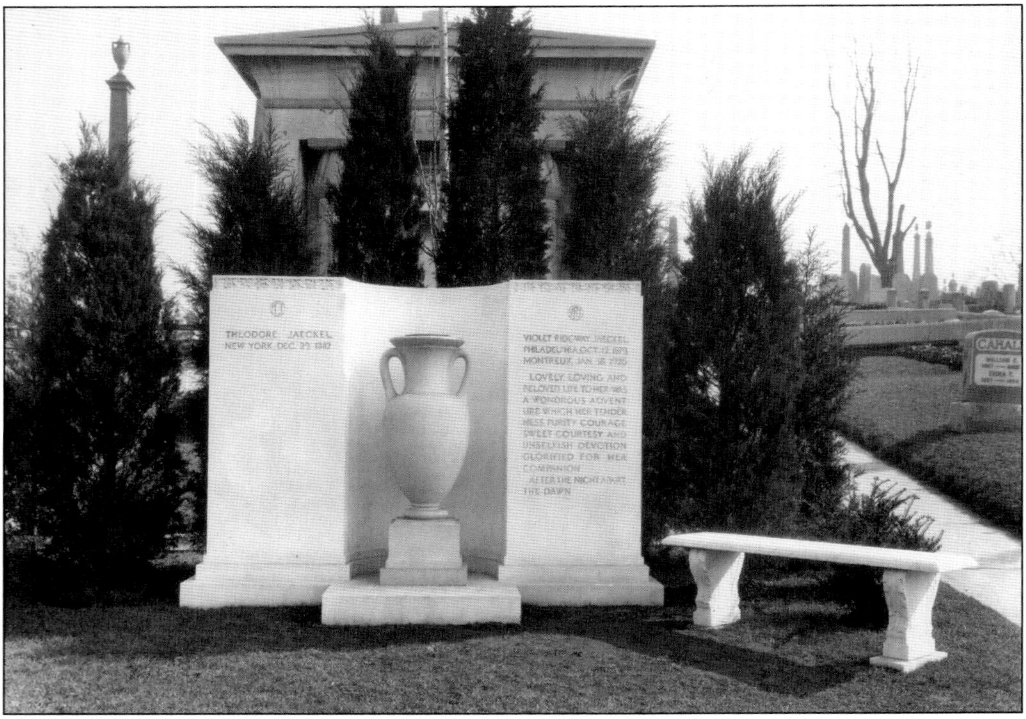

Jaeckel Monument, 1926. The memorial to Theodore and Violet Jaeckel tells a romantic love story. Theodore Jaeckel worked for the US Department of State, and while the couple was living in Switzerland, Violet died. Her cremated remains were placed in the memorial's urn. The epitaph describes her personality and his love for her. When Theodore died, he too was cremated, and his ashes were combined with his wife's.

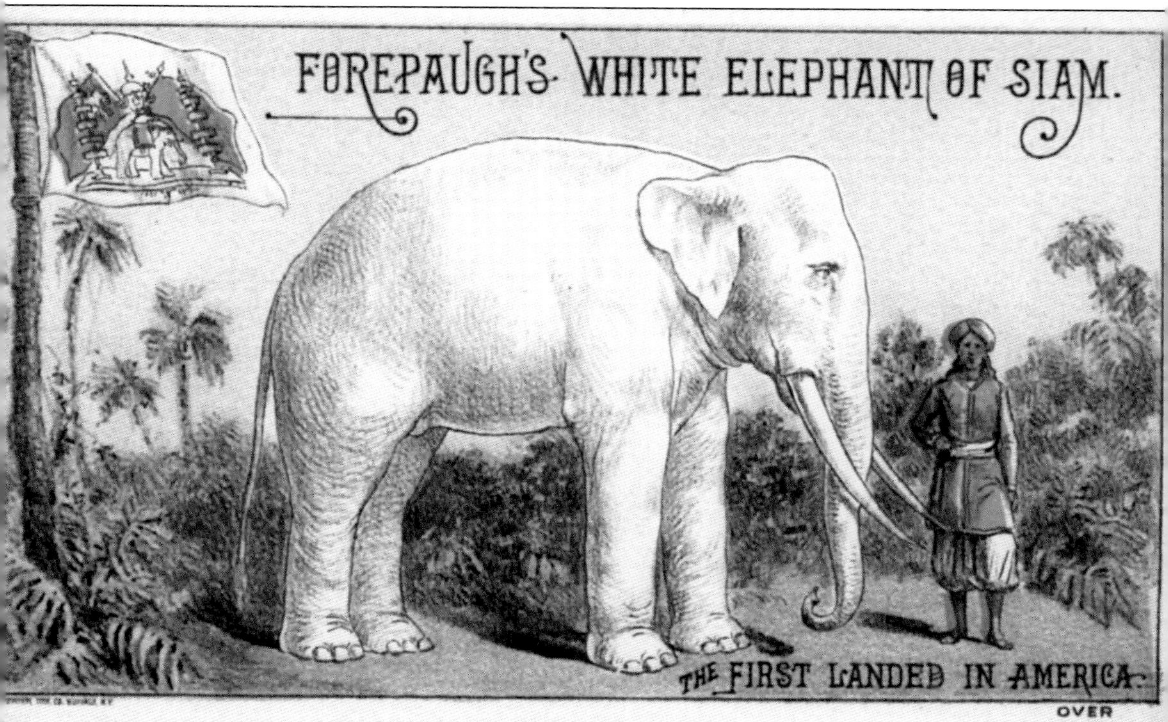

ADAM FOREPAUGH TRADE CARD. Adam Forepaugh made his fortune selling horses to the US government during the Civil War. In 1864, he assumed partial ownership of the Tom King Excelsior Circus. The next year, he and a partner purchased a menagerie and combined it with the circus, which Forepaugh divided into two circuses, selling one and keeping the other. Through the 1870s and 1880s, Forepaugh and P.T. Barnum owned the two largest circuses in America. In 1889, Forepaugh sold his circus acts to the Cooper & Bailey Circus and his railroad cars to Ringling Brothers, which transformed Ringling from a small regional production into a national circus extravaganza.

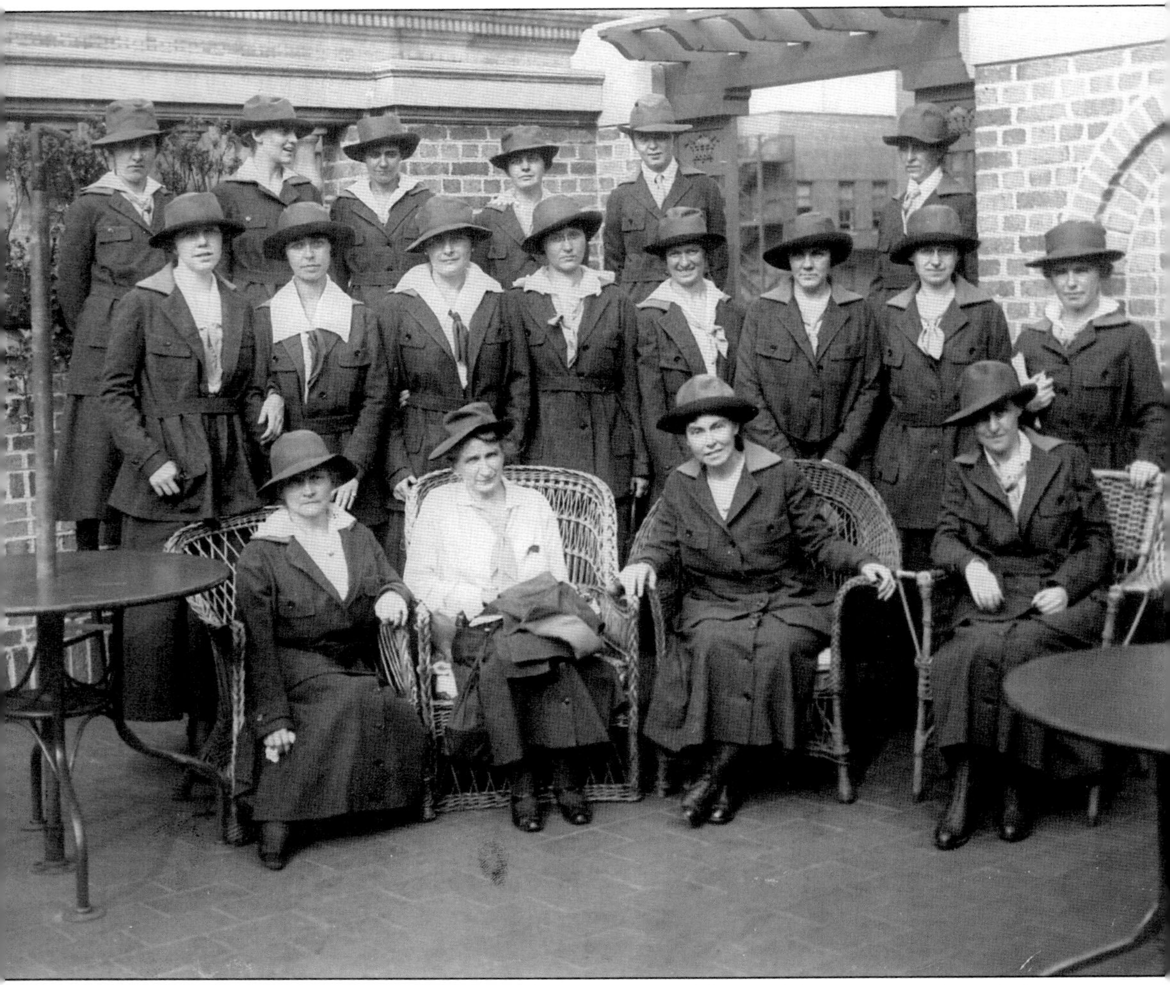

Maude Kelly, Smith College Relief Unit, 1917. Dr. Maude Kelly (first row, far right) was part of the Smith College Relief Unit, a group of women who went to France during World War I with supplies and medical aid. Kelly, who for a time worked at the Women's Medical College, was awarded the Croix de Guerre in 1919. She and Dr. Alice Tallant were the only women awarded the rank of major by the French army. By her own request, Dr. Kelly was buried in her French army uniform. (Smith College Archives, Smith College.)

Five

Central Laurel Hill

The final piece of expansion and the purchase that united the isolated tracts of North Laurel Hill and South Laurel Hill came in 1861. For years, cemetery managers sought to acquire merchant George Pepper's country estate, known as Fairy Hill. With Pepper's death, they finally had the opportunity to purchase the 21-acre parcel.

Griffith M. Hopkins, later known for publishing local city maps and atlases, surveyed and laid out the lots in Central Laurel Hill, with John Jay Smith once again supervising the plantings and landscape changes. Cemetery managers hired contractors Dolan and Shields to build a bridge connecting Central Laurel Hill to South Laurel Hill across Nicetown Lane (now Hunting Park Avenue). For the superintendent of the new section, John Jay Smith's cousin, R. Morris Smith, designed a cottage, which was built a short distance from the Central Laurel Hill side of the bridge. Once lot sales began in 1865, the scenic views proved desirable locations for Civil War–era industrial magnates looking for appropriate spots to erect memorials that would reflect their status and power. Laurel Hill's Millionaire's Row eventually took shape along a curving road in Central Laurel Hill, where row after row of elaborate, private family mausoleums still dot the landscape.

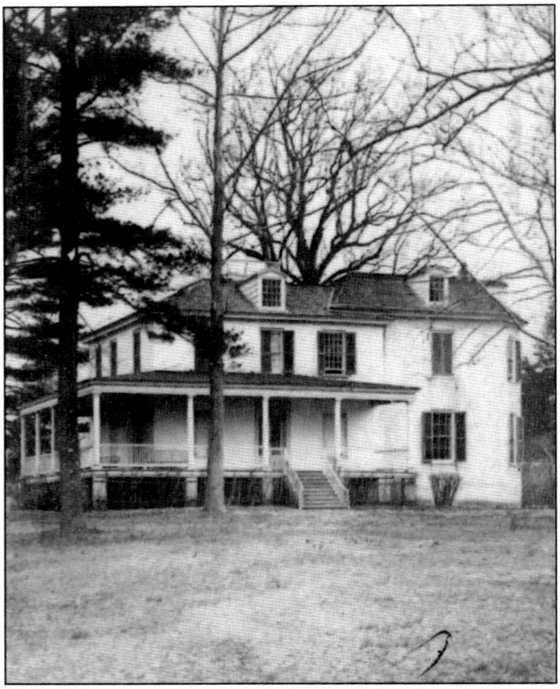

George Pepper's Fairy Hill Mansion. From 1813 to 1846, Fairy Hill, or "Fancy Hill," mansion was the summer retreat of Philadelphia brewer and businessman George Pepper. This mansion was located on wooded, rugged land featuring scenic river overlooks. Upon the death of Pepper, the Laurel Hill managers finally had the opportunity to purchase the estate, and the mansion was torn down shortly thereafter.

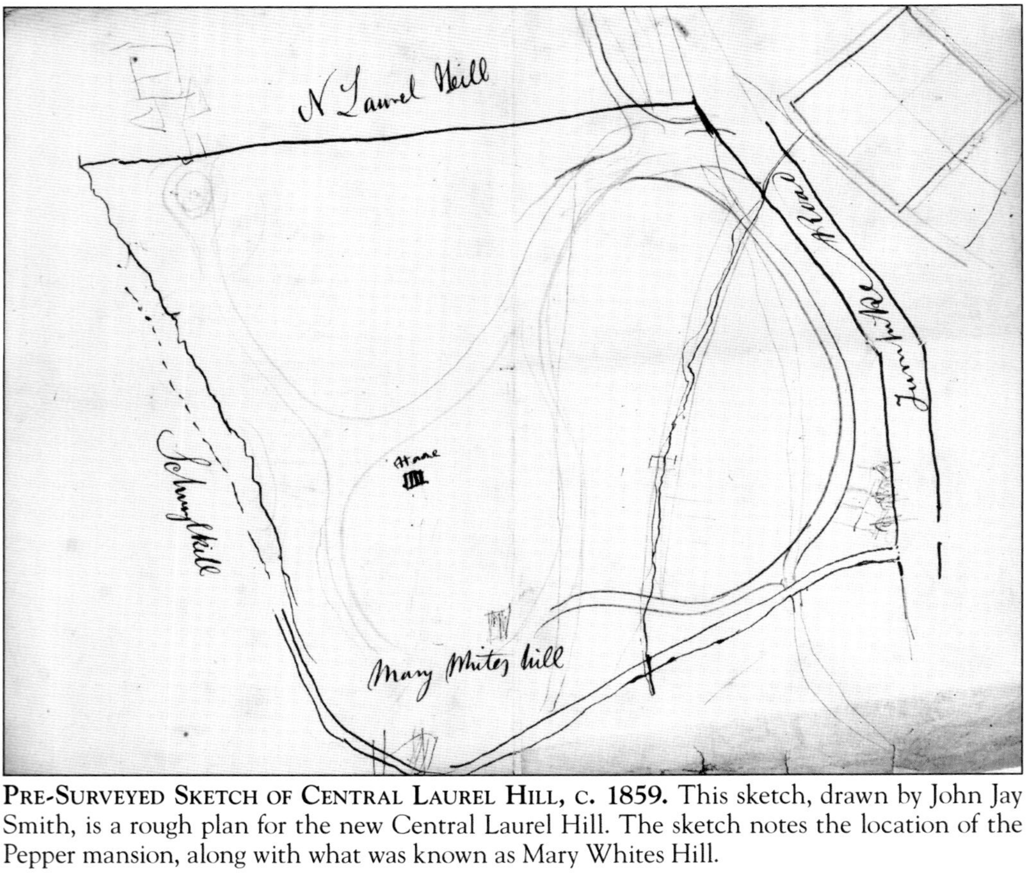

Pre-Surveyed Sketch of Central Laurel Hill, c. 1859. This sketch, drawn by John Jay Smith, is a rough plan for the new Central Laurel Hill. The sketch notes the location of the Pepper mansion, along with what was known as Mary Whites Hill.

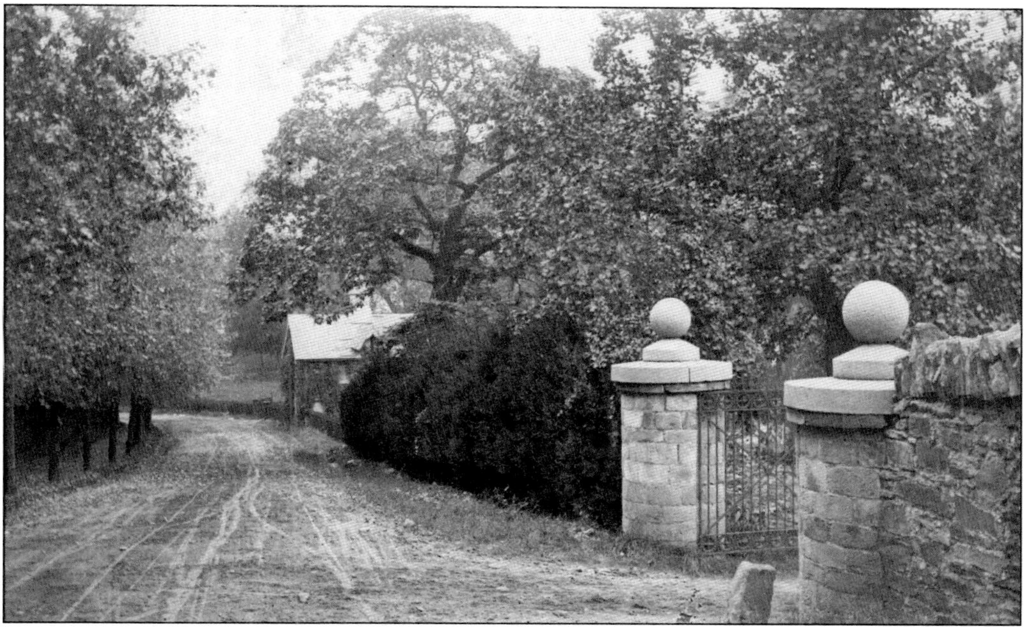

CENTRAL LAUREL HILL ENTRANCE, 1878. This photograph shows the entrance to Central Laurel Hill from Nicetown Lane (now Hunting Park Avenue). This road led to the Schuylkill River, and the pathway led to the cemetery office.

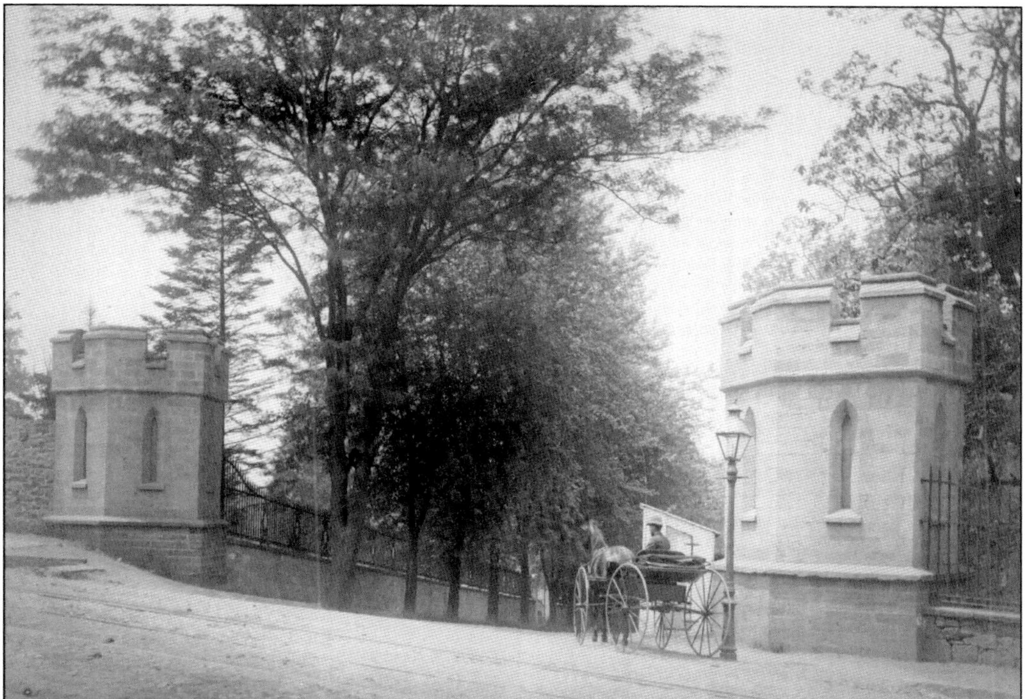

TOWERS BETWEEN SOUTH AND CENTRAL LAUREL HILL. This image shows the intersection of Ridge Pike and Nicetown Lane. The castle-like towers suggest the image of security and protection the cemetery wanted to project. The towers were a traffic hazard, however, and were removed in 1924.

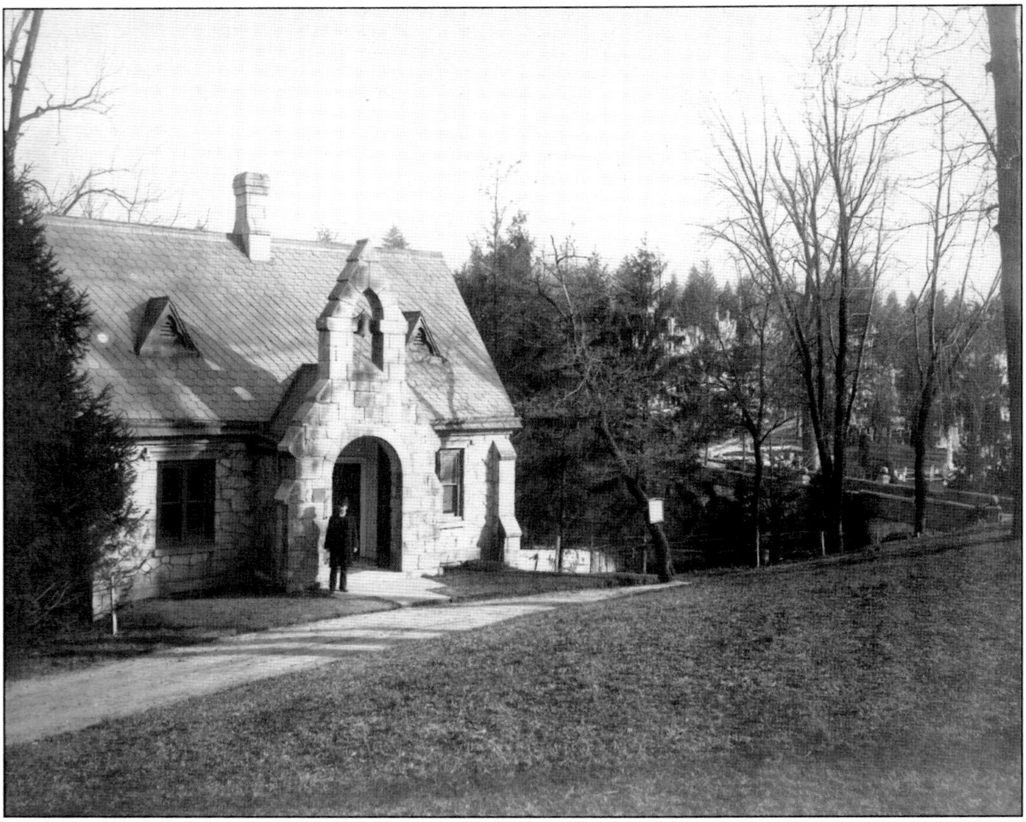

SUPERINTENDENT'S COTTAGE, CENTRAL LAUREL HILL. Just as North and South Laurel Hill maintained separate entrances and superintendents, Central Laurel Hill had its own superintendent's cottage as well. This office, designed by John Jay Smith's cousin, R. Morris Smith, was located in the Bridge Section. It was removed in 1899 to make more room for burial space. With its demolition, the three-superintendent system came to an end.

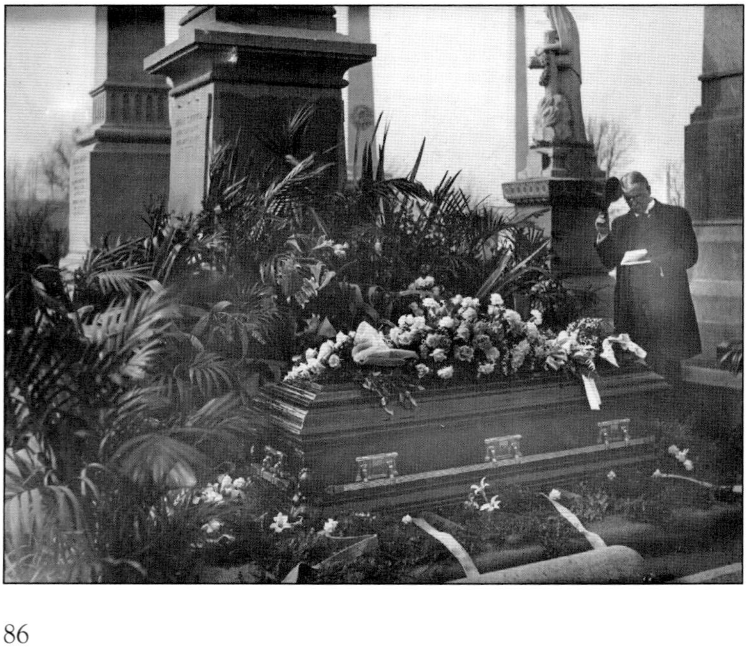

FUNERAL FOR LOUISA J. KUNKEL, MARCH 21, 1907. For a well-known society matron like Louisa Kunkel, elaborate floral tributes were an essential part of a burial. This image from her interment in Section T shows clergy presiding over the casket, which is surrounded by flowers and palms.

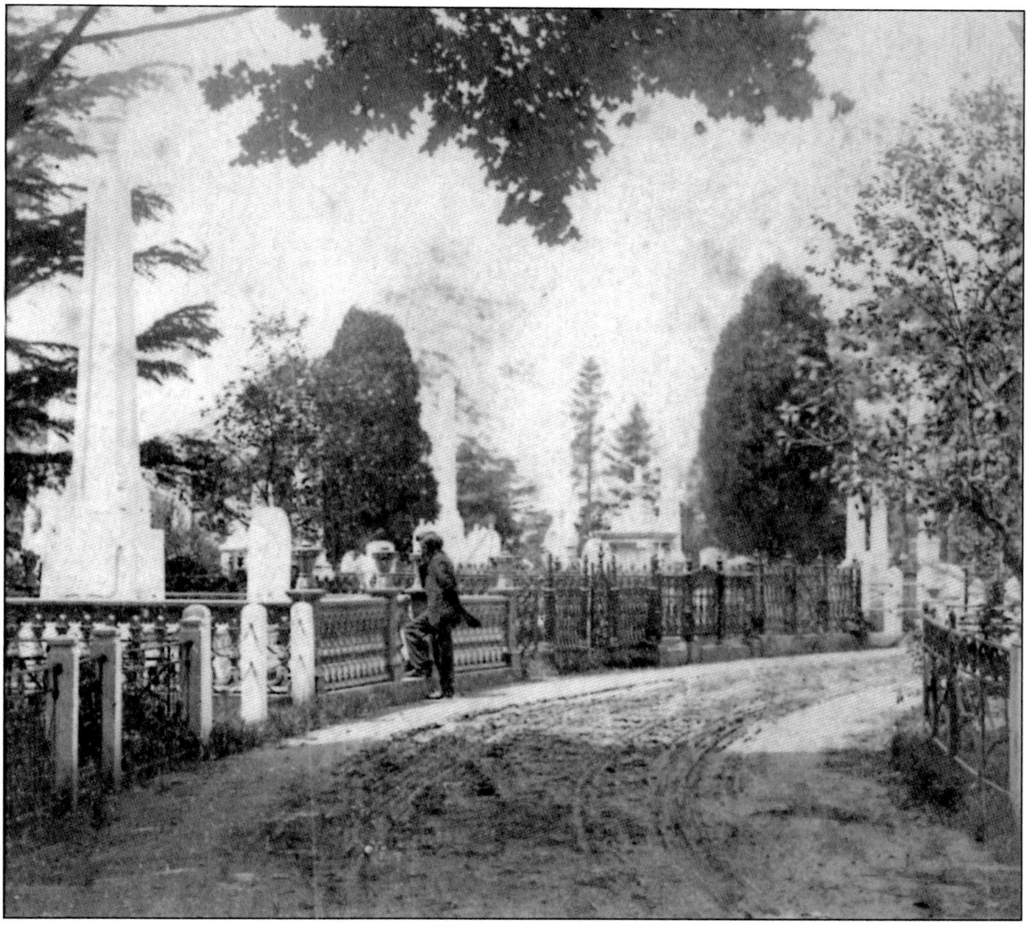

Laurel Hill Stereoviews, c. 1885. Laurel Hill was such a famous destination that stereoviews of the cemetery became very popular items worldwide. Those who could not actually visit Philadelphia could still enjoy the beauty of the cemetery in the privacy of their own homes. These photographs show the cemetery being used for recreation, reading, and meditation. (Below, LCP.)

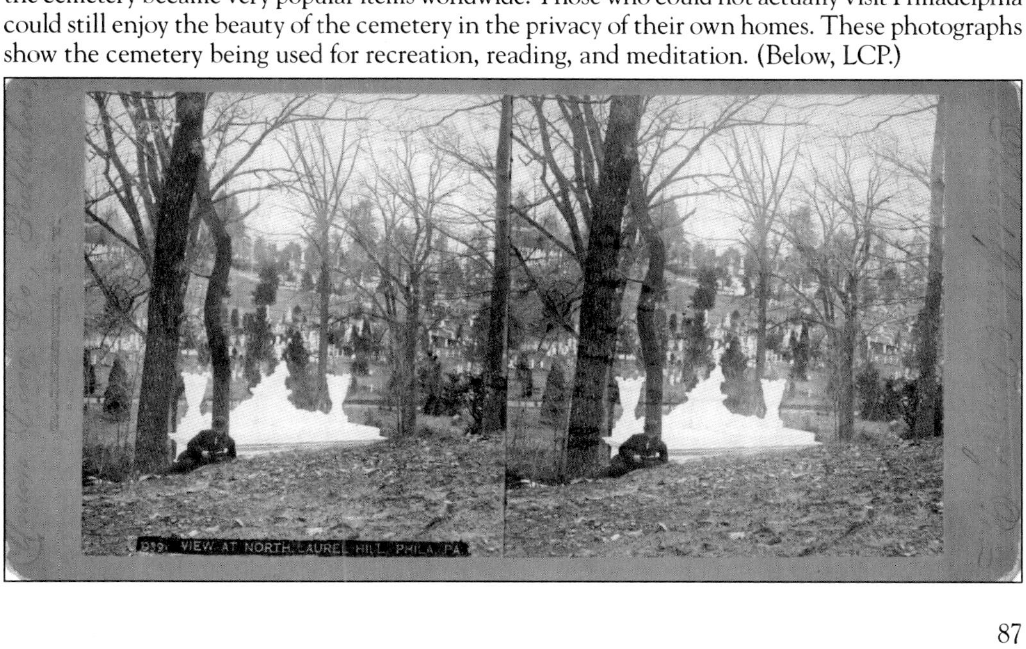

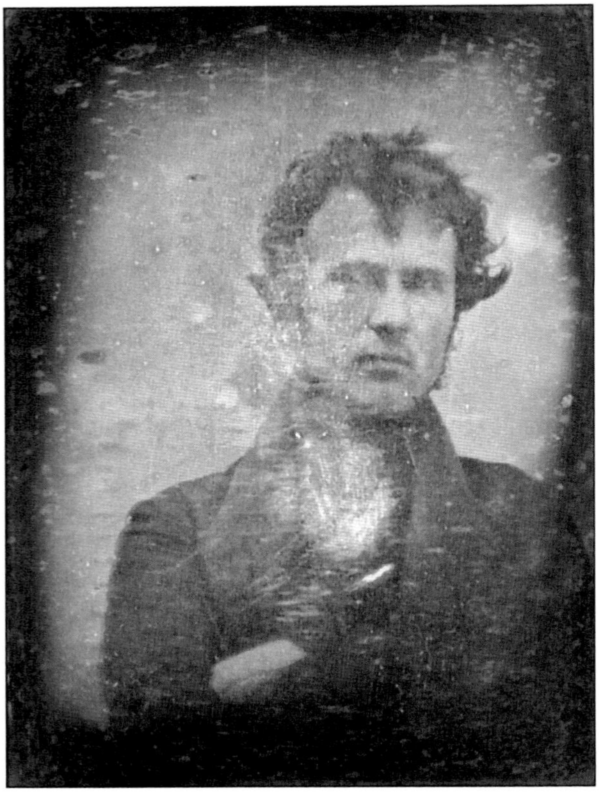

Robert Cornelius and First "Selfie," 1839. This image of Robert Cornelius is possibly the first self-portrait. Cornelius was a chemist, inventor, and amateur photographer when he set a camera up in the back of his parents' Philadelphia store. Cornelius opened one of the first photographic studios in the United States. (LOC.)

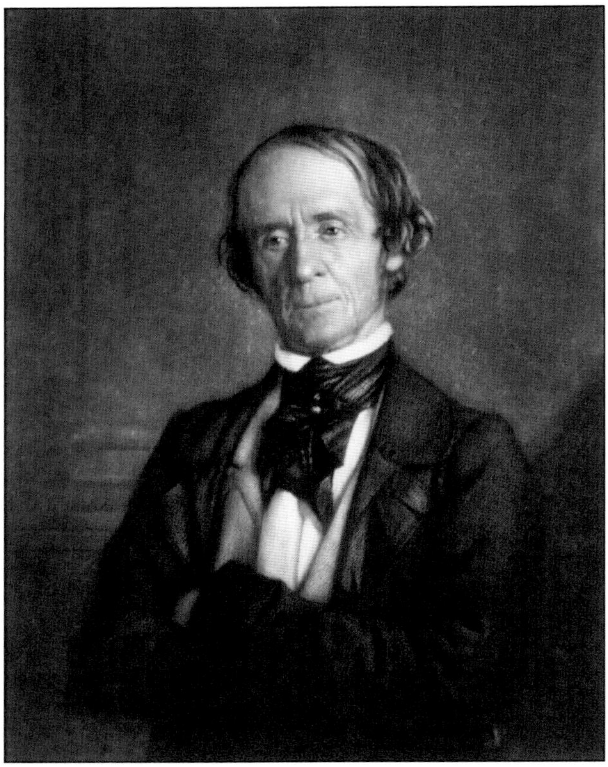

Charles D. Meigs, MD, c. 1846. Born in Bermuda in 1792, Meigs graduated from the University of Pennsylvania in 1815. Well known and respected in the field of obstetrics, he is nonetheless remembered for his paternalistic views, his objections to the use of anesthesia, and his disbelief in the transmission of germs from doctor to patient. He spent the final 19 years of his career at Jefferson Medical College as a professor of midwifery. (LOC.)

THOMAS BUCHANAN READ AND "SHERIDAN'S RIDE." Thomas Buchanan Read was a portrait painter and a poet. In his poem "Sheridan's Ride," written in 1864, he described Gen. Philip Sheridan's appearance at the Battle of Cedar Creek in Virginia, which inspired the troops to rally and turn the tide of battle in favor of the Union. (NYPL.)

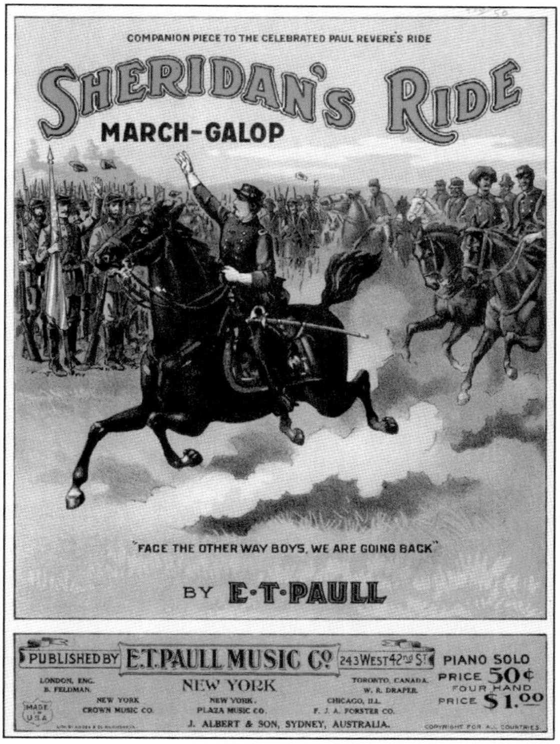

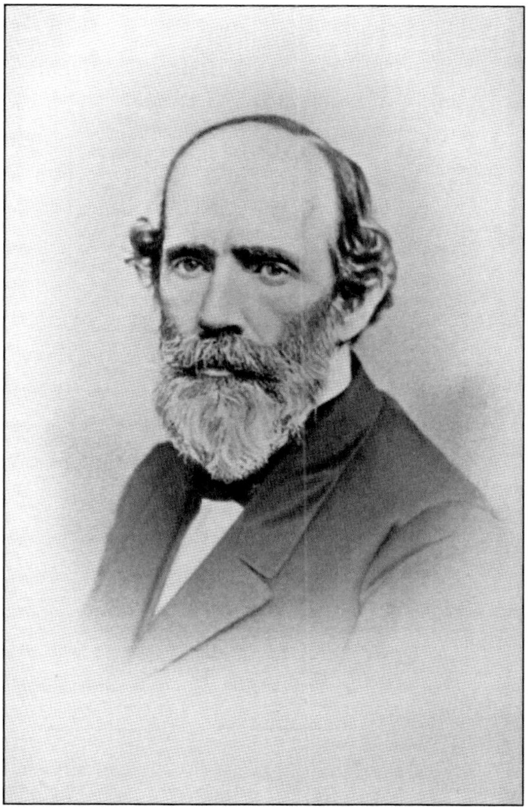

JOHN CASSIN PORTRAIT. John Cassin showed an interest in science at an early age. He received the position of honorary curator at the Philadelphia Academy of Natural Sciences in 1842 and spent years cataloguing thousands of bird specimens in the collection. Cassin believed in studying bird specimens over field study. Five North American birds have been named in his honor. (HSP.)

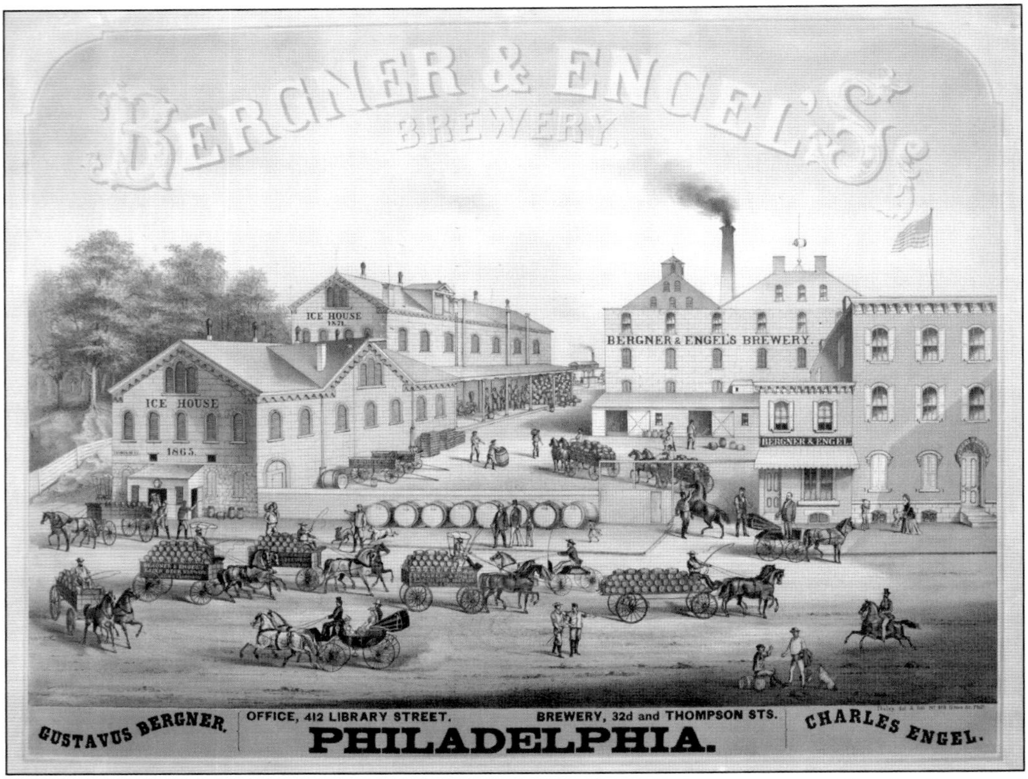

Bergner & Engel's Brewery, c. 1873. Buried side by side are business partners Charles Engel and Gustavus Bergner. Bergner & Engel's Brewery, founded in 1870, was one of the largest in the country and gained an international reputation by winning the grand prize at the Centennial Exposition in Philadelphia in 1876 and then again at the Paris Exposition in 1878. This Brewerytown-based company did not survive Prohibition. (LCP.)

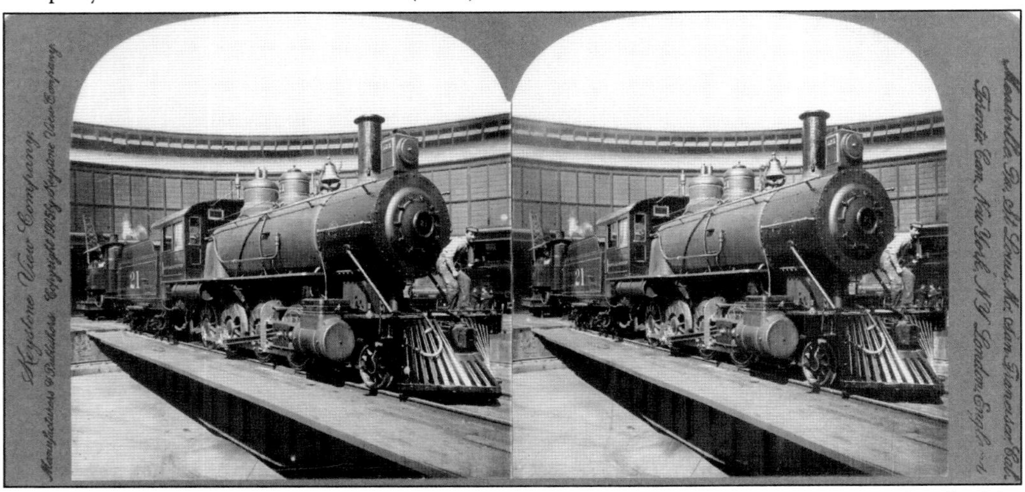

Baldwin Locomotive Works, c. 1905. In 1831, Matthias Baldwin was contracted to build a miniature railroad for a Philadelphia Museum exhibit. This inspired him to create his lasting contribution to the world of transportation, and by 1840, his company had produced more than 150 steam locomotives. Baldwin Locomotive Works became one of the most successful steam locomotive manufacturers in the world. (LOC.)

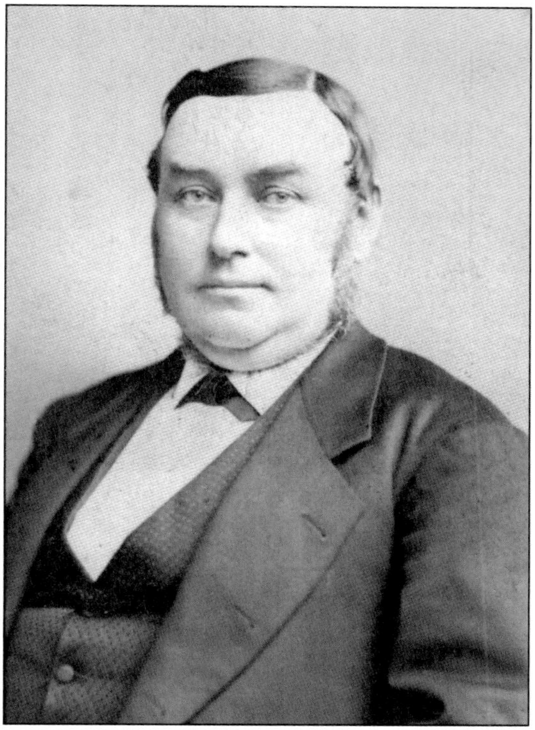

George Childs Portrait and Family Mausoleum. George and Emma Childs were prominent members of Philadelphia society. They entertained politicians, businessmen, and writers such as Walt Whitman and Mark Twain. Childs was publisher of the *Philadelphia Ledger*, close friends with Anthony J. Drexel, and became the second president of the board of trustees of Drexel University. Childs was known not just in the world of publishing, but for his philanthropy. Upon his death in 1894, Emma Peterson Childs continued this pattern, donating large tracts of land to the Commonwealth of Pennsylvania. (Right, LOC.)

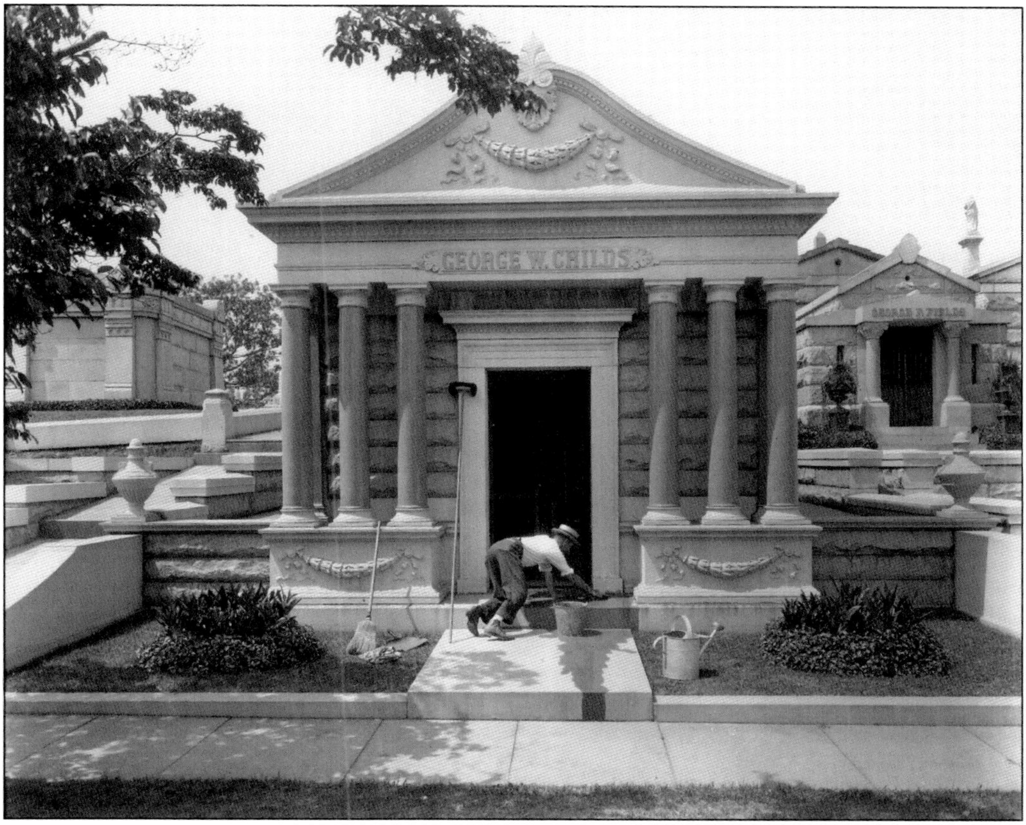

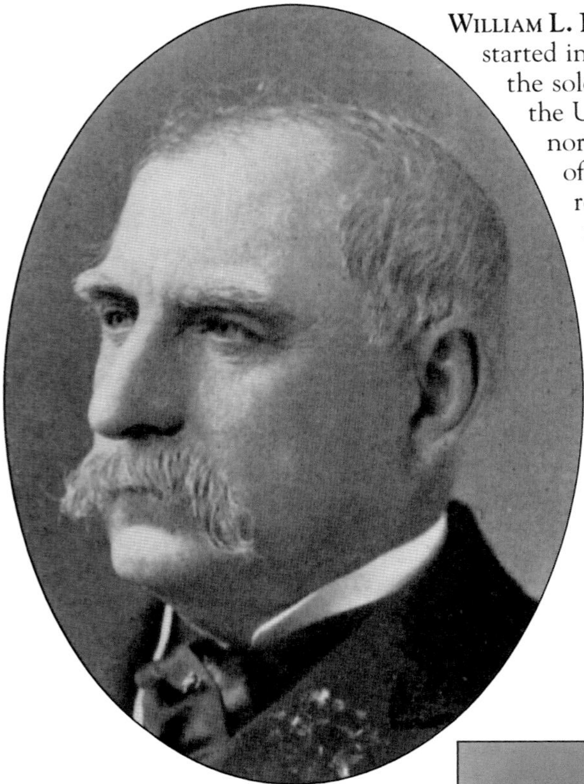

William L. Elkins Portrait. William Lukens Elkins started in the produce business, and by 1860 was the sole owner of the largest produce store in the United States. He bought oil interests in northwestern Pennsylvania and built one of the first refineries in Philadelphia. His refinery produced the first gasoline ever made, which led to a partnership with Standard Oil. In 1873, he met Peter A.B Widener, who became his business and investment partner.

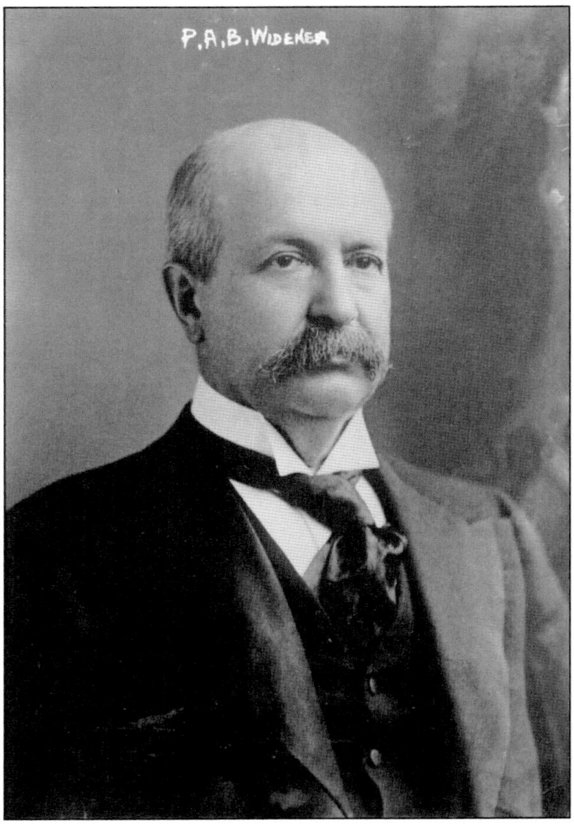

Peter A.B. Widener, 1911. Peter A.B. Widener began his career supplying meat to the Union army. In 1883, he and William Elkins founded the Philadelphia Traction Company. Widener helped found US Steel and the American Tobacco Company and had extensive holdings in Standard Oil. He used his wealth to buy art, and his collection was eventually given to the National Gallery in Washington, DC, by his son. (LOC.)

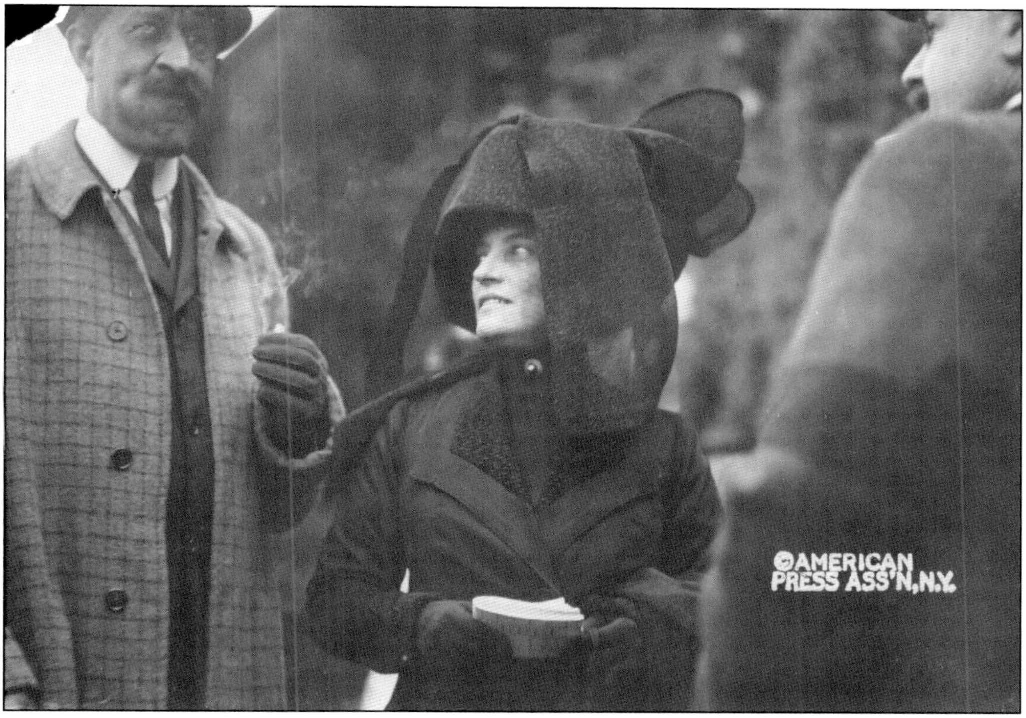

Eleanore Elkins Widener Rice and the Harry Elkins Widener Library. Eleanore Elkins Widener Rice was the daughter of Peter Widener's business partner, William Elkins. She married Widener's son George in 1883. In 1912, George, Eleanore, their son Harry, and two servants were aboard the *Titanic* when the ship went down. Only Eleanore and her maid survived. Soon after, she donated the Harry Elkins Widener Library to Harvard University. Harry Widener had been a Harvard graduate and avid rare book collector. Eleanore remarried in 1915 to Alexander Hamilton Rice Jr., a surgeon and noted South American explorer. She accompanied him on his explorations, which frequently made national news. She died in a Paris store in 1937. (LOC.)

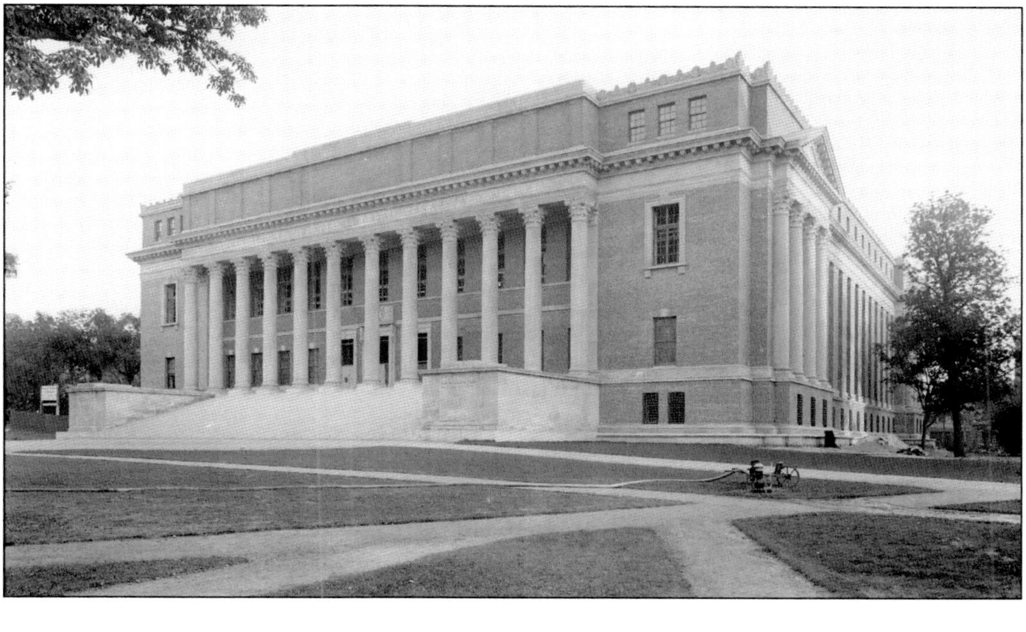

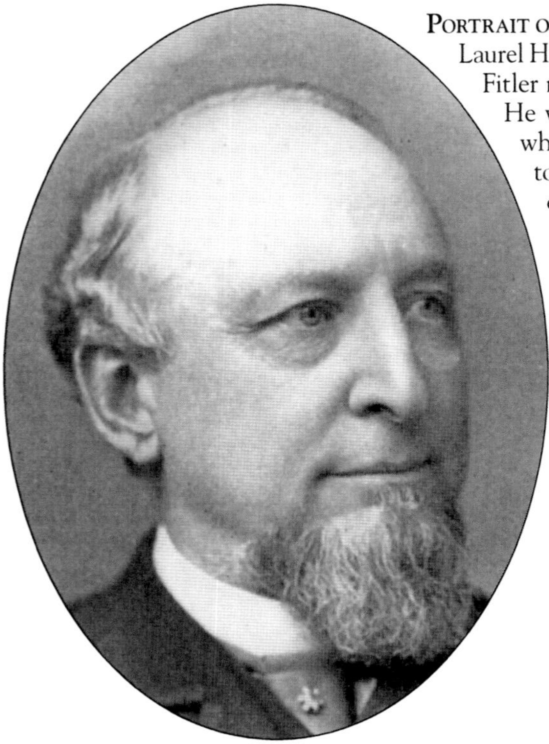

Portrait of Edwin Henry Fitler. The tallest obelisk in Laurel Hill belongs to Philadelphia mayor Edwin Fitler. Fitler made his fortune as a cordage manufacturer. He was a well-liked employer and businessman who served as Philadelphia's mayor from 1887 to 1891. In 1888, he was nominated for the office of president of the United States by the Philadelphia delegation at the Republican Convention.

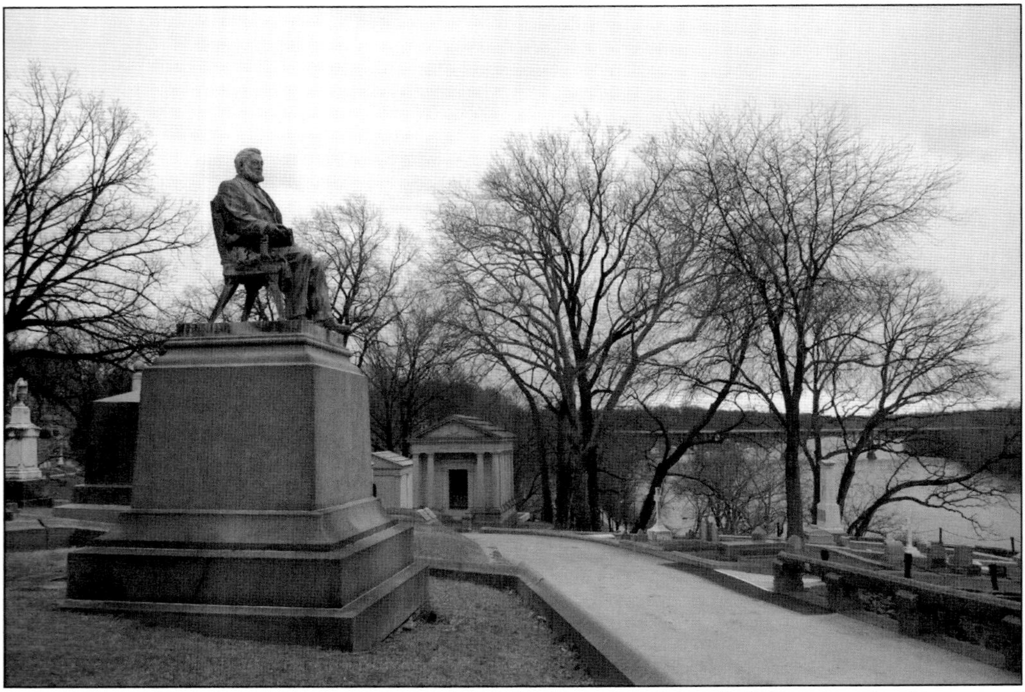

William F. Hughes Monument. Seated overlooking the Schuylkill River is the likeness of William F. Hughes. This bronze sculpture by Joseph A. Bailly is one of the few depictions of an actual person in Laurel Hill. Hughes owned the Southwark Hay Market, at one time the largest of its kind in the United States. (Emma Stern.)

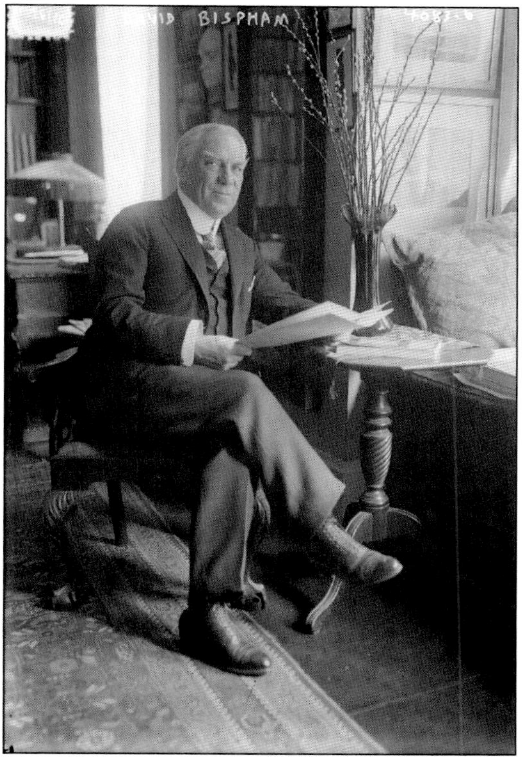

PORTRAIT OF DAVID BISPHAM, C. 1915–1920. At the time of his death in 1921, David Bispham was among the most prominent operatic singers in America. Born into a family of Quakers, Bispham was prohibited from training as a singer by his mother and only began to do so as a young adult. Bispham studied in Europe, making his operatic debut in 1891. (LOC.)

GIRARD COLLEGE LOT, 1910. Girard College was established in 1833 with funds from the fortune of Stephen Girard. This lot in Laurel Hill was purchased in 1881 as a place to bury former students and children who died during their time at the school. In 1882, a group of bodies was moved here from the school campus.

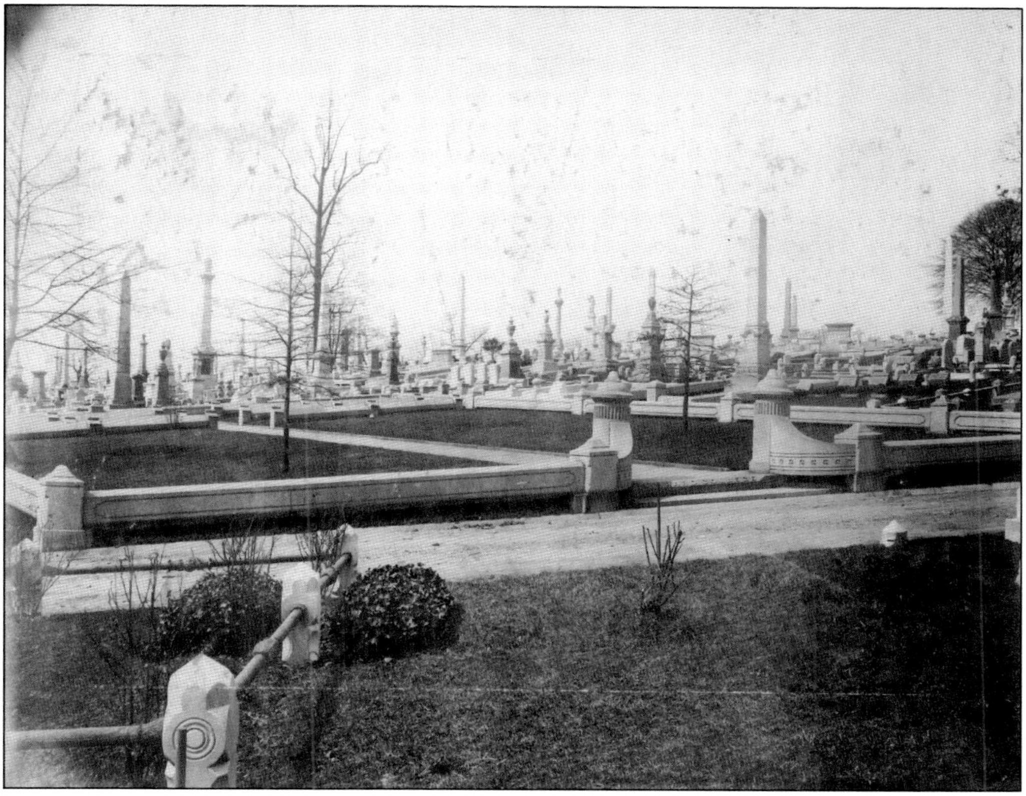

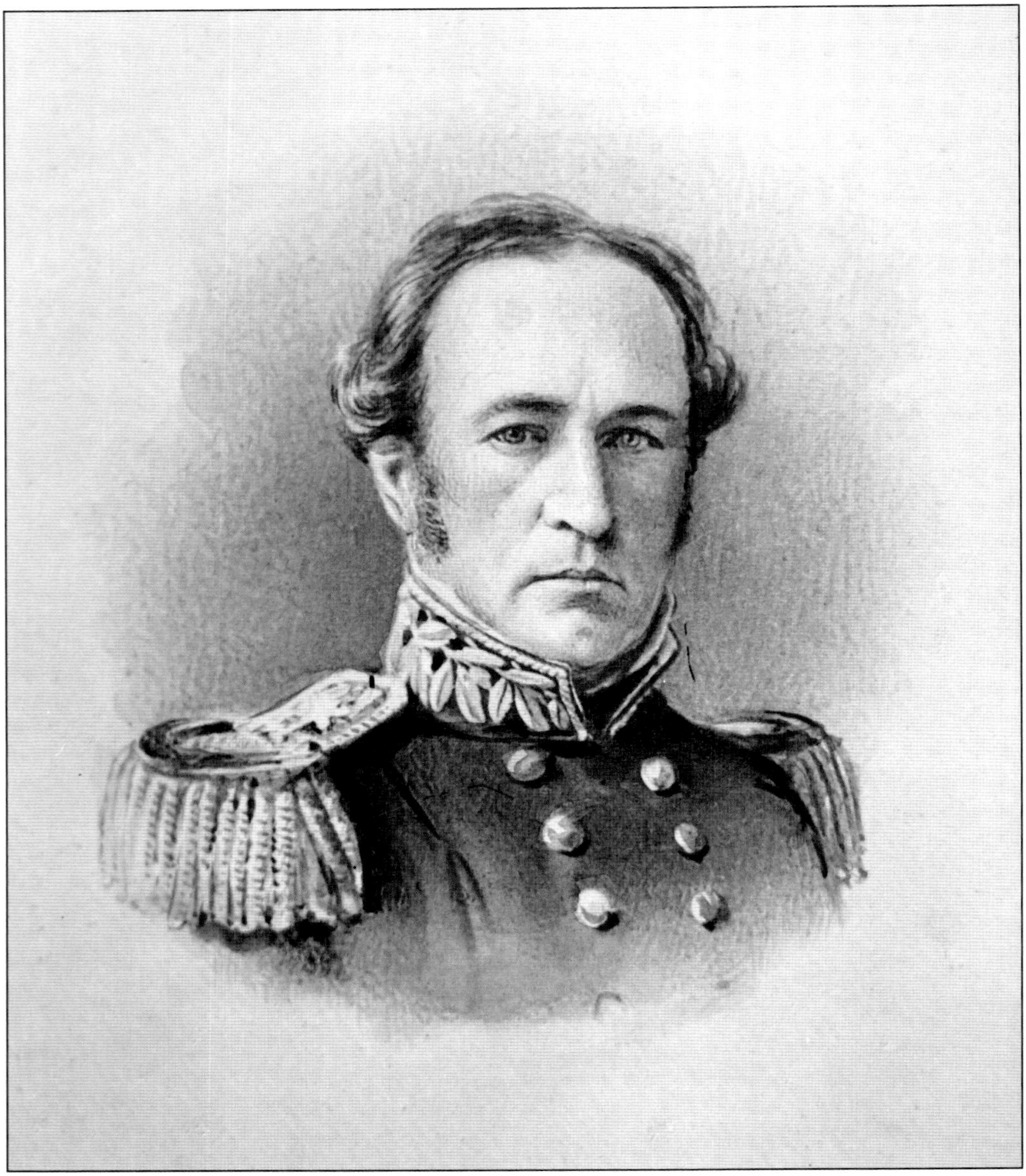

Portrait of Gen. Robert Patterson. Robert Patterson was a veteran of the War of 1812, the Mexican War, and the Civil War. Born in Ireland, he came to America in 1799. He received much criticism after the First Battle of Bull Run, and due to his actions, he was mustered out of the Army in July 1861. Patterson's monument documents his military service, as it depicts a lion sitting atop armaments. An inscription gives the dates of Patterson's service. (LOC.)

Francis and Robert Patterson Monuments. One of the most distinctive monuments in Central Laurel Hill is that of Civil War general Francis E. Patterson. The sculpture, by Joseph A. Bailly, shows a half-nude female holding a funeral urn. During the Civil War, Patterson faced criticism and a possible sanction after he withdrew his troops from their posts without authorization. Prior to the start of the inquiry, Patterson was found dead in his tent, and while the gunshot wound was ruled accidental, rumors of suicide persisted.

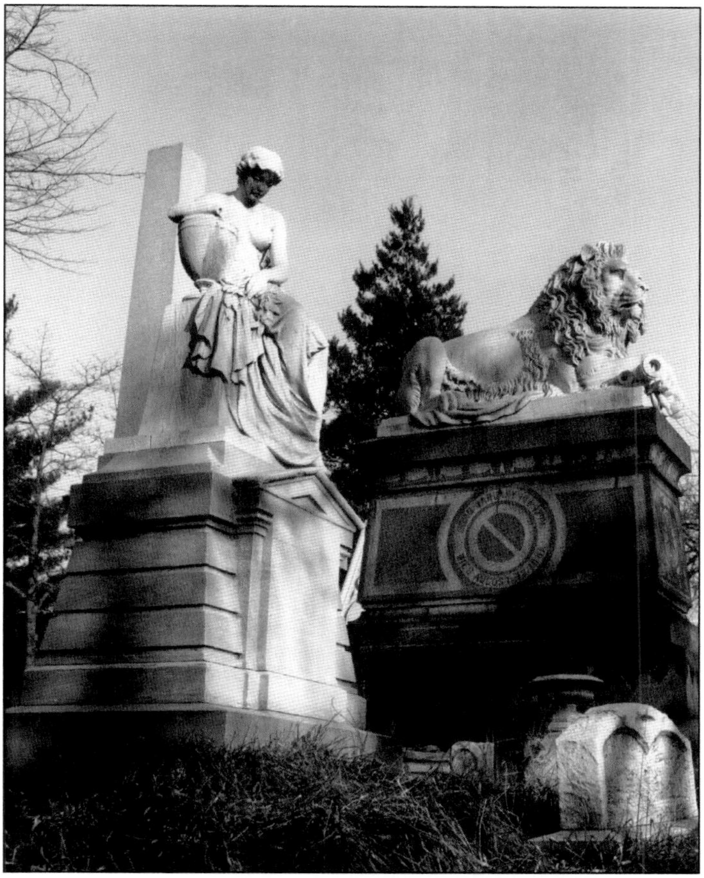

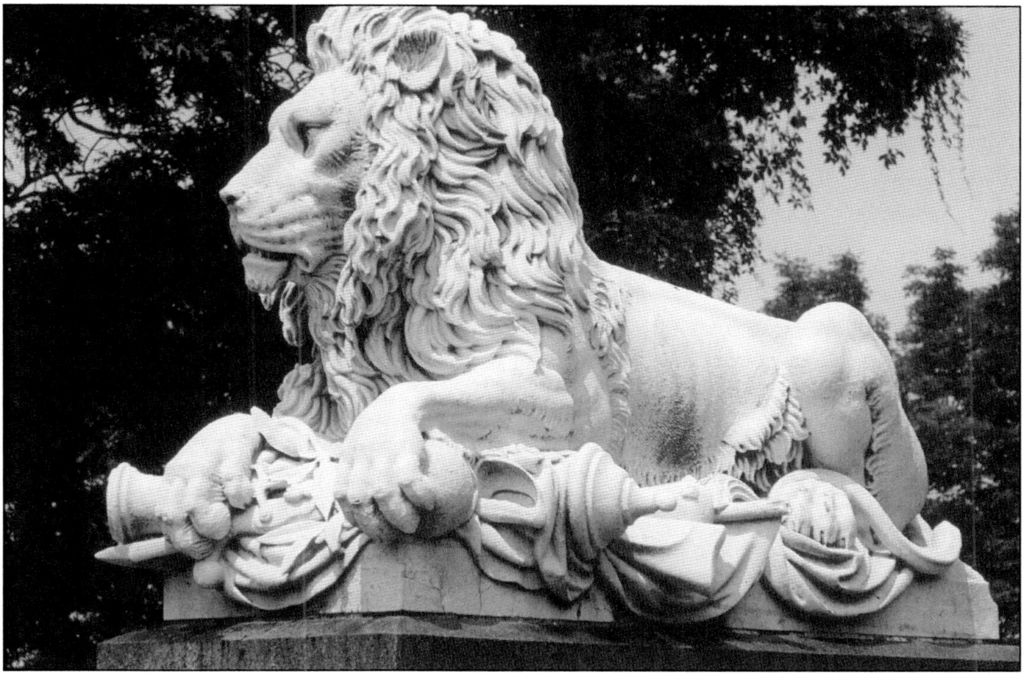

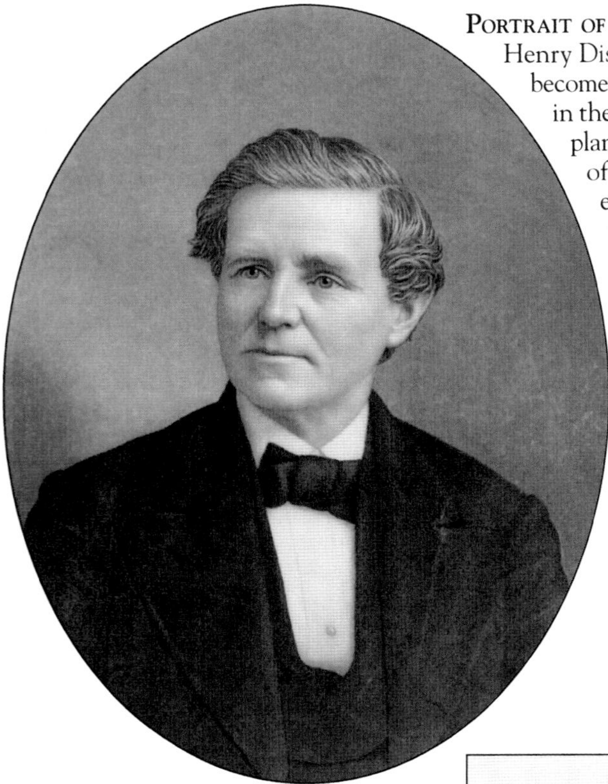

Portrait of Henry Disston, 1887. In the 1840s, Henry Disston founded the company that would become one of the largest handsaw manufacturers in the United States. Disston's manufacturing plant occupied 64 acres in the Tacony section of Philadelphia. Known as a generous employer, Disston worked to improve the workers' community surrounding his factory by building employee housing, a school, and a library. (Historical Society of Tacony.)

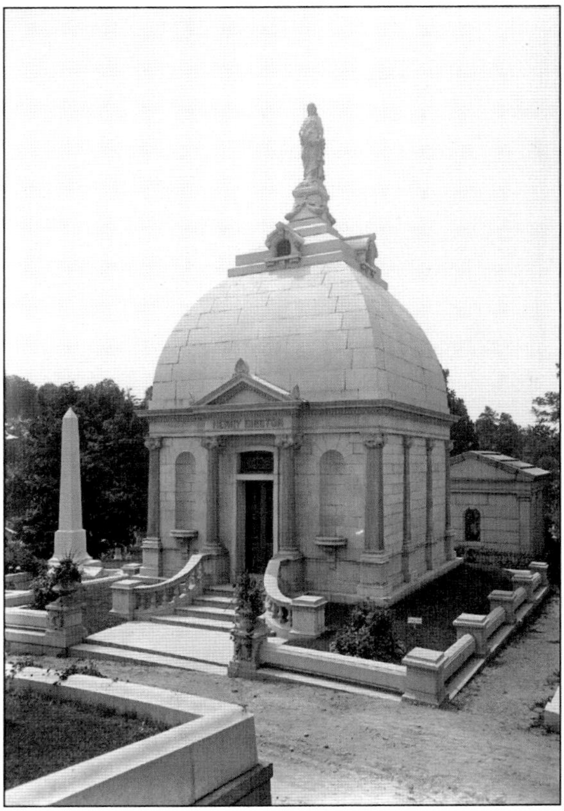

Disston Mausoleum, c. 1910. The largest private aboveground mausoleum in Laurel Hill, the Disston mausoleum is the final resting place of Henry and Mary Steelman Disston and their descendants. A native of New Jersey, Mary Disston secretly built and furnished a house in Atlantic City for her husband. He liked Atlantic City so much that he bought more property and helped turn the town into a shore destination.

Owen Wister Portrait. Owen Wister grew up in Germantown. Educated at Harvard, he wanted to pursue a career in music but ended up going into law. On advice from his physician, Wister headed west to Wyoming. His travels inspired him to write *The Virginian*, which was published in 1902. This novel was one of the first mass-market bestsellers and helped cement the popular idea of the American cowboy. (LOC.)

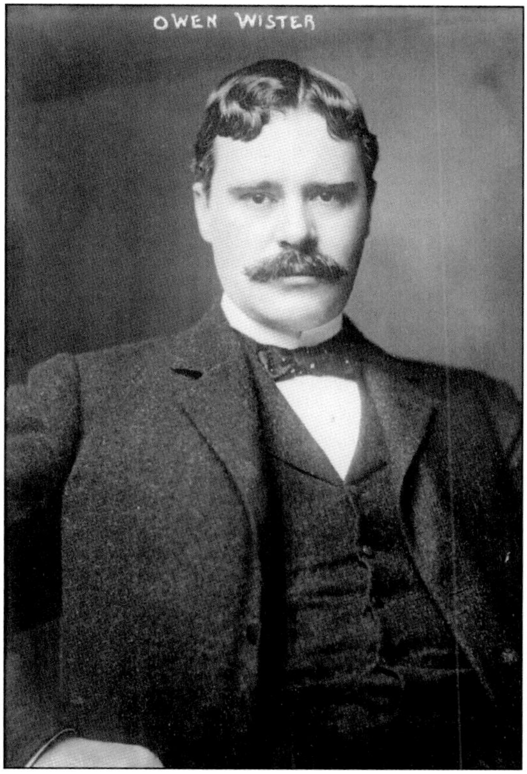

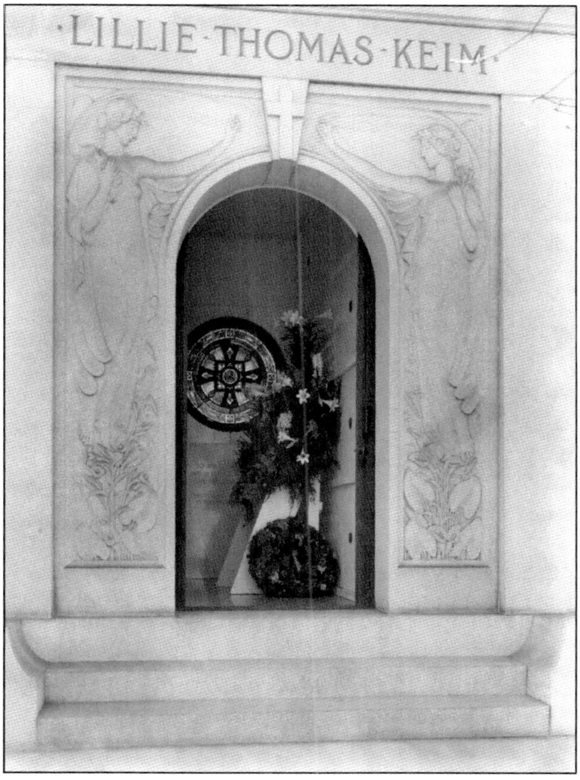

Lillie Keim Mausoleum. One of the most beautiful mausoleums in Laurel Hill is the Lillie Thomas Keim mausoleum. It was ordered by Lillie's son George in honor of his "precious mother" and was erected in 1926 by William J. Crawford & Co. of Buffalo, New York.

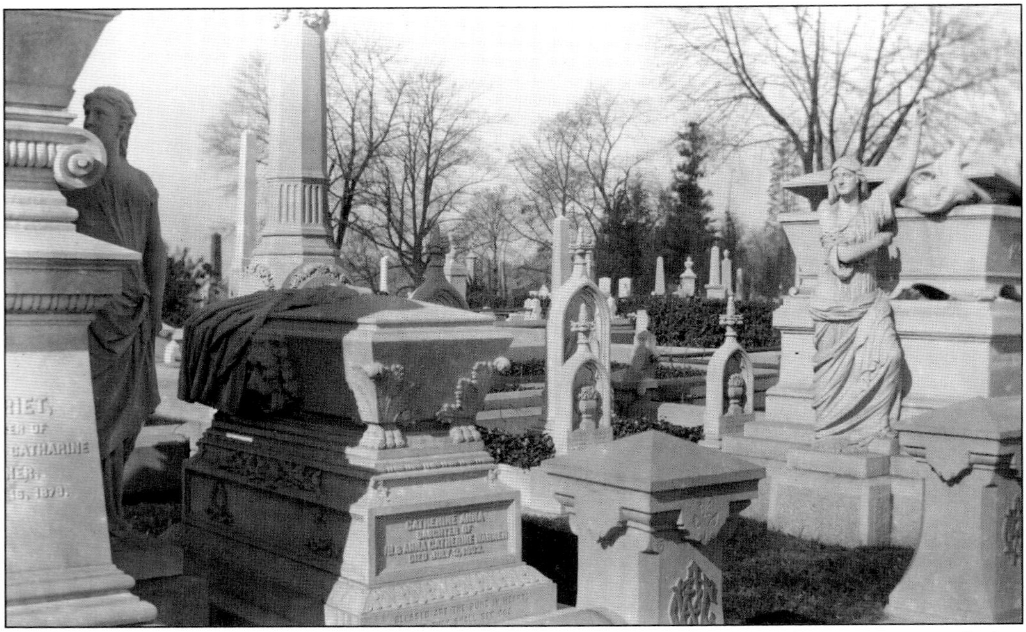

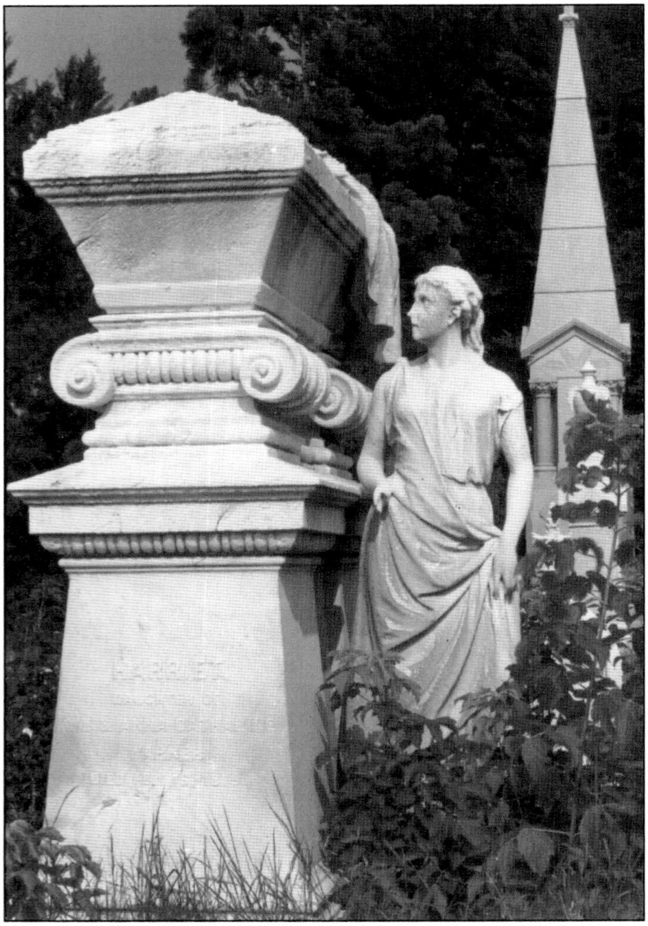

Warner Monument, c. 1910. Among the most distinctive memorials in Laurel Hill is the monument marking the lot of coal magnate William Warner. While little is known about Warner, his memorial is a notable example of American funerary art. Carved in granite by Scottish sculptor Alexander Milne Calder (best known for his sculptures on Philadelphia's City Hall), the Warner monument features a female figure and an open casket. The figure's arms are now missing, but originally, one hand was pointing to heaven, and the other was pointing at the sarcophagus, to Warner's escaping soul. A similar monument in marble stands opposite the Calder work.

SARA YORKE STEVENSON ENGRAVING. Born in Paris, Sara Yorke Stevenson was a writer, archeologist, and Egyptologist, who was also one of the founders of the Archaeological Association of the University of Pennsylvania (which later became the University Museum). She was the first curator of its Egyptian and Mediterranean sections. In 1894, Stevenson became the first woman to receive an honorary degree from the University of Pennsylvania.

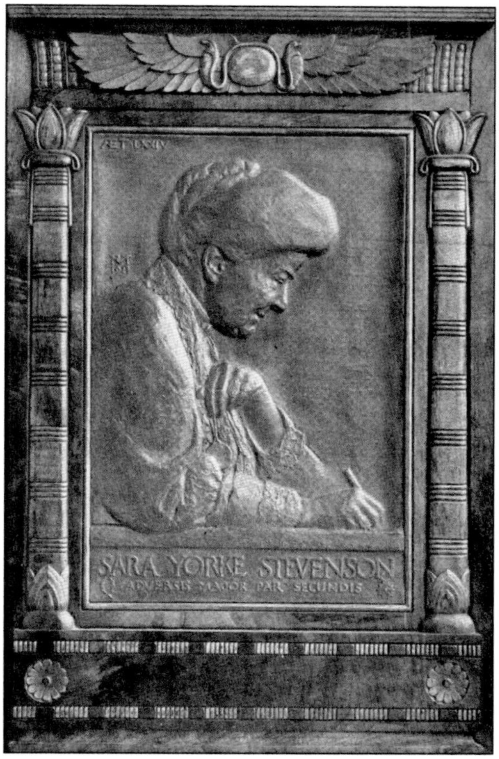

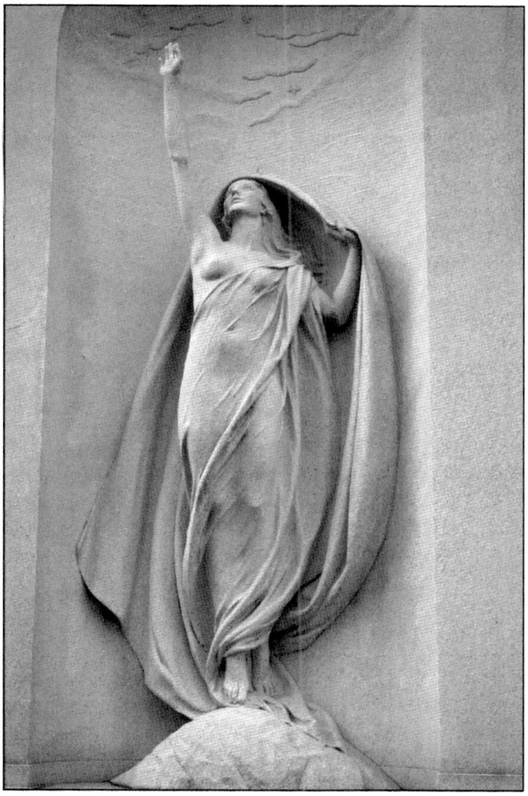

BERWIND MEMORIAL "ASPIRATION." Constructed in 1933, the memorial for Harry Berwind, president of the Berwind-White Coal Company, is the granite version of Harriet Whitney Frishmuth's bronze *Aspiration* sculpture. Frishmuth, who is also buried in Laurel Hill Cemetery, was born in Philadelphia in 1880. She studied in Paris and Berlin before returning to America. Frishmuth had a long and successful career and died in 1980. (Emma Stern.)

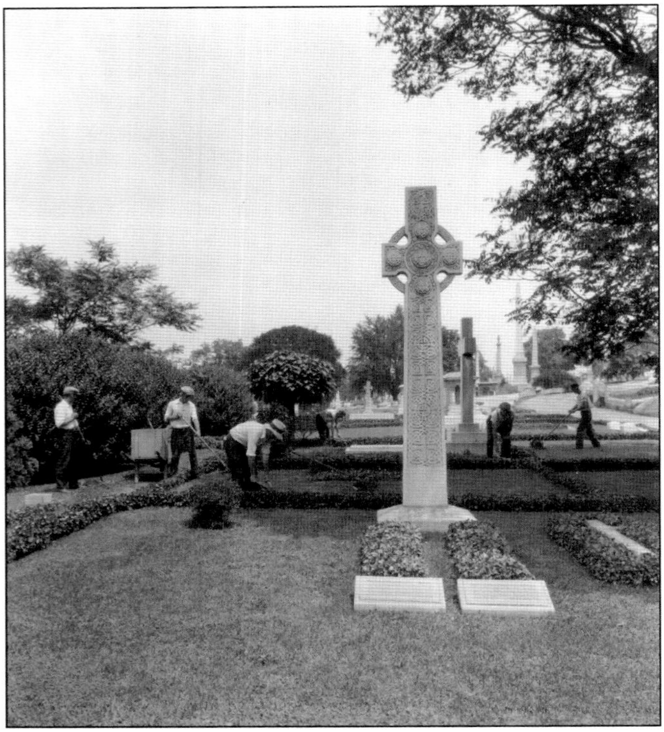

Celtic Cross, 1930. This Celtic cross is one of the most detailed of all the Celtic crosses in Laurel Hill. It cost $1,090 when it was erected in 1913 and is made of Red Westerly granite. It is approximately 12 feet tall and weighs around 2,200 pounds.

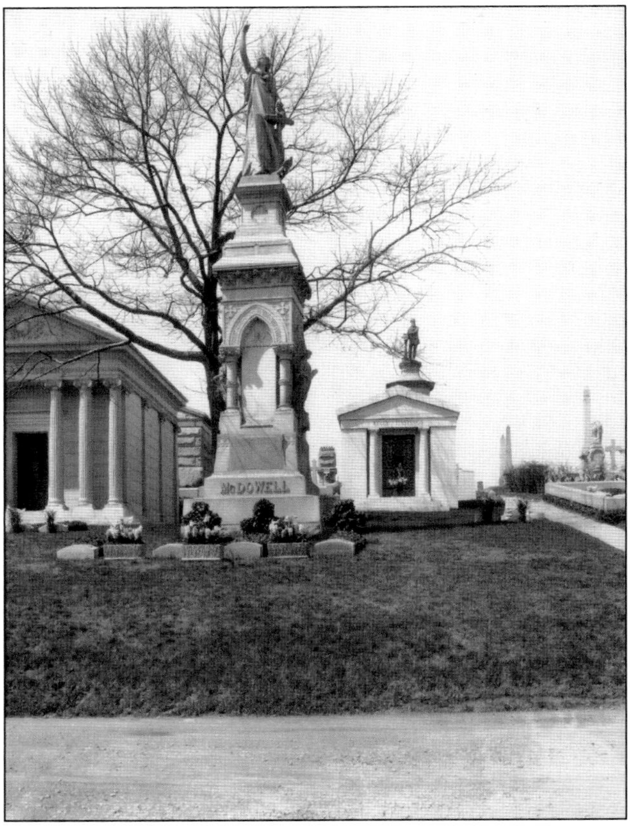

McDowell Memorial, 1931. Despite the pleas of cemetery managers for diversity in memorial selection, Laurel Hill was not immune to the duplication of memorials. Even one as elaborate as the McDowell monument has a twin in the cemetery. In the background is the statue of James Dougherty, whose fortune came from manufacturing the screws for train wheels.

GLASS TOMB TOP, 1931. Laurel Hill has approximately 300 underground mausoleums. Some are unnoticeable from the surface, while others offer a glimpse into the underground. The glass panes in this tomb top allowed visitors to see the crypts. Central Laurel Hill has the greatest number of above ground and underground mausoleums.

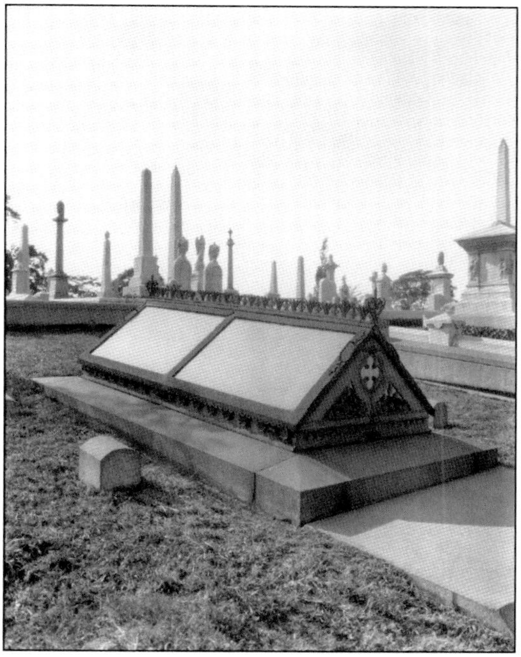

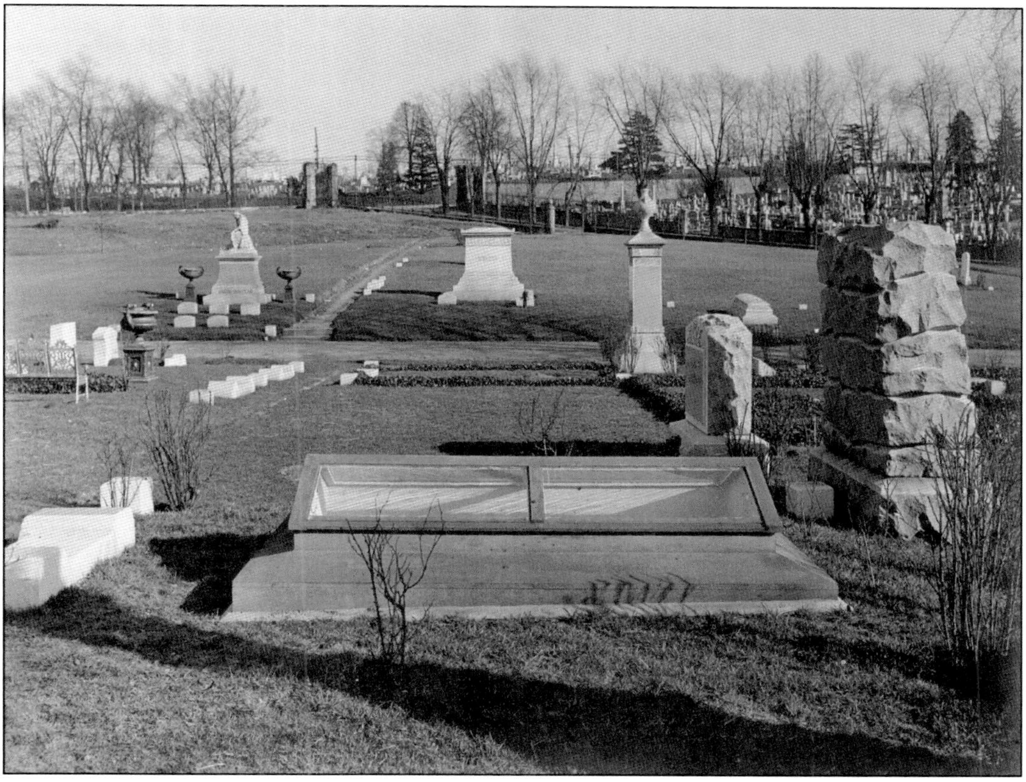

SECTION U, 1912. This photograph shows the glass tomb top to an underground mausoleum in the then newly developed Section U. Nicetown Lane and South Laurel Hill are in the background on the right. Note that the towers at the head of Nicetown Lane were not complete structures, but facades. Unfortunately, most of the bronze urns (such as those seen here) have disappeared.

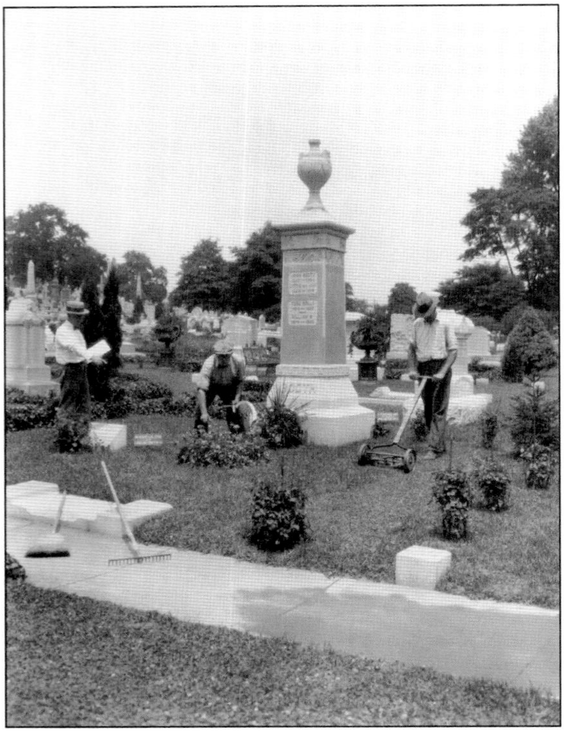

Workers in Section U, 1930. Laurel Hill banned outside gardeners in 1913. Although anger over this policy ultimately led to a fight in court, the move toward professional, paid groundskeepers (as opposed to private families caring for their lots) continued. This image shows workers caring for the Booth property in Central Laurel Hill. The small plaque in the foreground advertises the perpetual care fund for the property.

Workers in the Stevenson Lot, 1917. It took a great deal of manpower to maintain a lot as pristine as the Stevenson property. Cutting the grass, planting fresh flowers, removing dead flowers, and trimming hedges demanded regular care. Howard Stevenson left $2,500 in a trust fund to care for his lot. The cemetery was instructed to use the income from the fund to maintain the lot and place cut flowers at holidays.

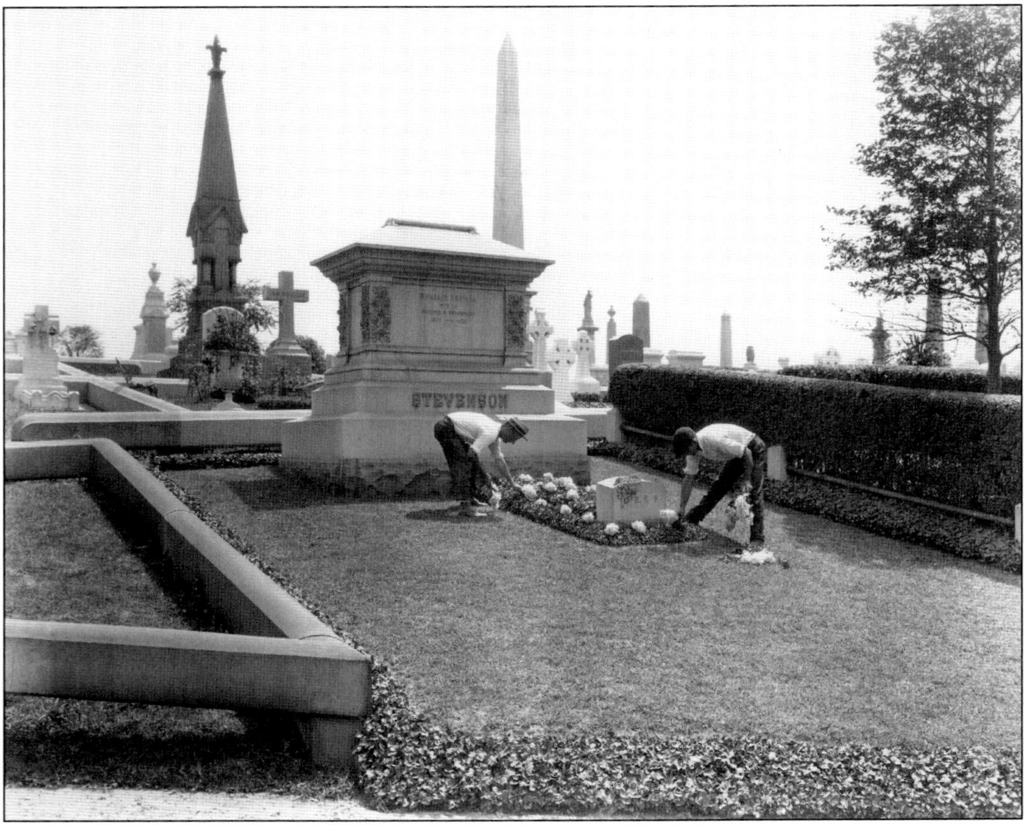

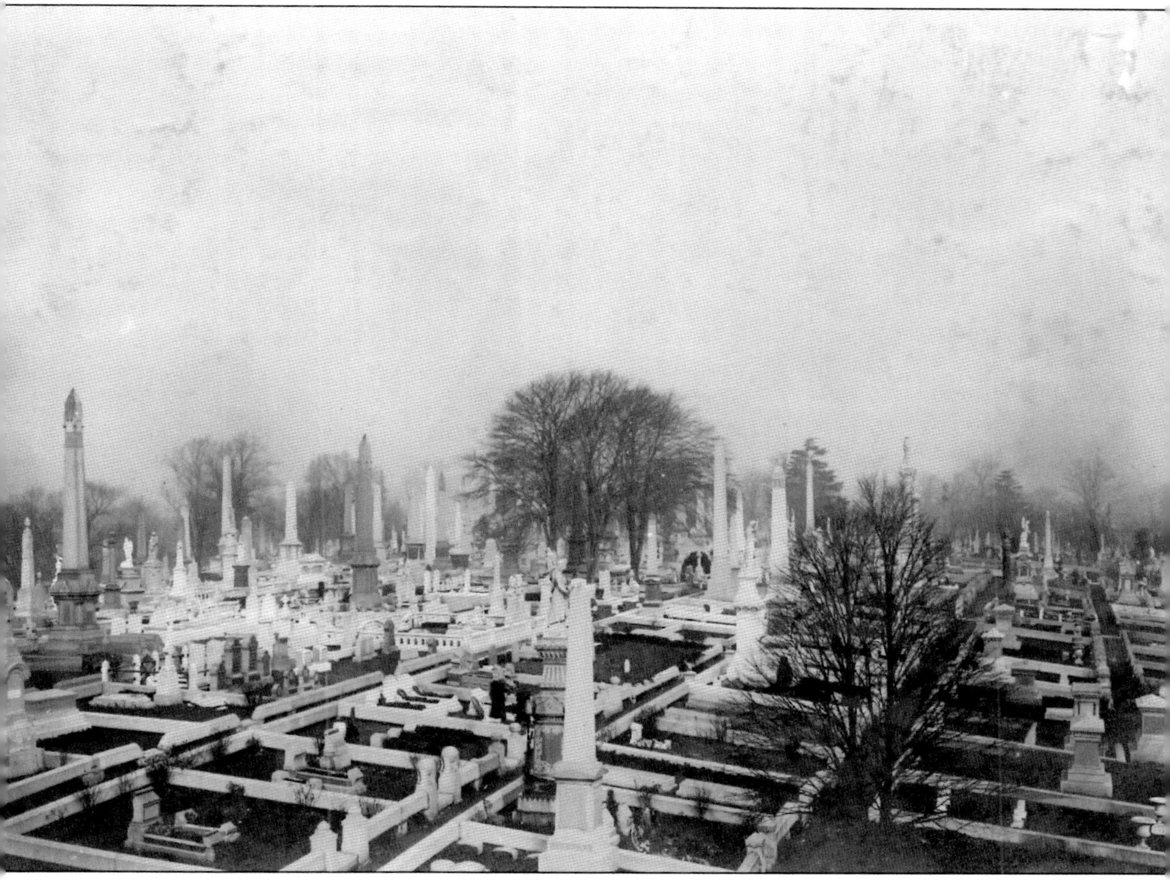

SECTION T, C. 1910. When rural cemeteries began to fall out of favor after the Civil War, one of the complaints against them was that they were too cluttered. The new landscape lawn plan, developed by Spring Grove Cemetery's Adolph Strauch, advocated open lawns and fewer monuments. This view of Section T illustrates this cluttered look, with nearly every family lot surrounded by a fence or granite coping.

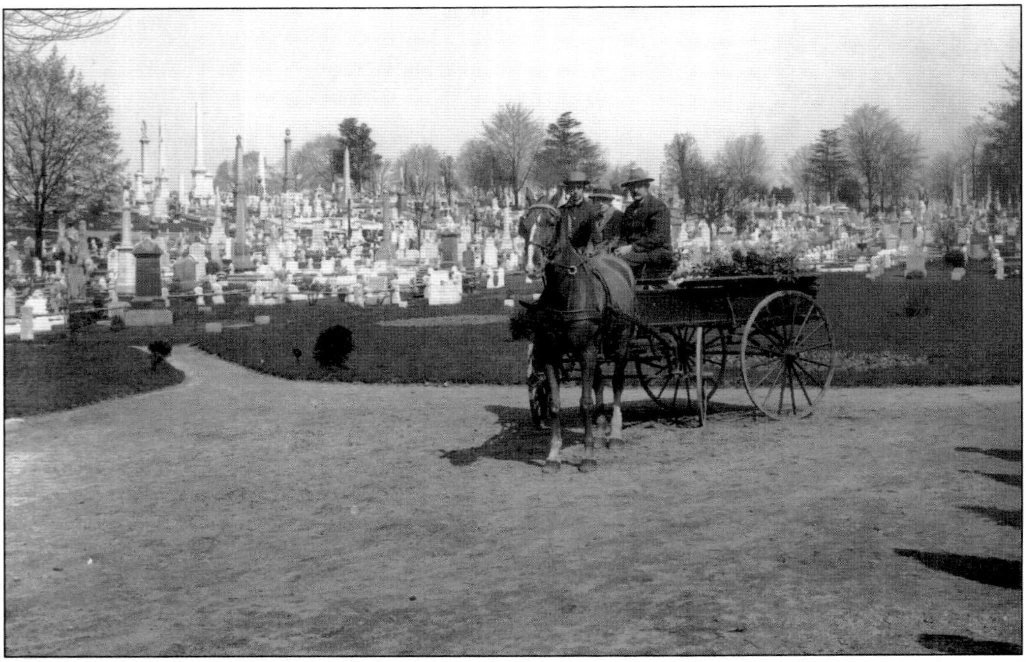

Workers deliver flowers in Section U, c. 1910. The use of horses was an integral part of cemetery work in the 19th century. Laurel Hill had several stables to house this workforce. By 1911, management began to discuss automobiles entering the grounds. There was no objection because "so far they do not appear to have developed the same appetite for shrubbery and grass that the horse is noted for."

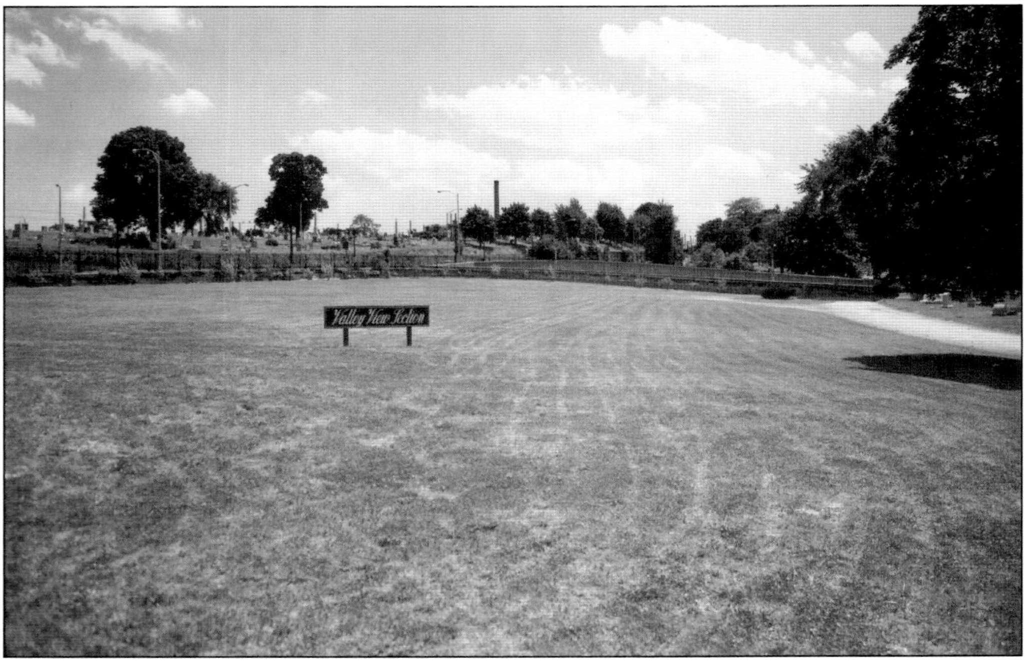

Valley View Section. Created after the greenhouses were demolished, the last available section of open grave space was the Valley View Section. As this area had traditionally been associated with maintenance of the cemetery, it was perceived as a less desirable area of Central Laurel Hill.

Six

Decline and Renewal

In the years following the Civil War, industry continued to creep farther into the countryside surrounding Laurel Hill. Cemetery managers had been on the lookout for additional opportunities to expand, but in 1869, they lost the option to acquire any more adjoining property when the Fairmount Park Commission seized lands surrounding the cemetery. Not content to abandon his interest in cemetery development, John Jay Smith purchased acreage across the river in Montgomery County and established West Laurel Hill Cemetery in 1869. He resigned from the Laurel Hill board in 1874.

While owned and managed by the same people who created Laurel Hill, West Laurel Hill differed from its older sister. It was farther outside the city, and burials came to the cemetery by railroad. It also differed in appearance. The first-generation rural cemeteries with their "cluttered" appearance and overly decorated landscapes were beginning to fall out of favor. The landscape lawn system, first developed by Adolph Strauch of Cincinnati's Spring Grove Cemetery, advocated more open, grassy areas, fewer plantings, and a more uniform and "scientific" approach to design. It was this model that West Laurel Hill more closely followed.

Even though Laurel Hill continued to sell lots after West Laurel Hill opened, without additional room to expand and sell new property, Laurel Hill's financial future was not assured. West Laurel Hill, with its acres of open space, was a competitor that benefitted from the Laurel Hill name and legacy. Several prominent families relocated to the new cemetery. The next generation of Philadelphia's wealthy citizens would be purchasing their lots at the newer and more fashionable site. By the early decades of the 20th century, Laurel Hill was beginning its decline. The permanent fund did not generate enough income to even maintain grass cutting, and vandalism and theft resulted in the destruction of countless monuments. It was not until the latter part of the 20th century that Laurel Hill began to experience a period of renewed interest. Several local educators brought classes to and gave tours in the cemetery. The creation of the Friends of Laurel Hill Cemetery and the cemetery's designation as a National Historic Landmark brought hope of a renewed future. Instead of selling new property, the cemetery now relies on grants and programming. The 21st century has witnessed a revitalized cemetery where once again visitors come to learn, stroll, and admire the scenery.

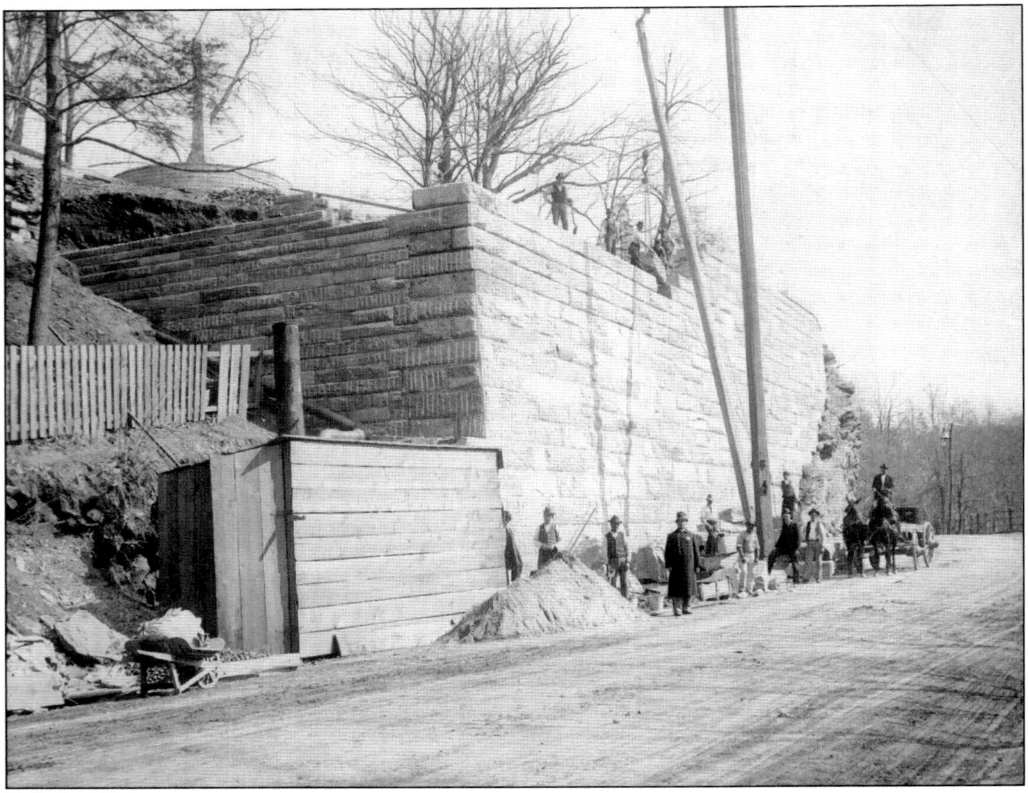

WORKERS BUILDING NEW WALL IN RIVER SECTION, 1895. The second half of the 19th century brought significant infrastructure updates and changes to the cemetery. Quarrying began in 1874 for a wall to isolate the cemetery from East River Drive. Construction went on for the next two decades, and resulted in some much-needed new grave space. This photograph shows the wall under construction and the Thomson obelisk at upper left.

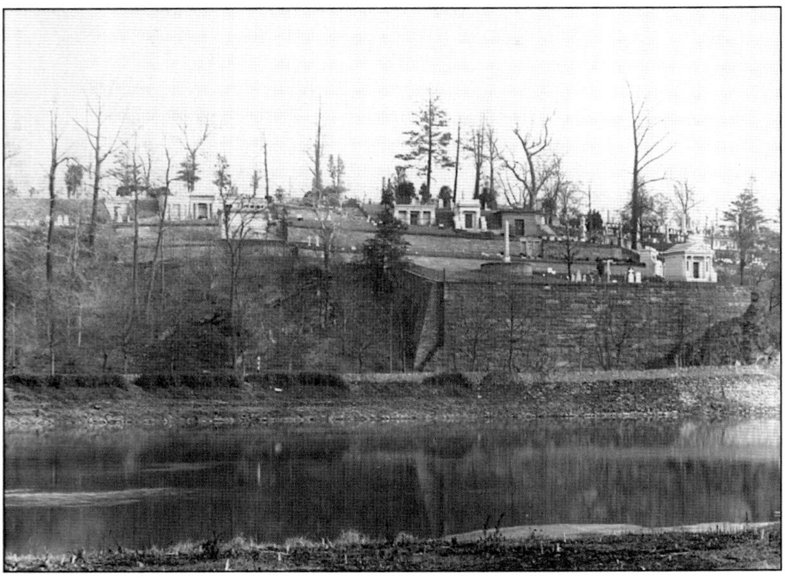

VIEW OF NORTH LAUREL HILL FROM ACROSS THE SCHUYLKILL RIVER, C. 1910. This view of North Laurel Hill shows the wall after completion. The Thomson obelisk can be seen near the center.

Tree Removal in Section U, 1905. By the beginning of the 20th century, Laurel Hill was dealing with the need for increased maintenance, as the cemetery's buildings, roads, trees, and monuments aged. This image shows a scaffold, 80 feet in height, erected to remove an unsafe tree. Today, this work would be done with a mechanized crane.

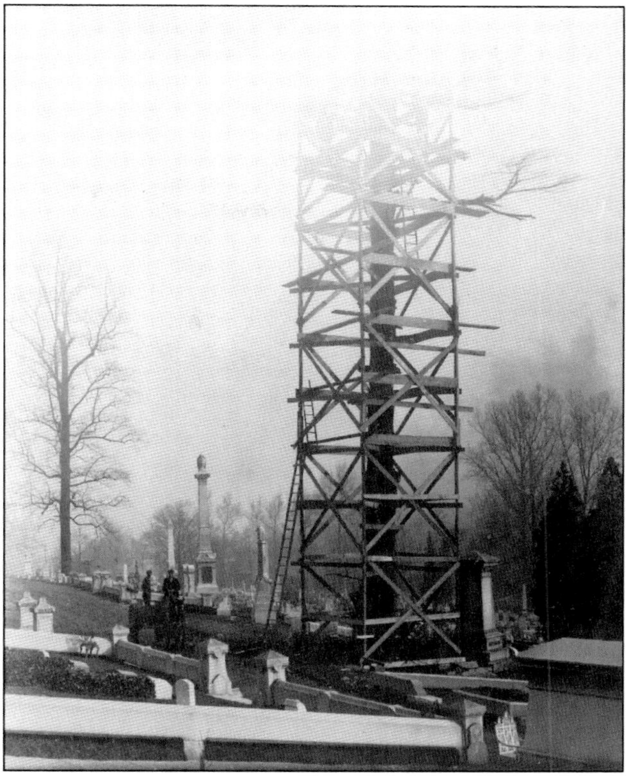

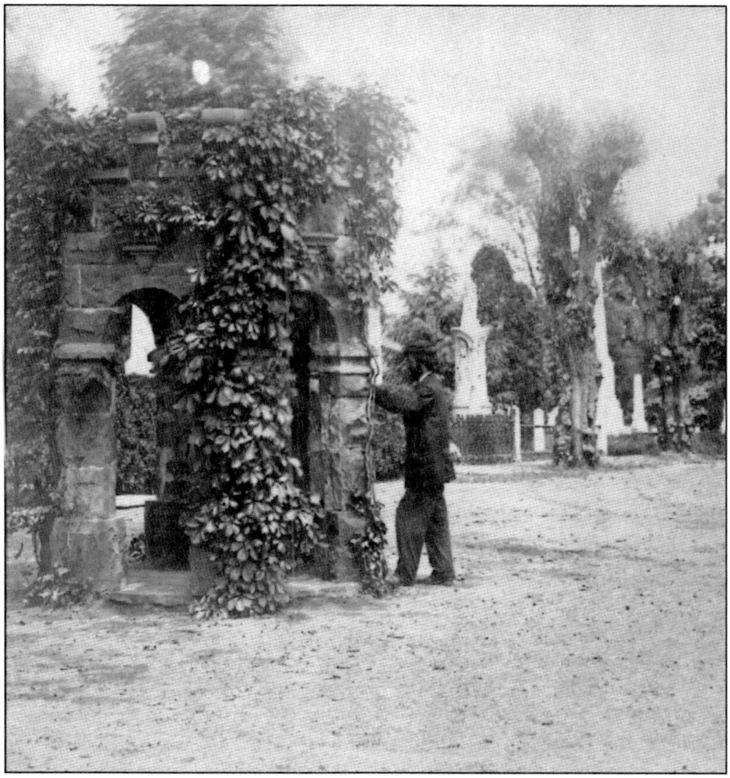

Man at Water Pump. During the 19th century, the cemetery constructed water pumps for use by visitors. Access to water was essential for the care of one's cemetery lot. In the 20th century, and with the prohibition of outside gardeners, the cemetery began to control the use of water by those not employed by the cemetery.

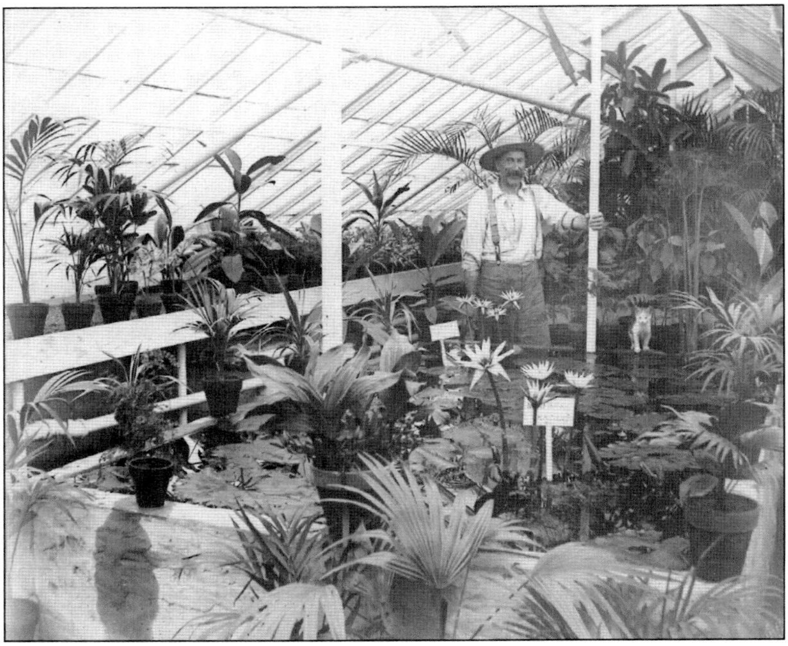

Man and Cat in Greenhouse. From as early as 1836, when the cemetery company leased land to florist John Sherwood, flowers and greenhouses were part of the cemetery business. Initially, flowers were sold across the street from Laurel Hill, but later, greenhouses were built inside the cemetery.

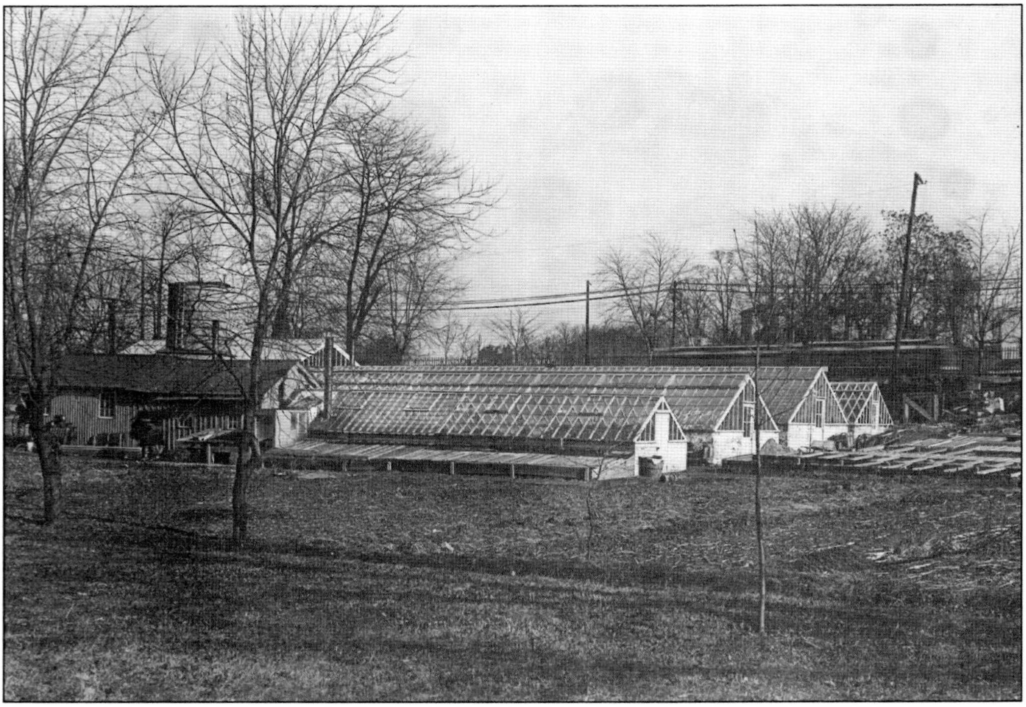

Greenhouse, c. 1910. At various times, greenhouses stood in every section of Laurel Hill. By the 20th century, however, with grave space at a premium, the greenhouses were located only in Central Laurel Hill, near today's Valley View Section.

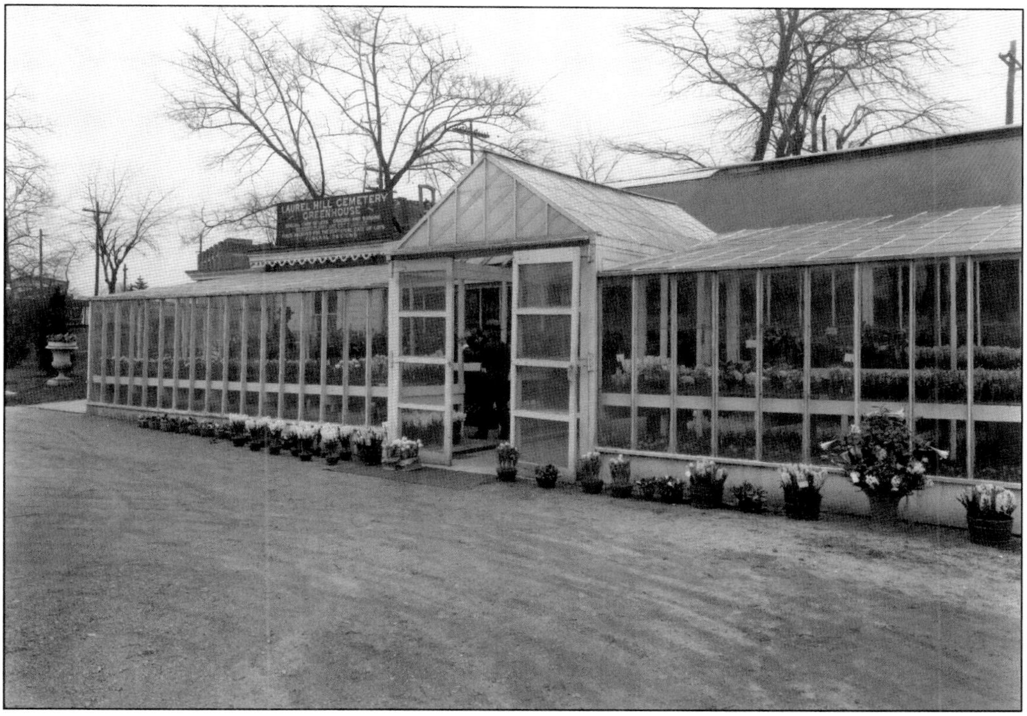

Greenhouse Exterior and Interior, c. 1931. Flowers were an important part of decorating a family lot, and by 1907, the main greenhouse had a large showroom. But as the cemetery's financial circumstances became dire following World War II, discussions arose about closing and removing the greenhouses entirely.

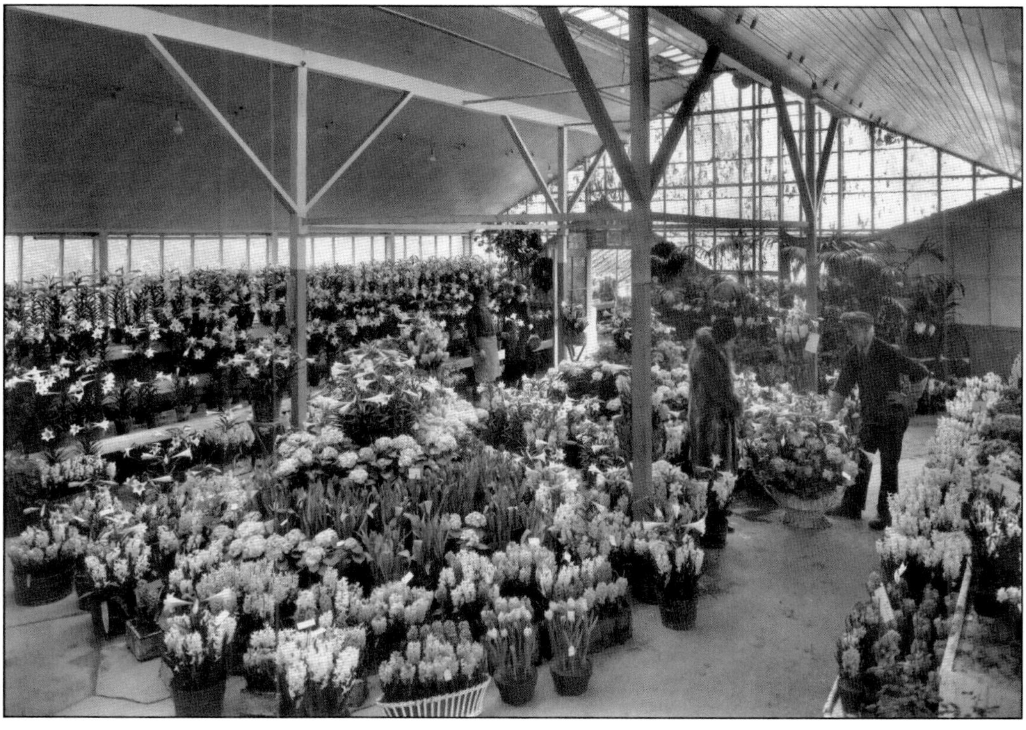

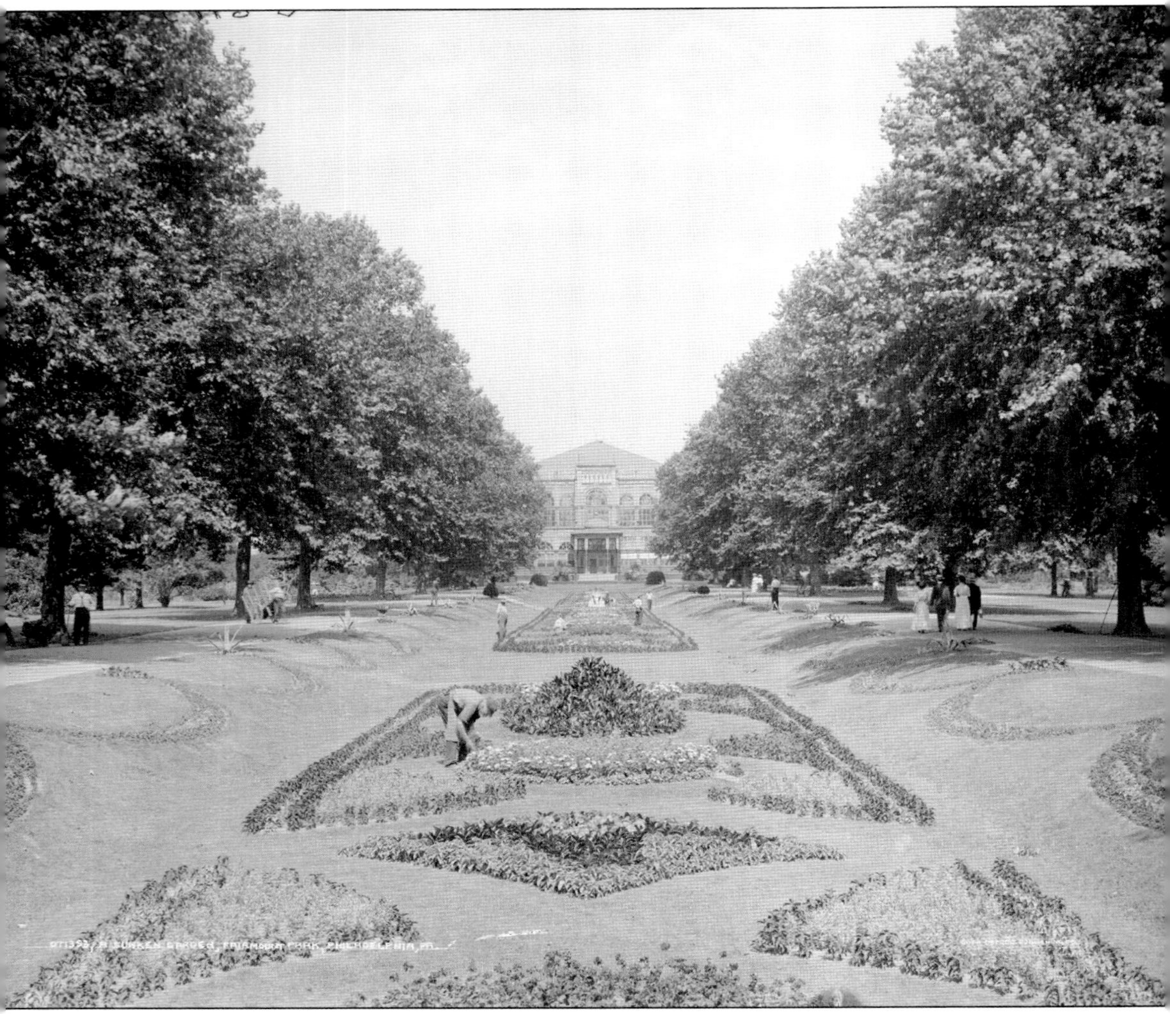

FAIRMOUNT PARK'S SUNKEN GARDENS, C. 1900–1920. The creation of Fairmount Park had dire consequences for Laurel Hill. The cemetery was confined by the park and the river with no new vacant land to be had for expansion. The Fairmount Park Commission actually took some of Laurel Hill's land by eminent domain. Fairmount Park provided Philadelphians with a grand municipal park to replace their rural cemetery. (LOC.)

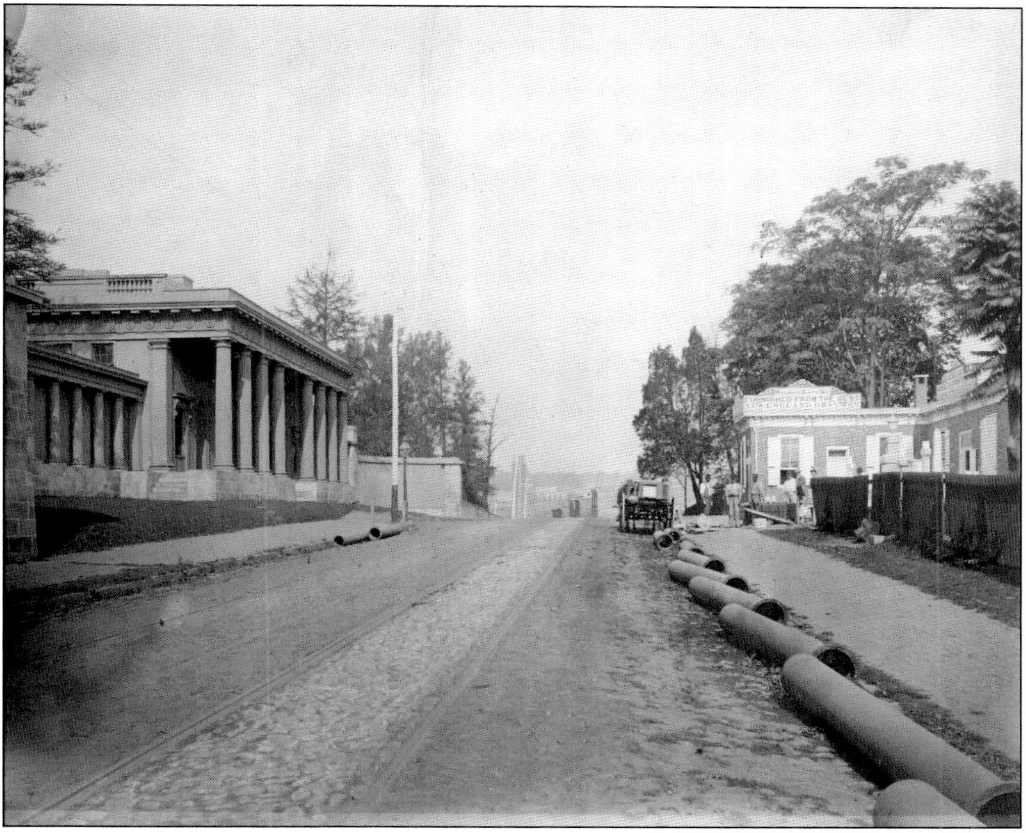

View of Ridge Pike Looking North, c. 1883. The 1880s witnessed further expansion of homes and businesses around Laurel Hill. This view shows the Delahunty monument yard that opened around 1880 directly across the street from the cemetery.

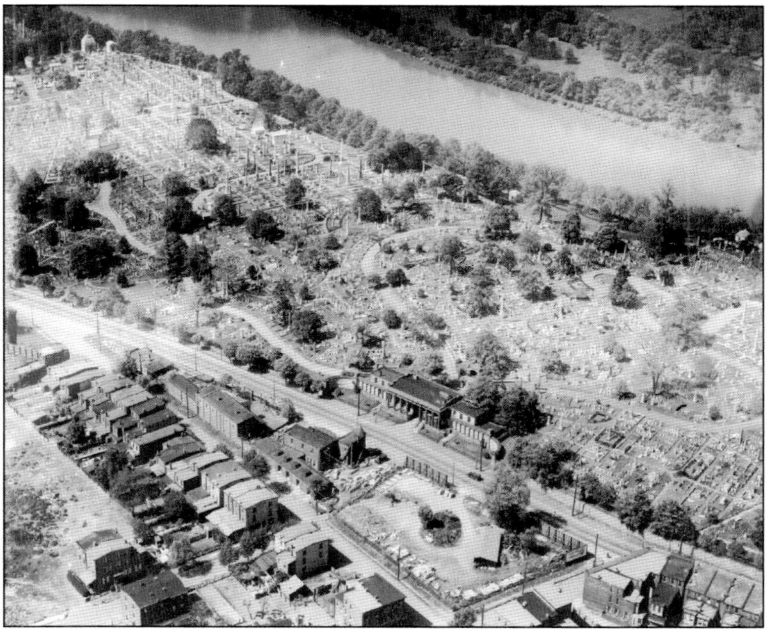

Aerial View of Laurel Hill Cemetery, 1924. By the 20th century, not only was the cemetery approaching capacity, but the surrounding neighborhoods had grown and developed. This image shows North and Central Laurel Hill stretching to the Schuylkill River.

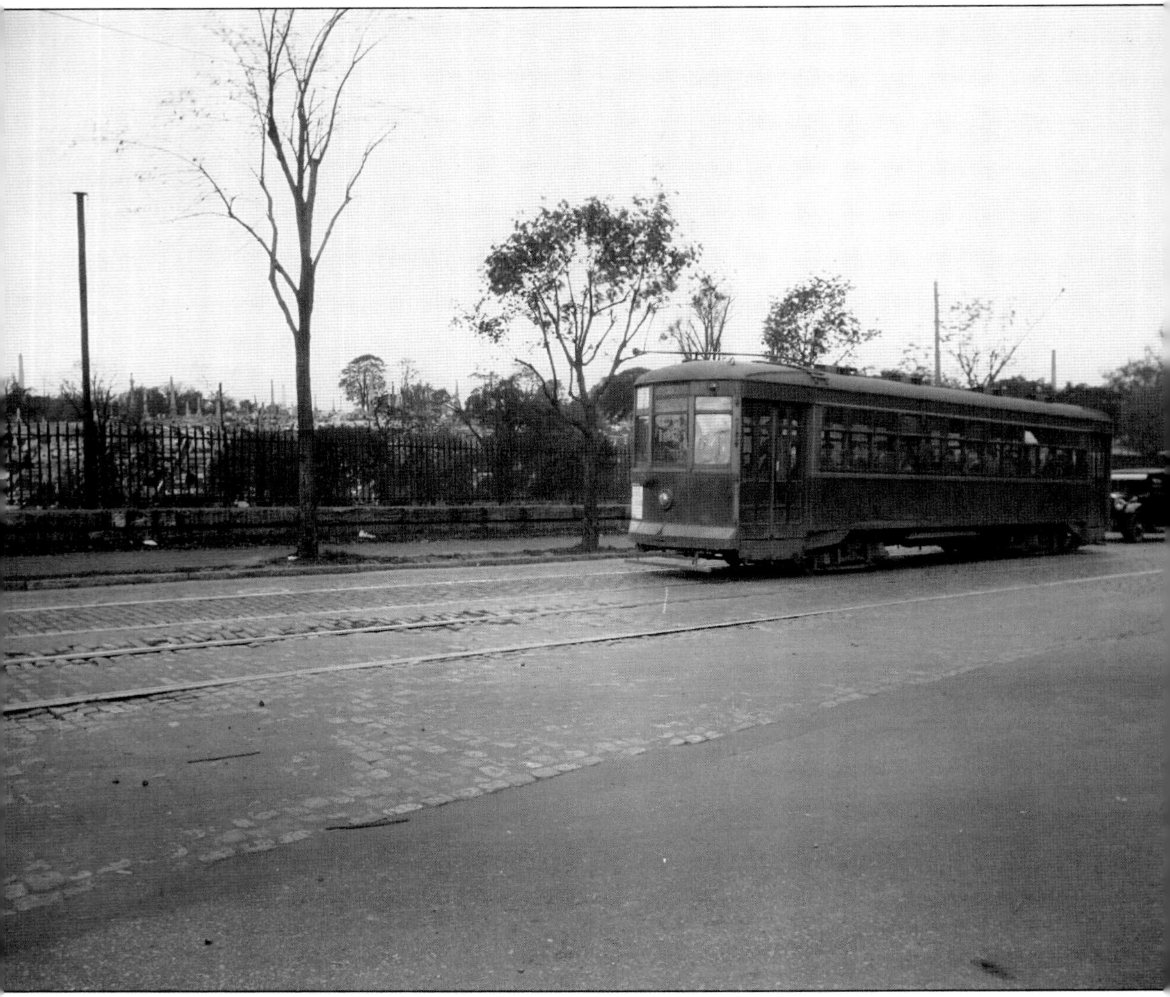

STREETCAR IN FRONT OF CENTRAL LAUREL HILL, 1928. Although it was never a popular way for funeral processions to reach the cemetery, visitors did take trolleys to Laurel Hill. This image shows a streetcar passing in front of Central Laurel Hill.

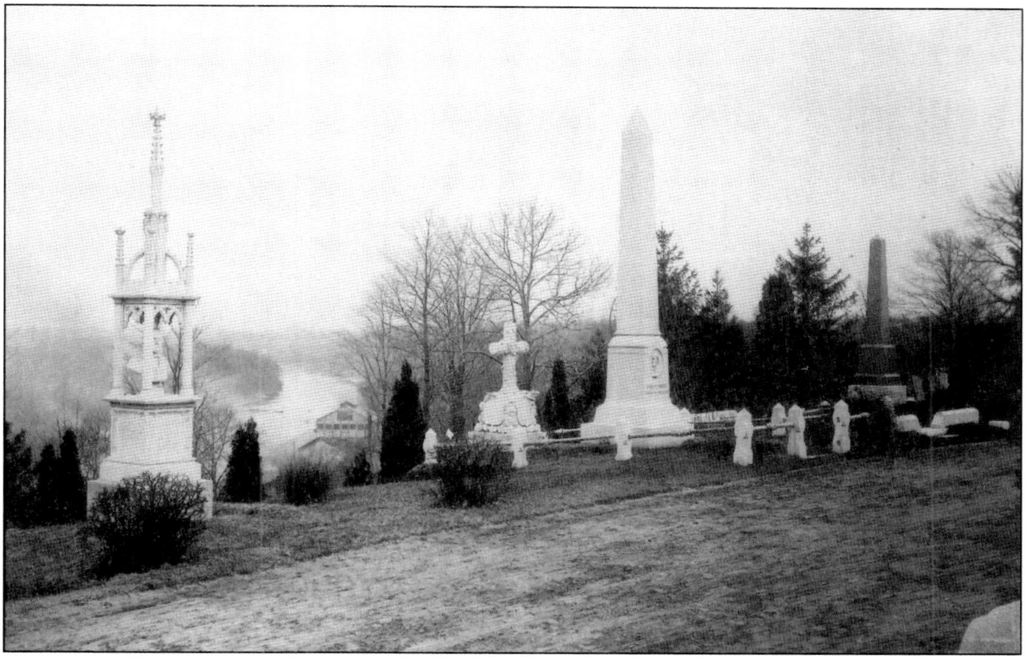

View of Schuylkill River in West Laurel Hill, c. 1890. The parcel of land John Jay Smith selected for West Laurel Hill Cemetery was farther from the city than Laurel Hill but featured equally striking views of the Schuylkill River. As with Laurel Hill, Smith supervised the selection of trees and plantings. This view looks north from West Laurel Hill's River Section. (WLHC.)

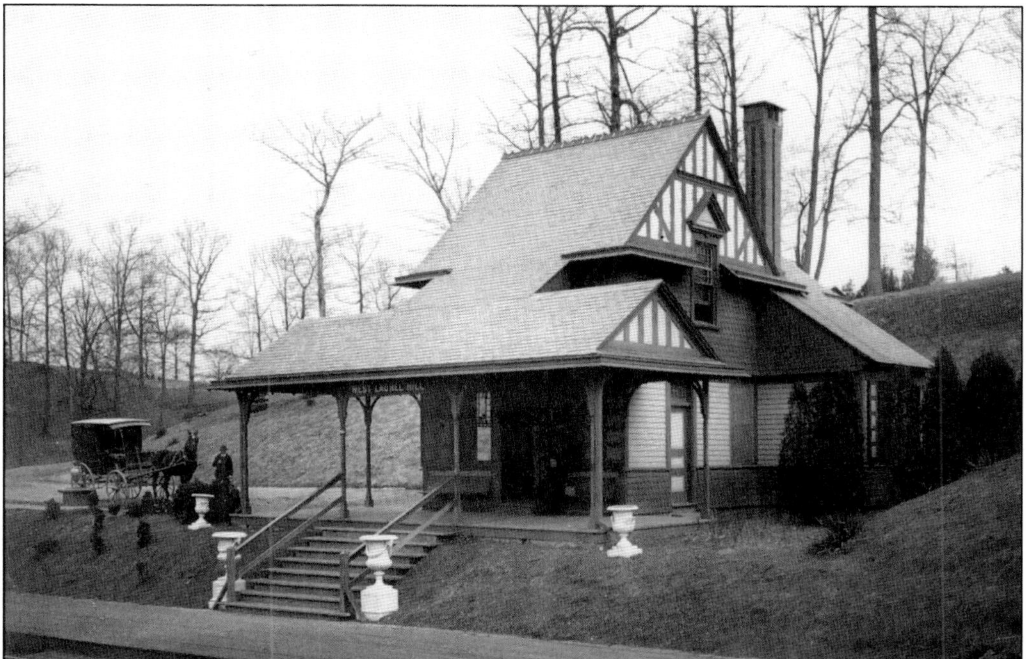

West Laurel Hill Train Station. At West Laurel Hill, funeral processions arrived via the railroad. Initially, the Pencoyd Station was the stop for processions journeying to the cemetery, but later, a station was built along the Pennsylvania Railroad specifically for West Laurel Hill. (WLHC.)

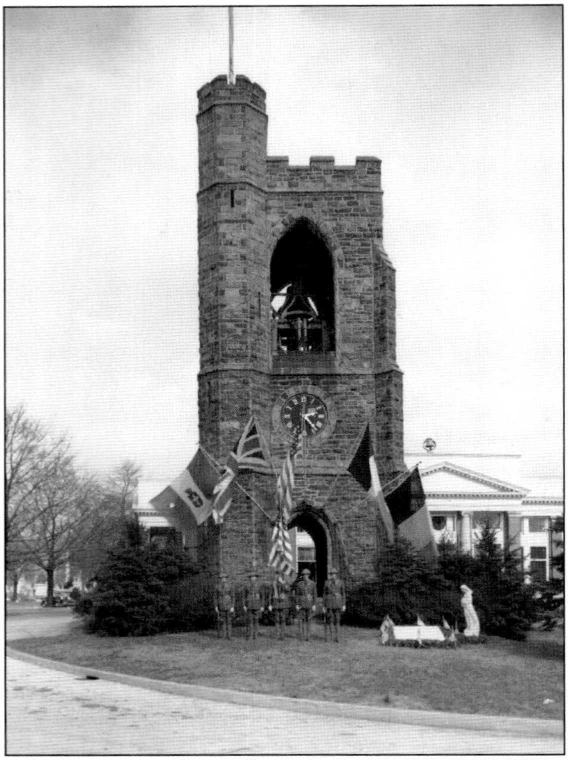

Bell Tower and Main Entrance, West Laurel Hill. Although West Laurel Hill was founded and managed by some of the same men who had run Laurel Hill, the two cemeteries were competitors, with the newer West Laurel Hill benefitting from the legacy of Laurel Hill. When Lloyd Smith, John Jay Smith's son and a manager at both Laurel Hill and West Laurel Hill, sent a note to Frederick Brown Jr. regarding a new cemetery opening with the name of East Laurel Hill, it was met with a sharp reply: "The Sidney's have the same right to the name 'East Laurel Hill' as you have to 'West Laurel Hill,' i.e. none at all." In its printed materials, Laurel Hill emphasized that it had "no connection with any other cemetery." Only toward the end of the 20th century would Laurel Hill begin to benefit from its younger "sister," as West Laurel Hill started partially subsidizing Laurel Hill. (Both, WLHC.)

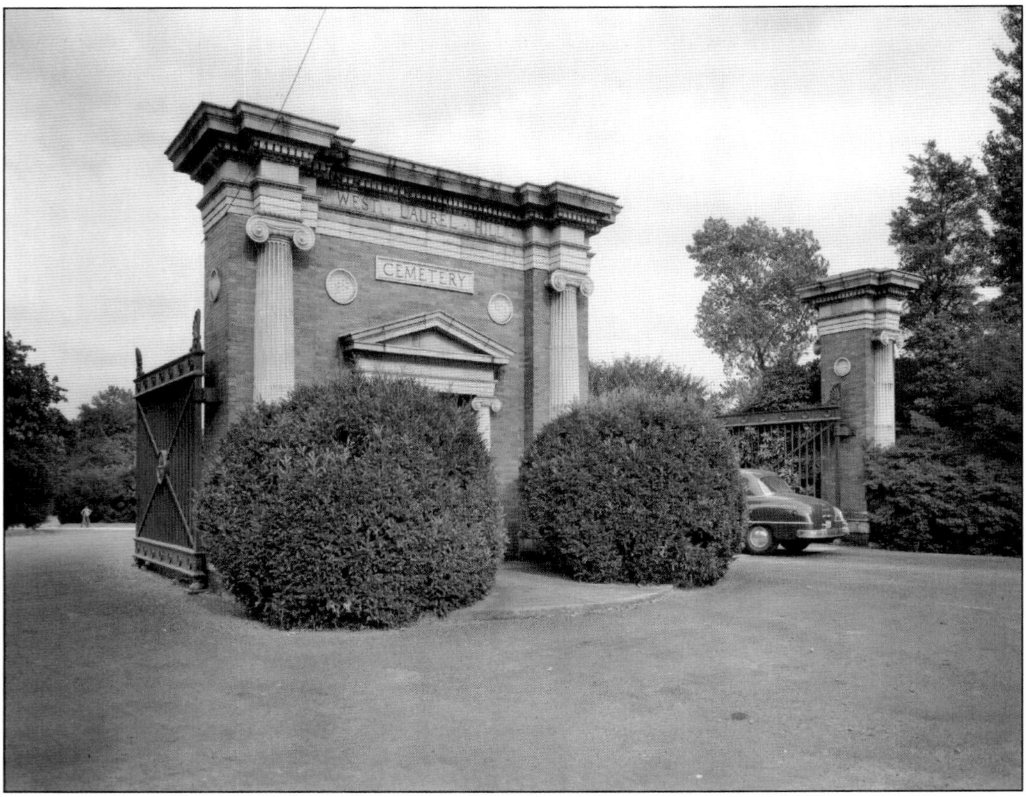

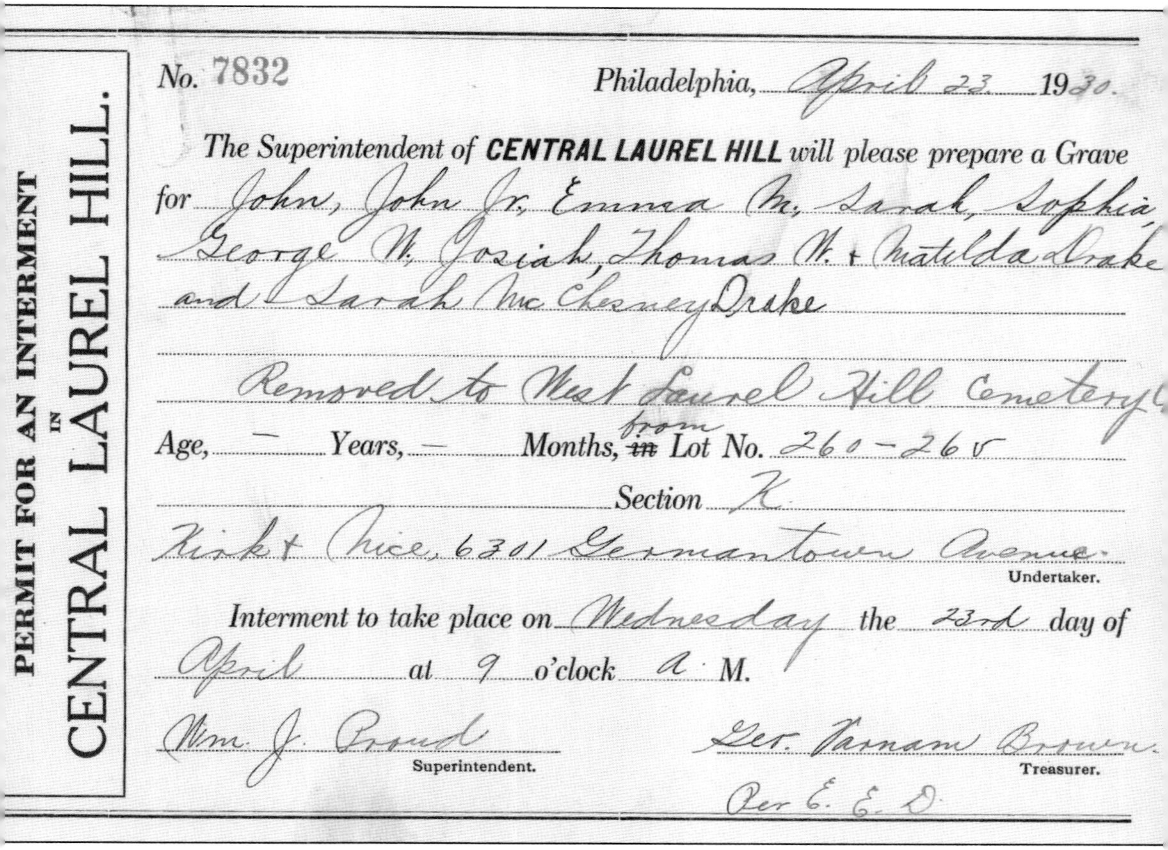
PERMIT FOR AN INTERMENT IN CENTRAL LAUREL HILL.

No. 7832 Philadelphia, April 23 1930.

The Superintendent of **CENTRAL LAUREL HILL** will please prepare a Grave for John, John Jr, Emma M, Sarah, Sophia, George W, Josiah, Thomas W. + Matilda Drake and Sarah McChesney Drake

Removed to West Laurel Hill Cemetery

Age, — Years, — Months, ~~in~~ from Lot No. 260-265

Section K.

Kirk + Nice, 6301 Germantown Avenue. Undertaker.

Interment to take place on Wednesday the 23rd day of April at 9 o'clock a. M.

Wm. J. Proud, Superintendent. Geo. Varnam Brown, Treasurer. Per E. E. D.

Central Laurel Hill Removal Permit, 1930. By the end of the 19th century, West Laurel Hill was the more fashionable of the two cemeteries. West Laurel Hill gave Philadelphians more than twice the amount of space from which to select a burial site. Germantown native and *Titanic* survivor Charlotte Drake Martinez Cardeza moved her entire family and the family mausoleum to West Laurel Hill. Correspondence indicating her annoyance with her neighbors in Central Laurel Hill and her selection of a property in West completely isolated from other lots provide clues to her reasons for relocating.

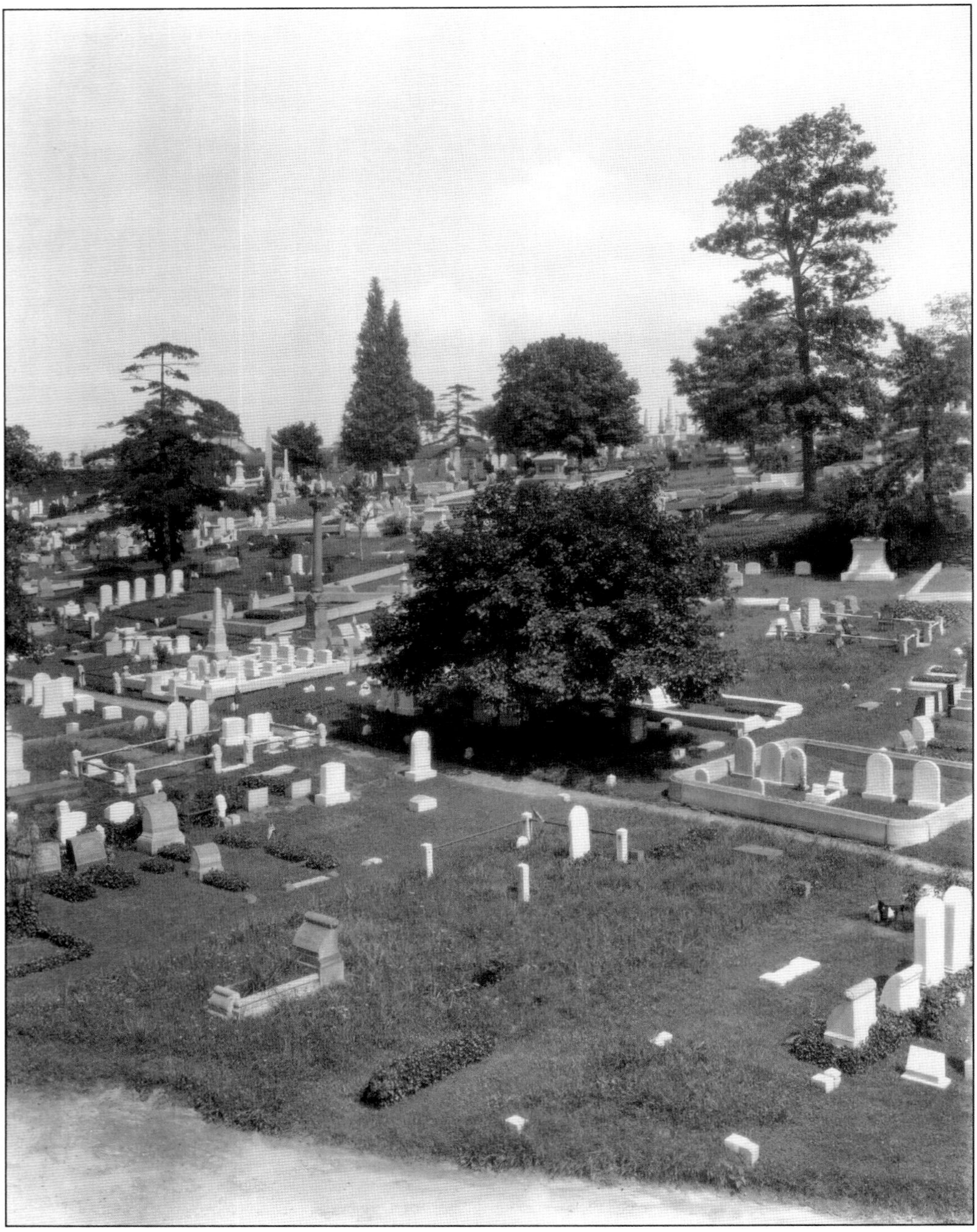

SECTION 16 IN SOUTH LAUREL HILL, 1931. With the permanent fund unable to cover expenses of cutting the grass, Laurel Hill's managers decided on the new tactic of only cutting the grass in lots where property owners paid for annual lot care. Unfortunately, with so many descendants unknown to the cemetery, the plan resulted in an inefficient way to maintain the cemetery, and only left paying lot owners angered.

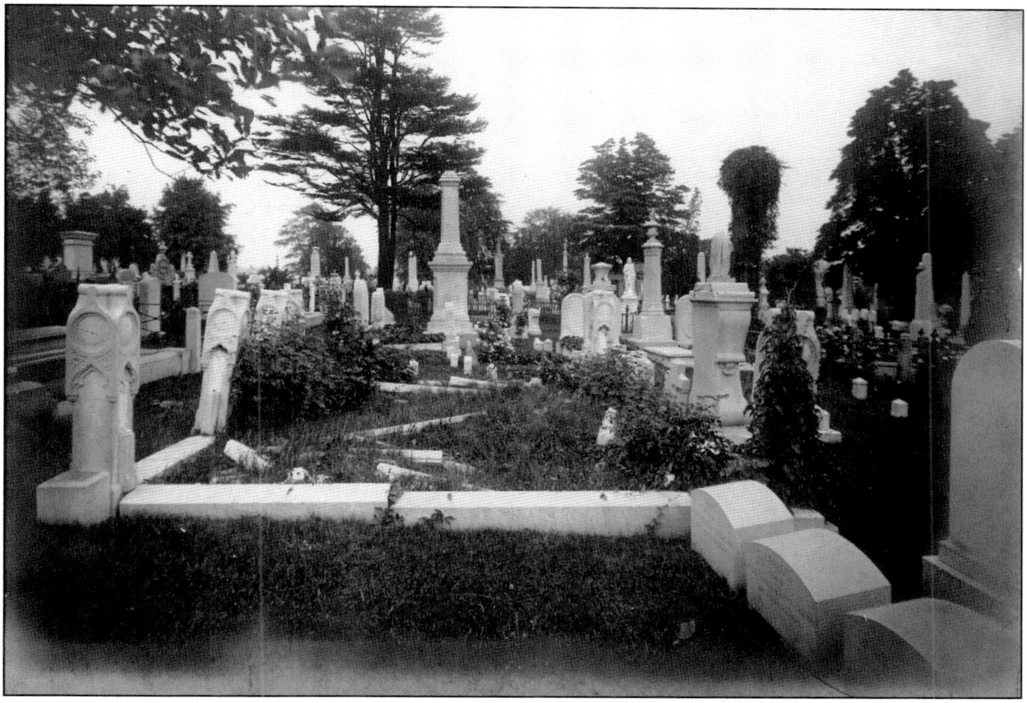

Lot in Disrepair, 1906 (above), and Vandalism, 1967 (below). The disrepair visible at the beginning of the 20th century only progressed. In the 1960s, a new form of deterioration became evident as vandals broke monuments and toppled stones, and thieves stole bronze pieces and stained-glass windows. The cemetery could not keep up with the amount of repair and maintenance needed, so it elected to bury fallen stones rather than reset them.

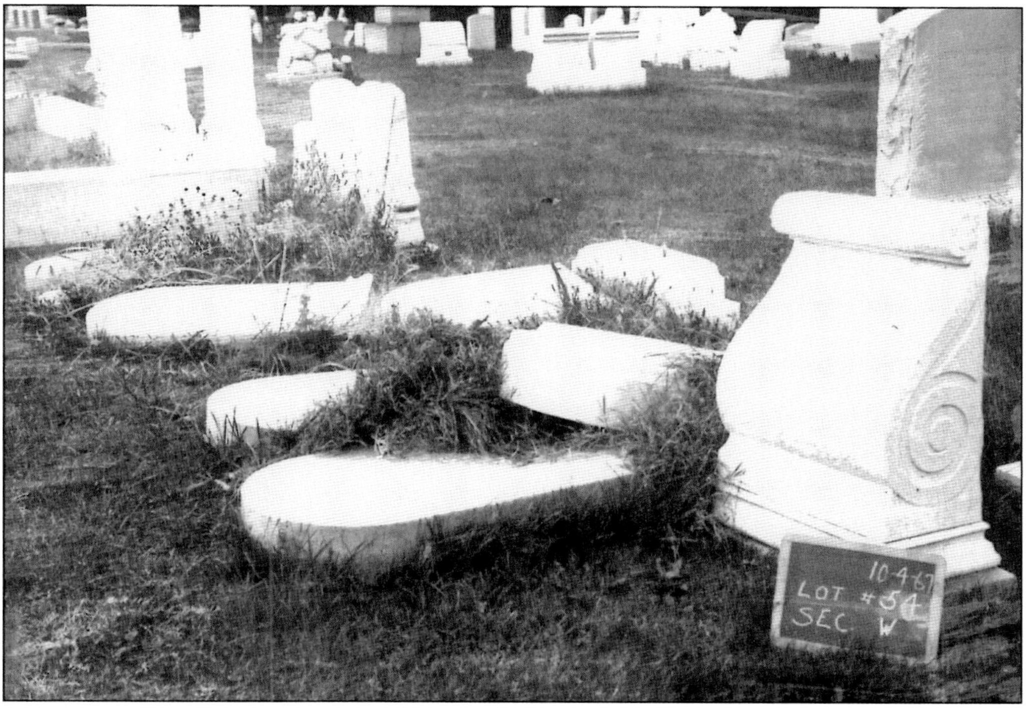

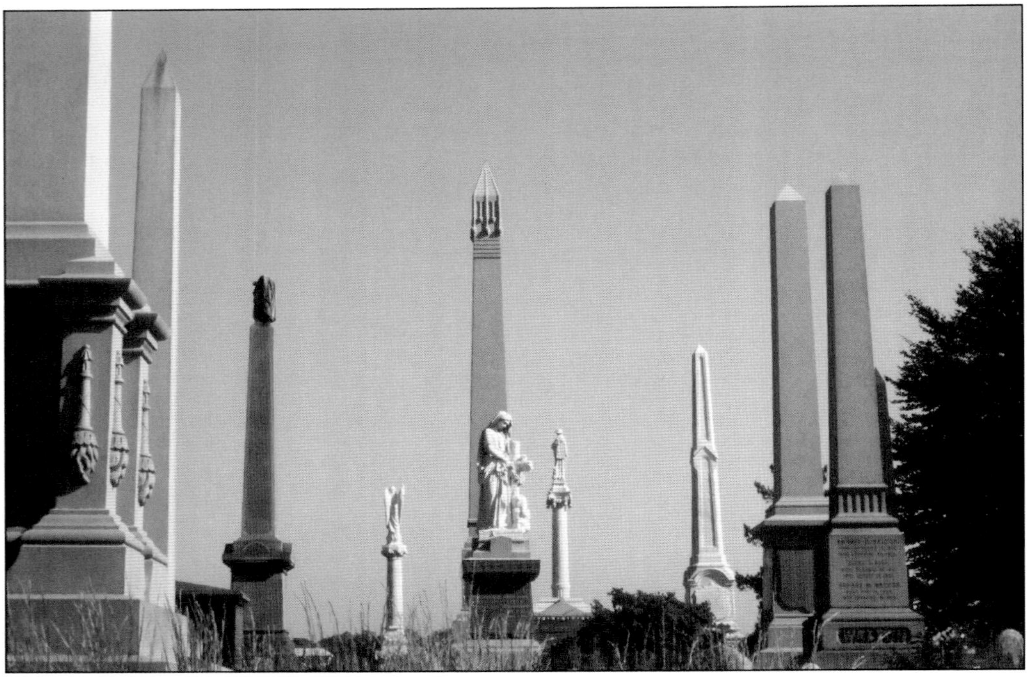

Overgrowth in Central Laurel Hill, 1977. By the 1970s, Laurel Hill was an overgrown jungle. Plants and grass obscured paths and monuments. Wild vines and shrubs covered buildings and statues. Nature was attempting to reclaim its space.

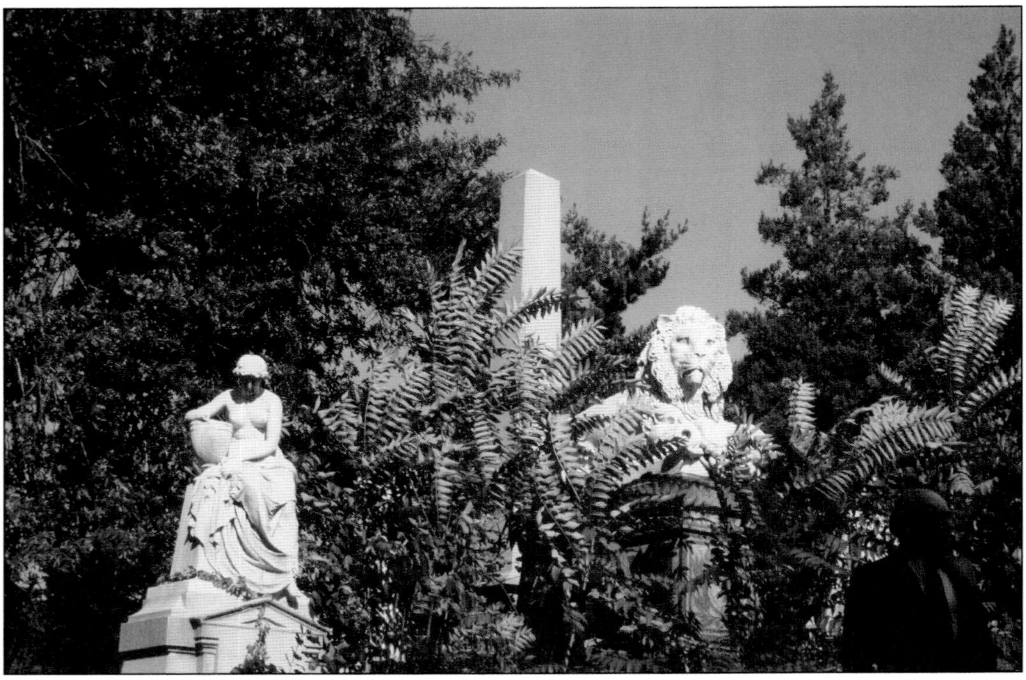

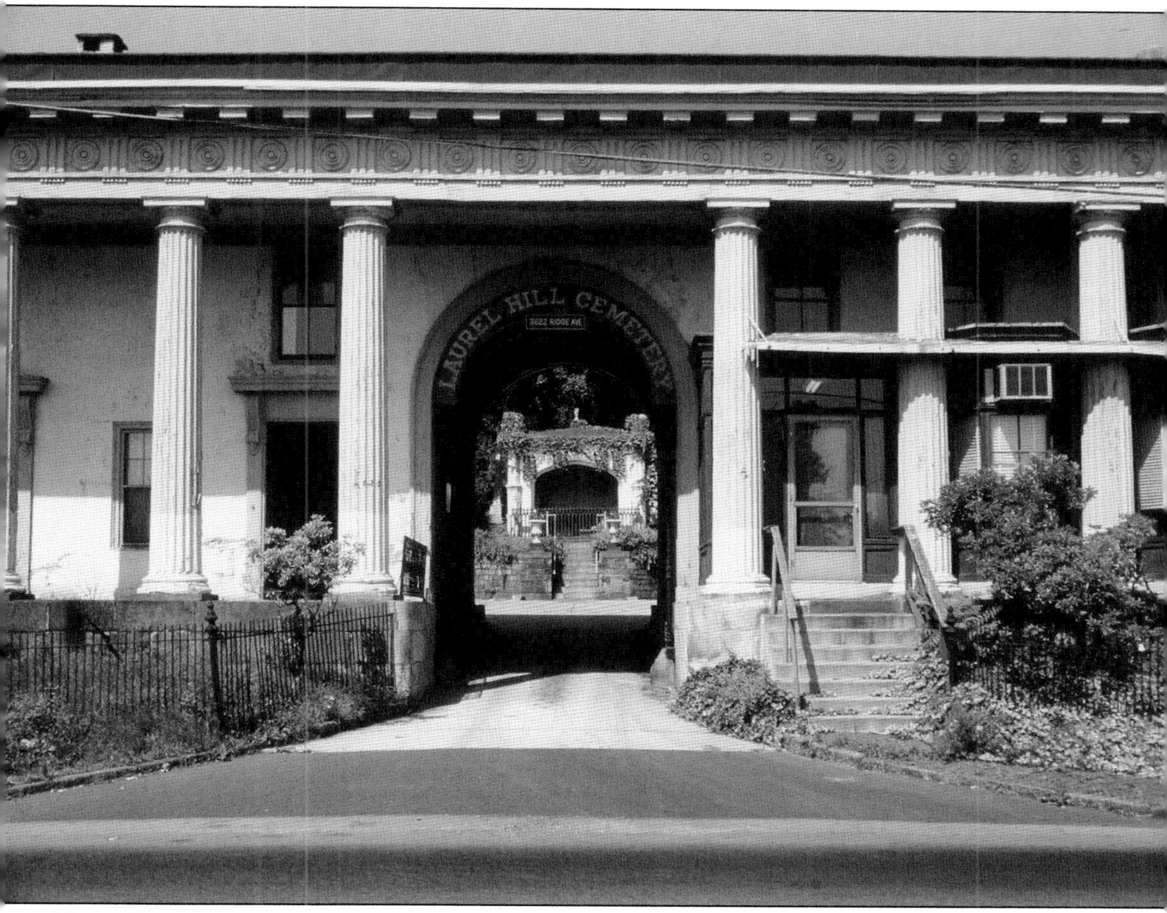

North Laurel Hill Gatehouse, 1979. John Notman's once-grand gatehouse also showed signs of deterioration. Overgrowth covered the exterior. Partially painted columns pointed to neglect, and the exterior walls showed obvious signs of wear. Even when the gate was unlocked to visitors, the glimpse inside to *Old Mortality* showed another neglected landmark.

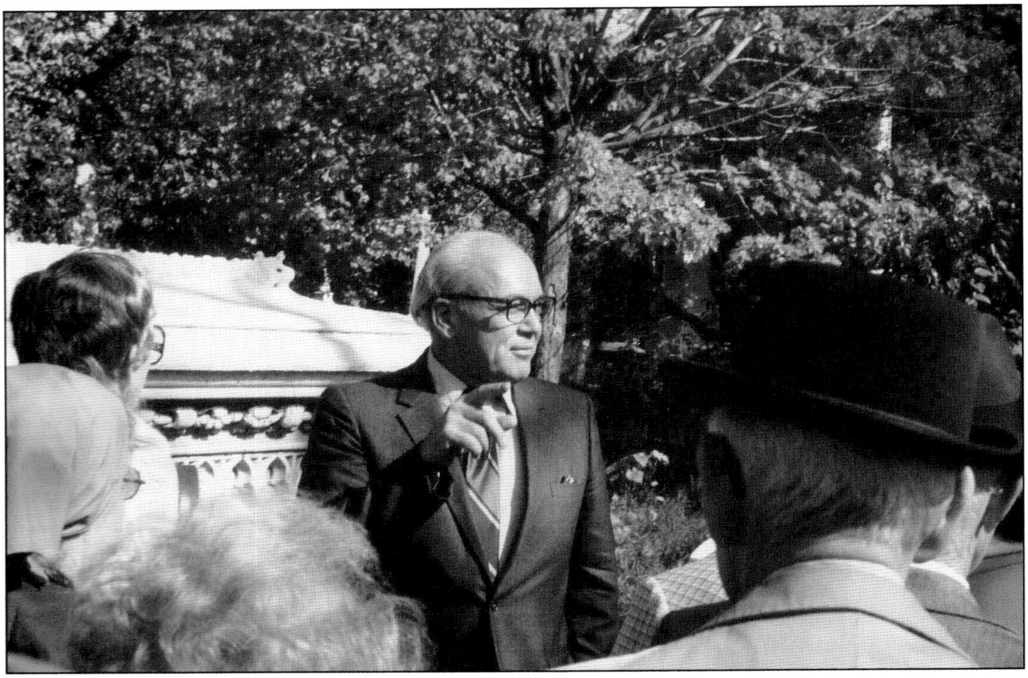

John Francis Marion Leading Tour Group, 1977. In spite of Laurel Hill's decline, there were still Philadelphians who valued its place in history. Author and historian John Francis Marion began giving tours of Laurel Hill in 1973. No matter the weather, he could be found walking the cemetery grounds, extolling the beauty of the landscape and retelling the histories of Laurel Hill's residents. He advertised his tours by way of his connections to the local newspapers, public radio, and television. In 1977, he wrote a book, *Famous and Curious Cemeteries*, in which Laurel Hill was prominently featured. Then, in 1978, he worked with Jane and Drayton Smith to establish the Friends of Laurel Hill Cemetery, the organization dedicated to restoring, preserving, and promoting the cemetery. Marion died in 1991 and was buried in Section S. No longer able to give tours, he is now a featured stop on them.

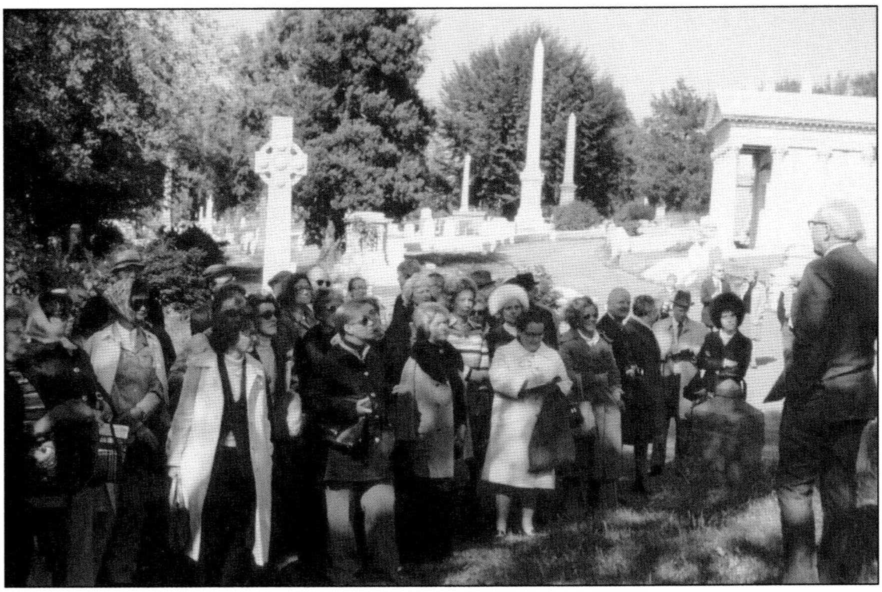

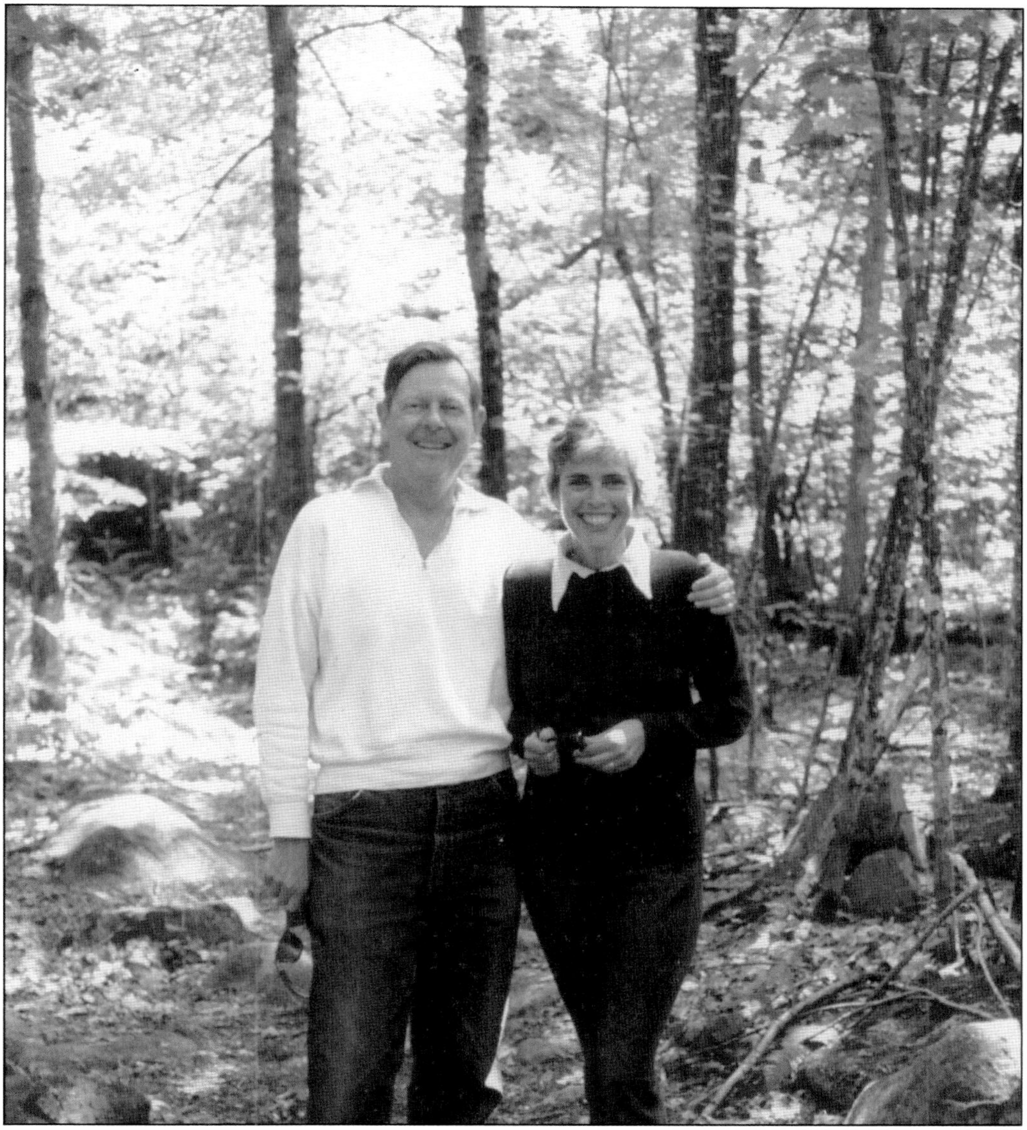

JANE AND DRAYTON SMITH. A direct descendant of founder John Jay Smith, Drayton Smith was very familiar with Laurel Hill. As president of the Laurel Hill Cemetery Company, he and his wife, Jane, saw the cemetery's poor condition, and wanted to restore its former glory. Working with John Francis Marion, Drayton and Jane established the Friends of Laurel Hill Cemetery in 1978. Although they did not live to see the organization's success, their family has worked to see their dream become a reality. (Smith family.)

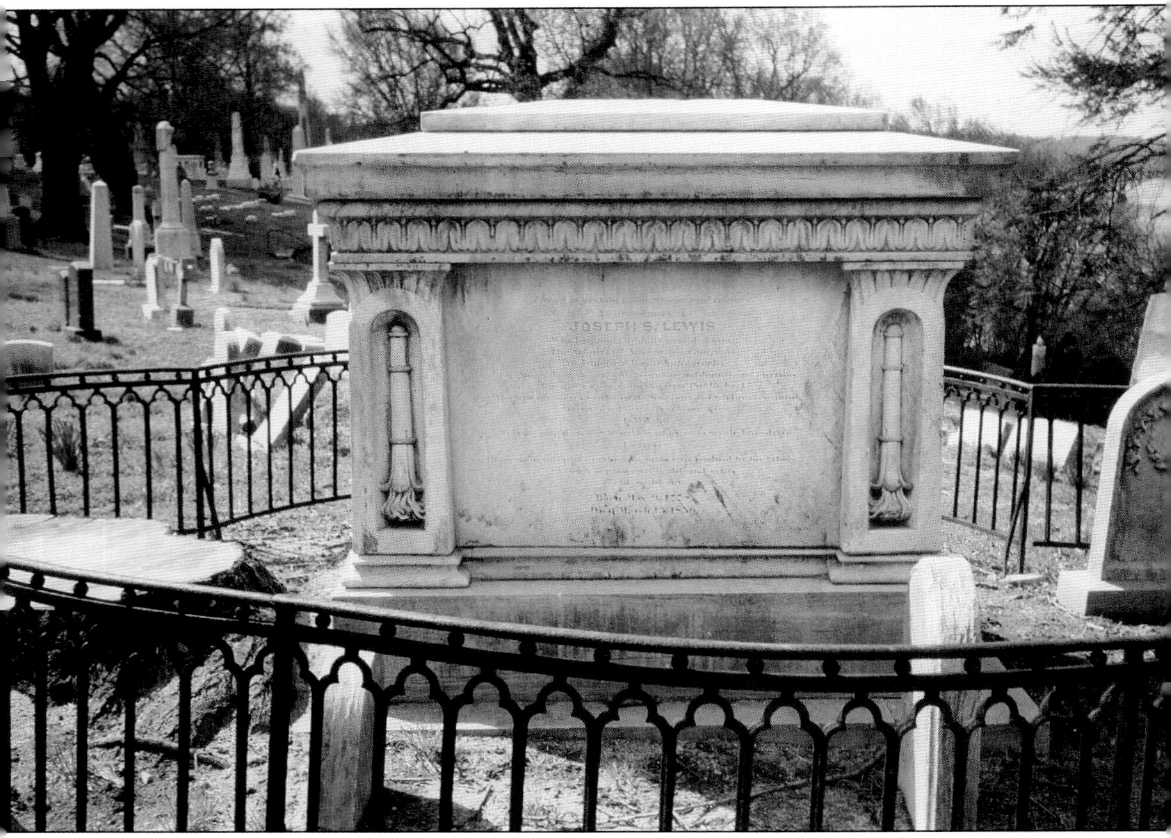

JOSEPH LEWIS MONUMENT RESTORATION, 1988. The first restoration project undertaken by the Friends of Laurel Hill was the monument of Joseph Lewis, the man who had funded much of the construction of the Fairmount Water Works. This project involved removing a tree from the lot, resetting headstones, and rebuilding the entire Lewis monument.

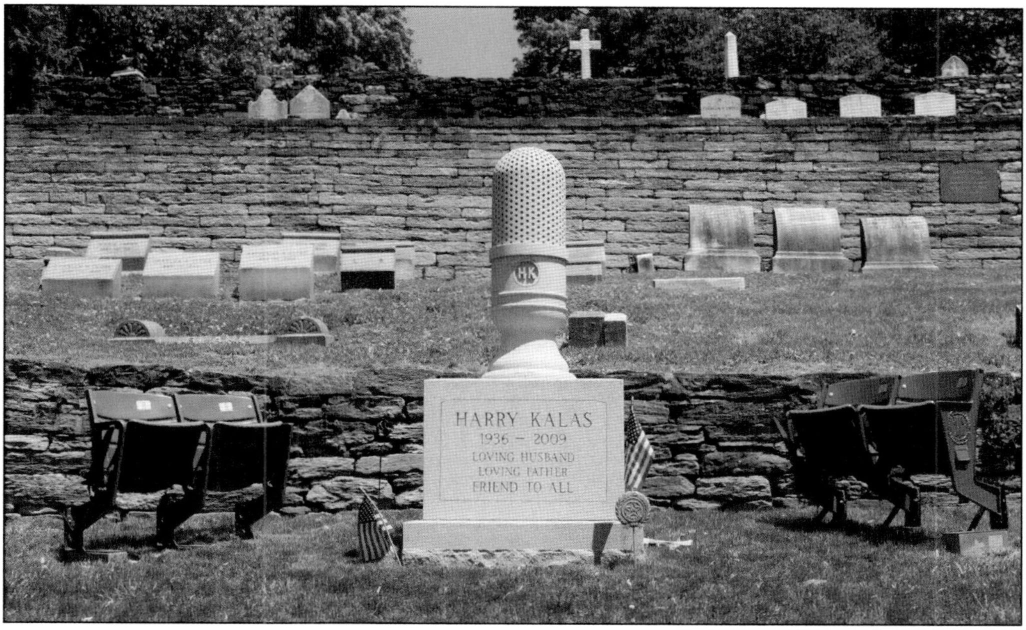

Harry Kalas Monument. An indication of Laurel Hill's rejuvenation came in 2009 with the unexpected death of legendary Philadelphia Phillies broadcaster Harry Kalas. His family chose to purchase property in Laurel Hill Cemetery because they wanted the nicest, most iconic cemetery in Philadelphia. They chose a beautiful spot overlooking the Schuylkill River. Today, seats from Veterans Stadium flank the microphone monument to Philadelphia's beloved sports announcer. (Emma Stern.)

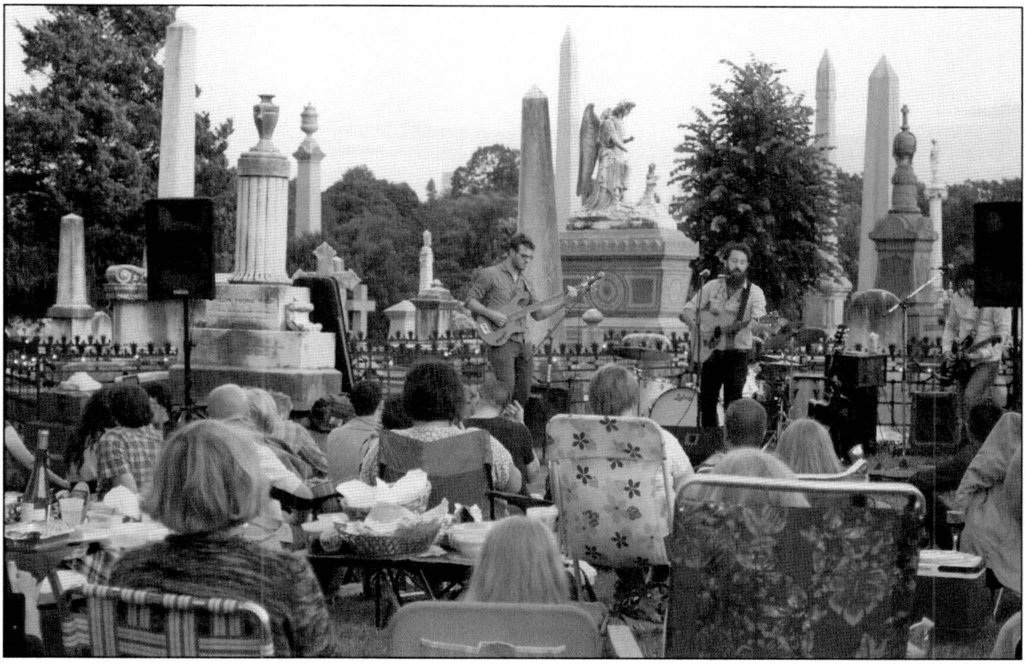

Bailey Hounds Concert in Laurel Hill. In the 21st century, Laurel Hill uses tours and programs to attract visitors and generate income. Once again, Philadelphians are utilizing the space for recreation, reflection, and education. (Emma Stern.)

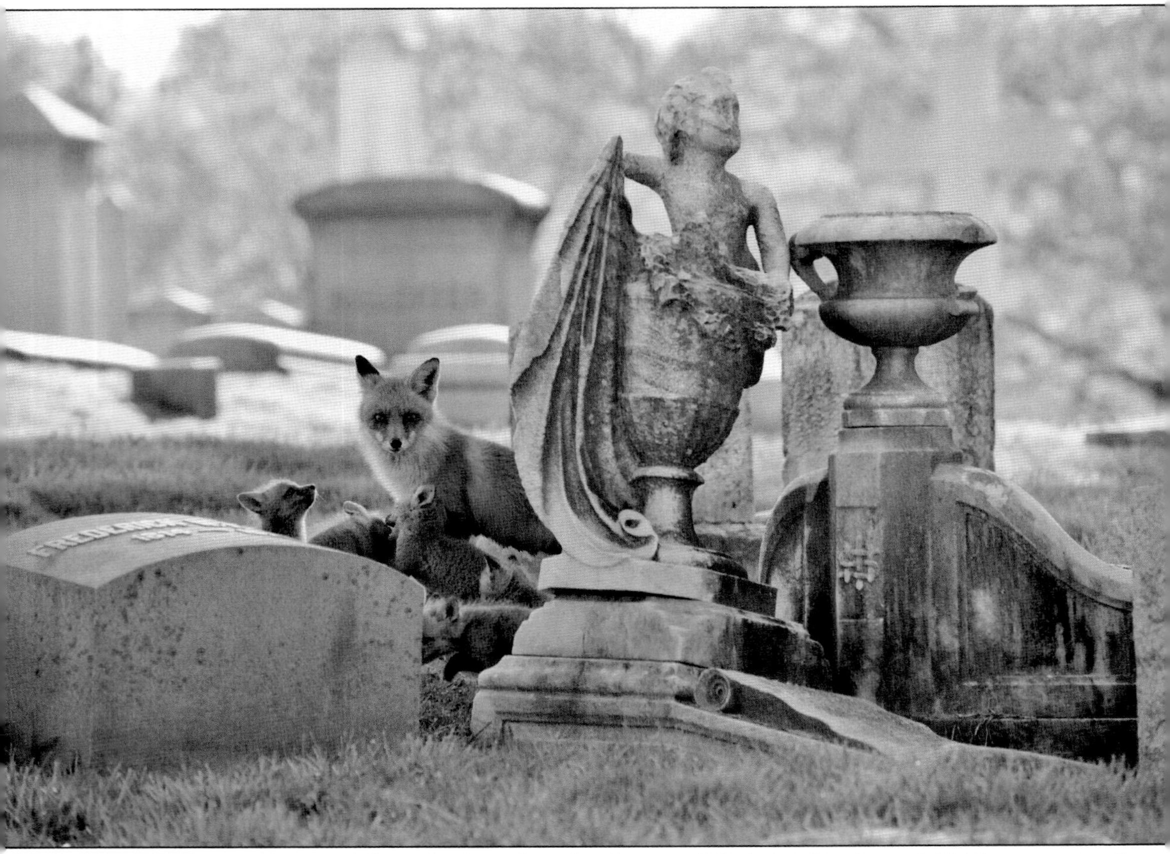

Fox Family in Laurel Hill. In the urban landscape of Philadelphia, Laurel Hill is an oasis of green space. In the new century, the cemetery has returned to its origins as a park-like space. (Frank Rausch.)

About the Organization

In 1978, the Friends of Laurel Hill Cemetery was founded by Drayton Smith (a direct descendant of one of the cemetery's four founders, John Jay Smith), his wife, Jane, and author and historian John Francis Marion. The Friends of Laurel Hill Cemetery was established as a 501(c)(3) organization for the purpose of preserving and promoting the historical character of the cemetery.

The organization's beginnings were modest, with public tours offered only at Halloween and in the spring. Professors from local colleges also brought their classes for private tours. Over time, interest in the cemetery grew, and the number of public and private tours increased until in 1998, Laurel Hill was awarded National Historic Landmark status, the first cemetery to receive such an honor.

The Friends of Laurel Hill Cemetery has received awards for its restoration projects. In 2011, the organization received a Construction Award for Special Historic Properties from Preservation Pennsylvania and a Preservation Achievement Grand Jury Award from the Preservation Alliance of Greater Philadelphia for the restoration of the *Old Mortality* sculpture group. In 2012, the Friends received a Construction Award for Special Historic Properties and a Preservation Achievement Grand Jury Award for the restoration of the Medallion Garden, the central rosette in the oldest portion of the cemetery. Then, in 2016, the Friends of Laurel Hill Cemetery received a Preservation Achievement Grand Jury Award for the pedestrian access restoration project, which restored access to the cemetery from the river and Kelly Drive.

Now, nearly 40 years since its founding, the Friends of Laurel Hill Cemetery offers programs of many types: concerts, movie nights, theatrical performances, photography workshops, car shows, ghost hunts, astronomy nights, and of course, walking tours. The cemetery has returned to its original purpose beyond burial of the dead; it is a green space in the city for relaxation and recreation.